D1552724

The Twilight of Amateur Diplomacy

AMERICAN DIPLOMATIC HISTORY
Lawrence S. Kaplan, *Editor*

Aftermath of War: Americans and the Remaking of Japan, 1945–1952
Howard B. Schonberger

*The Twilight of Amateur Diplomacy: The American Foreign Service and Its
Senior Officers in the 1890s*
Henry E. Mattox

The Twilight of Amateur Diplomacy

The American Foreign Service and Its Senior Officers in the 1890s

Henry E. Mattox

THE KENT STATE UNIVERSITY PRESS
Kent, Ohio, and London, England

© 1989 by The Kent State University Press, Kent, Ohio 44242
All rights reserved
Library of Congress Catalog Card Number 88–29022
ISBN 0–87338–375–3
Manufactured in the United States of America

Library of Congress Cataloging-in-Publication Data

Mattox, Henry E., 1930–
    The twilight of amateur diplomacy : the American Foreign Service
and its senior officers in the 1890s / Henry E. Mattox.
      p.   cm. — (American diplomatic history)
    Bibliography : p.
    Includes index.
    ISBN 0–87338–375–3 (alk. paper) ∞
    1. United States Foreign Service—History. 2. United States—
Diplomatic and consular service—History. 3. United States—
Foreign relations administration—History. 4. Diplomats—United
States—Biography. I. Title. II. Series.
JX1706.M17 1989
353.0089′09—dc19   88–29022
                                          CIP

British Library Cataloging-in-Publication data are available.

For Shelley

Contents

Preface and Acknowledgments

There is a history in all men's lives,
Figuring the nature of the times deceas'd. . . .
Shakespeare, Henry IV

This study, undertaken after I had served nearly a quarter of a century as an American Foreign Service officer, is an investigation of the rolls and roles of senior-level American diplomats just before the turn of the twentieth century. It is not a diplomatic history of fin de siècle America. That story has been told with varying interpretations by a number of scholars, from (alphabetically) Thomas A. Bailey to William Appleman Williams. Nor is this concerned primarily with the foreign policy of the period at the Washington level. It is, rather, expressly a monograph, an inquiry limited to one part of the American foreign affairs establishment in one time period; it is a study of the men who were chosen by the political leadership to be posted abroad in positions of the highest responsibility during the decade 1890–99. The study includes as well an account of the organization for which these men worked overseas.

The prime issue addressed here is the level of the preparation, aptitude, and general competency exhibited by the political-appointee chiefs of mission and consuls general of the late nineteenth century. How able, or otherwise, were they? How well or ill prepared? How good were they at their jobs abroad? As a former career diplomat, I expected at the outset that the inquiries would lead to support of the notion, prevalent in the historical literature on the period, that organizational professionalism—merit-based recruitment, selection, promotion, and assignment—was as much a need in the U.S. Diplomatic Service and Consular Service then, at the end of the nineteenth century, as now. (Throughout this

study, the uncapitalized words "foreign service" or "diplomatic and consular services" denote the two then-separate organizations; it was not
until 1924 that a combined Foreign Service of the United States
was created.)

Research leads to the conclusion, however, that the need for professionalism then was not so self-evident, that many of the persons chosen
through the political process were in fact among the best that America
had to offer. Ambrose Bierce made the contemporary observation that
American diplomats were failed politicians who were finally chosen for
office, on condition that they leave the country. The comment contains
the proverbial grain of truth. But the senior officer corps of the diplomatic and consular establishments evidently represented the United
States abroad in a manner adequate to the needs of the day, despite
administrative failings. Senior members of the service were not drawn
largely from the ranks of out-of-work Gilded Age ward heelers, as one
might gather from some scholarly studies of the period. To the contrary,
they compare favorably with their contemporary Americans and in some
cases with their colleagues in other foreign services.

"Professions are collective enterprises," in the words of Thomas L.
Haskell, "so their emergence and growth must be gauged in terms of
collective, not individual criteria."[1] The profession of diplomacy is represented in the following pages, a collective biography which presents
information on 226 individuals, almost all of the persons who served
abroad as American diplomatic or consular officers in charge of major
posts during the 1890s. Of these 226, nearly one-half, 110, held assignments to diplomatic posts as ambassadors or ministers. Another 90
served as consuls general. An additional 26 officers filled dual diplomatic
and consular positions, holding concurrently the titles of minister resident and consul general or secretary of legation and consul general. In a
few of these latter instances, the same individuals held different diplomatic and consular titles at different times within the decade.

In Thomas Carlyle's view, history is the essence of innumerable biographies. This book makes no pretensions to comprehensiveness; rather, it
attempts to illuminate a facet of United States foreign affairs of the era
through data on a finitely drawn group. As Lawrence Stone observes,
however, the premise of collective biographies is that "an understanding
of who the actors were will go far toward explaining the workings of the
institutions to which they belonged." "In the search for the truth," Elmer
Plischke further comments with regard to diplomatic history, "it is as
important to know *how* foreign policy is made and implemented and to
understand *how* external relations are conducted as it is to apprehend

and appreciate the substance of the foreign policy itself."[2] This study looks primarily at the overseas staffing and structure of the American foreign affairs agency, along briefly with the conduct of policies abroad in several geographic areas. It investigates how the nation's foreign policy was implemented, that is, not so much its substance.

In discussing these senior officers, one can do worse than to borrow as appropriate an assessment of British diplomats in early America: "These men . . . were not and were not intended to be portrayed as movers and shakers in diplomatic history." With one or two exceptions, their "impact was not on events, but rather on the attitudes of men . . . who shaped events."[3] Similarly, only a few of the American officers of the 1890s had an impact on diplomatic history; not many were "movers and shakers." This point should be emphasized here, and will be repeated later: American diplomats filled important roles then (as now) as reporters, observers, and negotiators, but the locus of policy formulation was in Washington.

It would be inappropriate in a prosopography to draw conclusions from a small selected group, either the best or the worst examples. Therefore, the study includes a near universe of people assigned to certain positions within a given time frame. The research considers well over two hundred diplomatic and consular officers, omitting fewer than a dozen who are identifiable but who left only very brief records of service at the beginning or end of the decade. Using this broad grouping of individuals permits a judgment about a spread of the good, bad, and indifferent officers in service overseas. As part of this overall evaluation, certain representatives are submitted to a functional assessment. Necessarily on an essentially subjective basis, the reporting from abroad and the official reputations of a limited number of the officers around the world are evaluated. (See the criteria for their selection in chapter 7.)

The concentration is on the years 1890 to 1899 because that was an important transitional period in America's outlook on the rest of the world, the rest of the world's perception of America, and in some few instances, the demands levied upon diplomats. Among other factors, it was the last decade before the reforms of the Progressive Era began to have a significant impact on how the diplomatic and consular establishments were staffed. It approached the end of the almost complete amateurism at all levels in the conduct of American foreign policy that had prevailed throughout the life of the Republic. Louis Galambos has called the years from about 1890 to 1910 "a crucial period in organizational terms." At that time, "the modern corporation, the modern craft union, and a variety of other forms of large-scale organization underwent decisive changes."[4] Although sentiment for change was stirring, the foreign service nonetheless was altered administratively but little in the decade under review.

From the information developed on these individuals a group portrait emerges of America's ambassadors extraordinary and ministers plenipotentiary—or ambassadors for short, a designation first granted to incumbents of certain posts in the 1890s—and of envoys extraordinary and ministers plenipotentiary—or ministers, the usual title of chiefs of diplomatic mission at the time. Ministers resident, the title of envoys sent to lesser diplomatic posts, also are included, as well as consuls general, a designation more prestigious than the rank of consul and one signifying at least in principle more supervisory responsibility.

Junior diplomats such as secretaries of legation are not investigated except in a few cases in which that title was combined with that of consul general as a budget-saving device and bestowed on one person. Also omitted are the numerous consular officers below the rank of consul general, that is, the vice or deputy consuls general, consuls, vice consuls, and consular or commercial agents. These lower-ranking officers had less impact on the conduct of foreign relations than their seniors because of the very nature of their assignments and responsibilities, even though some consuls, particularly at major seaports, drew substantial salaries.

The organization of the study is as follows: chapters 1 and 2 provide the context of the times, a discussion of the concept of professionalism, and a contemporary and historiographical critique of the view that America's foreign service was ripe for an overhaul by the 1890s. Chapter 3, in describing the selection process in the nineteenth century, concedes much of the argument that the system was unorganized and certainly politically based. The following chapter presents a group biography of the 226 men included in the study, a section which portrays their accomplishments and preparation, along with such items as age, geographic origins, and length of service. In all, a dozen attributes are looked at in each case. (Appendix A, a biographic register, provides personal and professional details on each of them.) Chapter 5 contains a discussion of senior officers' logistical and administrative difficulties in operating abroad. It makes a point similar to that made in chapter 3— the foreign service support system, like the means for selecting personnel, was not very "professional."

Chapter 6 recounts briefly the experiences at post of several of the prosopographical subjects. It would be infeasible to present the records of all, even in a work much longer than this one, but this section is intended to provide a sense of foreign service operations in the 1890s. The rationale for choosing one foreign service post over another is based on several factors: (1) although post reporting files were the basic research source, also consulted were the volumes of official records published in the *Foreign Relations* series of the Department of State which, while sometimes omitting documents on key issues, still are useful in giving at a minimum a picture of how posts dealt with routine problems through those years; (2) certain episodes such as Hawaiian annexation and the war with Spain are central to the nation's history during that era and could not very well be omitted; (3) a spread of geographic areas was essayed, even though Latin America was the focus of official attention during much of the decade; and (4) to avoid emphasizing the reputations of the nationally famous, the study attempts a mix of officers who are reasonably well known, including some who have less than favorable historical reputations, and others who are virtually unknown to history.

A penultimate chapter discusses the conclusion already briefly noted. Here there is speculation also that the political system and governmental machinery of the day, in combination with the United States' relatively limited responsibilities abroad until after 1898, were such that a professional corps of diplomats might not then necessarily have suited the nation best. That chapter and appendixes D and E present information on the subjects' socioeconomic standings and a tentative assessment of how these individuals might be rated as to foreign service-related competency.

The implications of these findings for the staffing of the present-day Foreign Service are not entirely clear and of course are arguable. Nevertheless, a final chapter suggests that amateurism, or better phrased, nonprofessionalism, can be defended in today's diplomacy. Possibly as an ex-Foreign Service officer thoroughly imbued in the past with the principles of professionalism, I can most convincingly suggest the merits of including amateurs among the nation's top diplomatic and consular officers. Even though long a careerist in the field, I believe that increased professionalism is not always the answer to organizational problems, including those of the Foreign Service. If this be bureaucratic treason, then let the careerists of the world make the most of it.

I owe thanks in the writing of this book to many. In general, I am indebted to colleagues in the Foreign Service of the United States and friends in the foreign affairs establishments of other countries for such understanding of the diplomatic and consular processes as I acquired over the years. Numerous teachers and students contributed to such familiarity with American history as I have developed over time. The staffs of libraries and manuscript collections at many institutions were helpful. Prominent among these institutions are the Walter Royal Davis and Louis Round Wilson Libraries at the University of North Carolina, Chapel Hill; the Duke University Library, Durham, N.C.; and the Appalachian State University Library, Boone, N.C.

Personnel in the Diplomatic Branch of the National Archives and the Manuscript Reading Room of the Library of Congress in particular provided unfailing support in the use of their massive collections of relevant materials. Among the archivists who went out of their way to assist me are Dr. Dane Hartgrove of the National Archives and Ms. Anne R. Kenney of the Western Historical Collection, University of Missouri, St. Louis.

Special appreciation is due to Professors Michael H. Hunt of the University of North Carolina at Chapel Hill and Peter F. Coogan of Hollins College for their criticism in detail of an earlier version of this study. The study profited as well from the suggestions of Professors John W. Coogan of Michigan State University, Lawrence E. Gelfand of the University of Iowa, and John T. Hubbell of Kent State University. I am grateful also to my wife, Shelley E. Mattox, for her support of the project and her editorial comments.

The errors of fact and interpretation which surely remain are my responsibility alone, of course.

1

The Need for Foreign Service Reform

*In the early 1880s diplomats and writers rarely spoke of the United
States in the same breath as the six recognized great powers—
Britain, France, Germany, Austria-Hungary, Russia, and Italy.
By the beginning of the twentieth century they included it almost
invariably.*

Ernest R. May, Imperial Democracy:
The Emergence of America as a Great Power *(1961)*

Throughout the nineteenth century, amateurs staffed the United
States diplomatic and consular services. Political appointees filled all ranks
of this foreign service until the early years of the twentieth century, with
only a few occasional and limited exceptions. No merit-based service existed at practically any rank. Ambassadorial and clerical positions abroad
alike reflected political influence, although other industrialized nations
had careerist diplomatic and consular systems in place by then.

Average Americans of that era, preoccupied with domestic opportunities and challenges, did not care about this; they concerned themselves
little with the nation's representatives abroad. They were generally paro-
chial in outlook, not greatly seized with questions of foreign policy or
international relations despite the occasional attention paid to hemi-
spheric events. This attitude was not so much isolationism, as we think
of it today, as a disinclination to accord high priority to overseas matters
far removed from most Americans' daily lives.

The subjects of the present inquiry, the United States' senior diplomatic and consular representatives abroad in the 1890s, lived and worked
in a setting of incipient change, however, whether or not many Americans fully appreciated that fact at the time. Even though history can
rarely if ever be divided into precise periods, scholars often call the decade just before the turn of the twentieth century a watershed in American history. Interpretations of the era vary widely,[1] but clearly the
United States' world view in 1900 was different from that of ten years

earlier. At least through 1890, so Robert L. Beisner has argued, even policymakers in Washington saw the world in a reactive, segmented fashion. Only in later years, particularly from 1898 onward, did this policy outlook consciously incorporate international power considerations. In the early 1890s, according to another scholar, "national politics still revolved around internal questions. Americans regarded the economic issues stemming from industrialization and immigration as essentially domestic ones, despite rising concerns for foreign trade. . . . Little of the nation's economic strength had been translated into the military or diplomatic power necessary for large-scale overseas intervention."[2]

Several changes impinged on foreign relations in those years: the perception that the Western frontier had disappeared by about 1890, with the accompanying faintly mystical belief that the United States needed such an outlet to complete its national development; the intellectual influence of social Darwinism, with its assertions of Anglo-Saxon, and hence American, superiority over other races and the need to "prove" national worth in the face of colonial competition from other advanced nations; the theories of strategist Alfred T. Mahan on the significance of naval forces in world history, including the belief that bases overseas were needed to control the sea lanes; the continuing development of a small but modern and powerful American navy from humble beginnings in the early 1880s; and the rise of sometimes exaggerated nationalistic feelings as the sectional enmities of the Civil War period faded.

Further, and importantly in the view of historians writing during the past three decades, change in foreign policy can be attributed to the worry of government and business leaders over surplus production and the need to find markets and investment opportunities abroad now that the country was becoming the leading manufacturer in the world. The United States was a large and wealthy nation of nearly sixty-three million people as the decade began, but the depression years of the nineties brought on by the Panic of 1893 spurred the belief, emphasized in the interpretation of scholars who focus on economic factors, that overproduction was a serious problem and that social unrest threatened if the problem was not addressed.

All of these changes on the national scene, from the conviction that overseas markets were needed to the fading of frontier opportunities in the American West, led to a sense of a "new" Manifest Destiny. The original concept held that the country was fated to overspread the North American continent, an idea that dated back to the 1840s. In its new form, America's role was seen as one of extracontinental expansion, in commercial terms if not necessarily in territorial acquisition, a role requiring gradually far more international involvement than previously. The nation gained no new possessions until toward the end of this watershed decade, but new and different influences operated on the foreign policy scene. Beisner terms the response to the changed circumstances beginning about 1890 a move from the old diplomacy to the new; "something quite different began to appear in U.S. diplomacy" at that time.[3]

Challenges and problems associated with these shifting views came in due course during the nineties. There was a crisis with Chile in 1891–92, a simmering rivalry with Germany over Samoa, a near-miss effort to annex Hawaii in 1893, and a brief but pointed confrontation with Great Britain over Venezuelan boundaries, among other issues that arose. The climax came in 1898. At the beginning of the year, the United States had only lightly populated Alaska and barren Midway Island in the Pacific as overseas dependencies. By the end of the same year, after a short, sharp war with Spain begun essentially over Cuban independence, America had annexed or had stationed troops in Cuba, Puerto Rico, Hawaii, Guam, and the Philippines. The following year, the United States divided the Samoan Islands with Germany and Britain and additionally issued the first of the two Open Door notes on China, asserting thereby American commercial interests in that country. By 1900 the changes in the foreign affairs framework were so profound that the nation found itself faced with many of the modern-day issues with which it has struggled ever since. The international outlook was different before and after the 1890s watershed; for America, the world had changed.

Not surprisingly, the foreign affairs agencies, in the manner of all bureaucracies, had not kept pace with the events of the decade. Many observers then and scholars in more recent days considered the fundamental failing to be the system of appointing amateurs to posts abroad through patronage, a procedure thought to be detrimental to the advancement of increasingly important American interests overseas. "The heritage of a generation determines in large part the conduct of its diplomacy," observes one historian, and as already noted, the outlook of Americans long had been other than internationalist. "The heritage continued to nourish parochialism"[4] despite changing circumstances in the 1890s.

For more than one reason this generational legacy incorporated a nonprofessional approach to carrying out the nation's policies abroad. Part of the reason was the fact that pressing international problems which would call for trained experts heretofore had arisen only intermittently. In 1889 Henry Cabot Lodge, then a member of the House of Representatives, wrote disapprovingly, "Our relations with foreign nations to-day fill but a slight place in American politics, and excite only a languid interest. We have separated ourselves so completely from the affairs of other people that it is difficult to realize how large a place they occupied when the government was founded."[5] Throughout much of the nineteenth century prior to the 1890s, the United States conducted its limited bilateral affairs in a setting that rarely cried out for first-rate experienced diplomats.

Further, a political tradition of amateurs in government had long standing, dating from the Jacksonian era. Andrew Jackson's tenet that practically anyone could hold down most government jobs played a part in the lack of interest in fostering a career foreign service. The two major parties as well had the requirement to reward the party faithful. The domestic sector provided most public jobs, but political supporters of the party in office could claim hundreds of positions abroad, from consular clerk to chief of diplomatic mission. These patronage payoffs were an institutionalized fact of political life and a rationale for amateur appointments to diplomatic and consular posts.

Viewed from one angle, the amateur principle in government represented Jacksonian egalitarianism and democratic ideals—anybody could be a consul or diplomat. But in another sense amateurism reflected the need for personal wealth and elite social status as a precondition to certain appointments, even those with subordinate titles and duties. Many positions, especially in the diplomatic ranks, paid little, or the expected expenditures were high. Only the well-to-do therefore could afford to accept them, and the Washington appointing powers sometimes thought only monied amateurs with the social graces would be suitable for diplomatic assignments. In 1892 New York socialite Ward McAllister expressed the common view that wealth was essential for appointment as an American minister in Europe—and incidentally that it was necessary for American envoys to dress well and be good after-dinner speakers.[6] The political leadership made appointments to some exalted but expensive positions not as party payoffs in financial terms, but rather as "psychic recompense" for past political services or support.

For at least three reasons, then, Americans in the latter part of the nineteenth century generally either held their foreign affairs establishment abroad in poor repute, viewed it as an object of suspicion, or at best treated it as a neglected arm of the government. First, Americans widely believed that patronage appointments went to unsuited, unqualified politicians. This belief was almost an article of faith among many intellectuals and those familiar with governmental operations—unless, in some instances, the appointments were from their own political party. Second, some thought that there was no real need for a trained foreign service corps, given the usually insular focus of American interests. And third, widely held ideas of egalitarianism clashed with the elitist cast and wealth requirements of many assignments, thereby raising the suspicions of the many who lacked elite backgrounds.

No concerted demand for a trained, experienced foreign service emerged prior to the early 1900s (see also chapter 2). To the contrary, in 1885 a senator from New York went so far as to call for a quarantine of returning American diplomats, holding that "this diplomatic service is working our ruin by creating a desire for foreign customs and foreign follies." Other members of Congress of the era propounded the notion that a diplomatic service was superfluous.[7] Many Americans attributed so little importance to foreign relations that Charles A. Dana's irreverent *New York Sun* in 1889 could half seriously call for the abolition of the Diplomatic Service as "a costly humbug and sham . . . no good to anybody." A few years later the conservative *Washington Post* similarly editorialized caustically that perhaps "there is no longer any need for men of affairs in our foreign service, and it had better be abolished." In 1893 Oscar Solomon Straus of New York, who was to be a three-time envoy to Turkey, observed that the public not surprisingly was "less familiar with the duties of our diplomatic and consular agents than any other branch of the public service."[8] His assertion was accurate whether or not those who wanted to quarantine or do away with the Diplomatic Service were entirely serious.

Reformist moves were in the offing, however. The several negative attitudes noted above only reinforced the belief, especially in the nation's nascent reform element, that the amateur foreign service of the day was staffed in a highly disorganized fashion by incompetents or worse, persons who presented a poor image of America abroad and who served the United States poorly. Reformers began explicitly to recognize the need for changes in the staffing of the diplomatic and consular services to overcome these problems.[9] In 1892 a leading business figure and minister to France, Thomas Jefferson Coolidge, made a discouraging judgment, typical of the mindset that led to calls for reform: "It is useless for us to attempt to stand on even terms in foreign countries [with European diplomats], when we send out every four years new men, who know nothing of the diplomatic relations of the countries, and who meet with men whose whole training has been in that one subject." On the subject of the Consular Service, Coolidge thought the United States suffered even more "by appointing Consuls, merely as a reward for political work, so that every few years a new man makes his appearance, who has hardly learned his business when he is turned out for another; whereas the

English, the French, and particularly the German consuls are men thoroughly trained, of long experience, and who understand the business relations of their country." Similar comments, although not yet especially numerous, can be found. In 1894 Oscar Straus wrote a twelve-page pamphlet for the National Civil Service Reform League in which he called for changes. In his view the patronage system's evils were "becoming more glaring than at any previous period of our history, because the party in control of the Government has changed three times [in ten years], so that our consuls have been on the march to and fro ever since."[10]

Another example of a call for improvements came from a participant in the system who noted that "saloon keepers, broken down preachers whose congregations were tired of them, and political henchmen were apt to be appointed" to the Consular Service. In 1895 Henry Cabot Lodge, by now a senator, supported a bill to take the Consular Service "out from the wretched condition of being the mere sport of politics." The service's responsibility, he pronounced on the floor of the Senate, was not "merely to attend to ordinary consular duties"; consular officers were abroad "to promote the business interests of the United States," a duty which he thought the service was not performing. He echoed Coolidge's remarks: "We are at a disadvantage with every other civilized nation in the organization of our service. Every four years, at every change of Administration, men who have just begun to learn their duties are thrown out and we are forced to begin all over again with a new set of men unfamiliar with the language of the country to which they are sent, unfamiliar with the business of the country, and with everything to learn."[11]

Lodge's was a standard complaint of the emerging reform-minded element to which he, Coolidge, and Straus belonged. In 1894, early in a new administration, a prominent former gentleman-amateur in diplomacy, Congressman Robert R. Hitt of Illinois, voiced similar sentiments on the House floor: "The British [consular] system is very different from ours. Their consuls are kept continuously in the service." Assuredly the United States got "some pretty queer people into [its] diplomatic and consular service," in the words of a *New York Times* correspondent in 1895.[12]

A number of American periodicals of note in the Gilded Age also beat the drums of governmental reform. *Harper's Weekly*, the leading illustrated publication, E. L. Godkin's *Nation*, *Harper's Monthly*, the *Atlantic Monthly*, the venerable *North American Review*, a quarterly—all are examples of civil service reform-oriented periodicals publishing in the closing decades of the nineteenth century. One scholar has noted that they "created a national intellectual community for the first time and provided a national forum where positive and concrete proposals for institutional reform could be aired and debated." In 1888 the *Forum*, a newcomer to the magazine field, printed a plea for reform of the Consular Service in which the point was made especially that pay scales needed to be more comparable to those of the European powers. Five years later former minister to Brazil Robert Adams, Jr., a Philadelphia lawyer who is included in this group biographic study, published an article in the *North American Review* titled, "Faults in our Consular Service." Drawing upon his experience abroad earlier in the decade, Adams, by then a congressman, recommended training for consular officers and the establishment of a career service. Francis Butler Loomis, also a subject of this study, served in the early 1890s as a consul in France and as minister successively to Venezuela and Portugal; some years later he published in the *North American Review* two articles on needed reforms.[13]

Reform sentiment arose in other areas of public life late in the nineteenth century. Some leading daily newspapers took the same tack as the periodicals. Reformist editorial sentiment grew in such journals as Godkin's crusading *New York Evening Post*, the *New York Times*, and the *Washington Evening Star*. Among the numerically fewer opponents of civil service merit plans were Whitelaw Reid's conservative Republican *New York Tribune* and the *Washington Post*. The latter two newspapers were more concerned editorially with partisan political rewards and control than with civil service reform. The *Washington Post* in mid-1889 called for the repeal of the 1883 Pendleton civil service reform act and the reinstitution of an unfettered spoils system so as to strengthen the Republican party, which during the previous year had won back the presidency from Grover Cleveland and the Democrats. Four years later the *Post* showed a consistent editorial position by defending patronage in the Consular Service even under a new Cleveland administration—unless, the *Post* editorialized, the changes went so far as to replace competent officers with incompetents.[14]

An antireform stand by a major newspaper was exceptional as the twentieth century approached. A series of *New York Times* editorials beginning in March 1889, the month of President Benjamin Harrison's inauguration, exemplified reform sentiment. The newspaper inveighed against the "mischievous nature" of the "hopelessly stupid" and "corrupt" patronage system. Editorialists praised Henry Cabot Lodge's quoted recommendation on "taking all the routine offices of Government out of politics." Referring specifically to the diplomatic and consular services, the *Times* denounced the practice of making political appointments to office because it encouraged job seekers to the detriment of the orderly work of government. Even consular assignments should be covered by a merit system: "The truth is that the prevailing eagerness for [diplomatic and consular] appointments is a *reductio ad absurdum* of our system of rotation in office." A journalist remarked on the "illusory glamour" of the Consular Service. The newspaper apparently saw the appeal of diplomatic posts as more real, but the *Times* pointed up several personal disadvantages to living abroad. Posing a question as to whether the American diplomat is happy abroad, the daily replied in the negative: "Our belief is that he usually is not."[15]

President Harrison's handling of appointments roused the ire of reformers. Earlier he had pledged, "In appointments of every grade and department fitness and not party service should be the essential and discriminating test, and fidelity and efficiency the only sure tenure of office."[16] Among the appointments he soon routinely made, however, was that of the wealthy Philadelphia merchant John Wanamaker as postmaster general. Wanamaker's substantial campaign contributions, which amounted to two hundred thousand dollars by his own count, obviously dictated the choice. In June the *New York Times* thereupon denounced "rotation and spoils," and by July, when Harrison was seen to be going the way of all previous patronage dispensers despite his promises to the contrary, the *Times* referred bluntly to his "treachery to the country" for failing to observe his and the Republican party's explicit pledges of reforms in government hiring.[17]

Many historians have repeated the contemporary judgments of these reform-minded critics. Twentieth-century scholars are unimpressed by the credentials and performances of appointees to the American foreign service of that era. Students of American diplomatic history usually consider the nation's diplomats and consular officers to be a poor lot in an absolute sense. Further, in their view those officers suffer in comparison with the Republic's early diplomatic appointees. Historians agree that the United States' first envoys, fortunately for the country, were adept at dealing with the maneuvers of the skilled European foreign offices. But beginning in 1829 with the two terms of the Jackson presidency and the onset of amateurism in government, the level of skills fell, in the judgment of many present-day scholars. "A deplorable drop in the abilities of American diplomats began," writes Robert H. Ferrell, "which lasted at least until the early twentieth century." Richard Hofstadter remarked that Jackson ushered in an era when "the expert, even the merely competent man, was being restricted . . . by the creed of rotation [in office]."[18]

Scholars therefore frequently take the position that foreign service reform was overdue by the 1890s, a conventional view expressed in many historical studies. In this interpretation America's emerging place on the world stage at the turn of the century dictated that its representatives abroad be able, well trained, and experienced, the better to advance national interests—not the products of a political spoils system. Some studies of recent years link foreign service institution building to conscious efforts of Washington leaders to expand America's world role. Richard H. Werking notes, for instance, that the pre–World War I foreign service was "first and foremost an instrument for the nation's commercial expansion." This end could hardly be met if the diplomatic and consular services were staffed largely by incompetent spoilsmen. Walter LaFeber incorporates the point in his work on American expansionism prior to 1898; he remarks that American business interests saw consular reform as a "must" in the United States' drive to world commercial leadership.[19]

Historians of various interpretive persuasions from left to right fit into a near-consensus on the need for substantive reform. Although there are a few favorable judgments on individuals in the foreign service, some of which will be brought out in the later sections of this study, the historiographical thrust in the field is negative. Ferrell's assessment that nineteenth-century American diplomats were "regularly inept . . . hangers-on . . . who achieved depths of incompetence" represents the judgment of many historians. According to him, President Grant made his worst appointments to the Consular Service, which is surely saying a lot. David H. Pletcher is not an especially strong critic; nonetheless he finds that the spoils system and low salaries "made for mediocre diplomatic and consular services." In yet another historian's view, a diplomatic or consular assignment of the era was "the equivalent of a modern-day government grant for promising or established literary figures." And H. Wayne Morgan notes that the late nineteenth-century foreign service was small, overworked, and "often unequal to its tasks." It generally did not meet the country's needs, nor did it measure up to its foreign counterparts. The Consular Service, according to Morgan, was a "burying ground for political liabilities"; low pay, undesirable posts, and tedious duties made consular work, as with the Catholic church, "fit only for celibates." Beisner comments devastatingly: With some exceptions, "the consular service consisted largely of time-serving functionaries, party hacks, bumptious fools, and petty corruptionists." Also with some exceptions, "American ministers . . . all too often earned more shame than respect for their country." Alfred L. P. Dennis presaged Morgan's "burying ground" remark with his earlier description of the foreign service at the turn of the century as "a refuge for elderly party workers." Morton I. Keller in a more recent study notes that the Department of State in the 1880s was lightly staffed and its emissaries abroad often "nondescript," although he softens this indictment by observing that these emissaries "were adequate to the minimal demands made upon them."[20]

The gist of such critical comments on American diplomats and consular officers is that the two services were and long had been dumping grounds for "worn-out, useless, second-rate politicians." "Party mendicants" were assigned to diplomatic positions. A diplomat was identified as a "ward politician with a frock coat."[21] As a foreign observer, English diplomat Harold Nicolson, assessed in the 1930s:

> In past years the reputation of America's foreign service suffered much from the political appointments made under the "spoils system." A political supporter who was accorded the perquisite of an Embassy or a Legation was all too often more concerned with maintaining his publicity-value in his hometown than with serving the rights and interests of his own country abroad. The capitals of Europe and Latin America echoed with the indiscretions of these amateur diplomatists and much damage was done to all concerned.[22]

This negative tone pervades studies of the latter part of the century. Critics in recent years have written approvingly of reform efforts, limited though they were, beginning at the turn of the century.

Twentieth-century historians have not simply echoed contemporary reformers' assessments of the 1890s foreign service, of course. In many instances they have drawn their judgments from a close reading of the records. But their times also have influenced them. This is so whether they lean toward a "realist" position, a traditionalist "consensus" view which held sway during and after World War II, an "idealist" viewpoint, a revisionist New Left interpretation with its intellectual debt to Charles A. Beard and Progressivism, or some version of postrevisionist scholarship. These schools of diplomatic historians, and other scholars who espouse neither conventional mainstream nor more radical Vietnam-era ideas, write implicitly or explicitly in favor of the professionalized conduct of diplomacy and consular affairs. It seems to be an unexceptionable idea, one that deserves support almost without question.

But are the negative evaluations of the diplomatic and consular officers concerned substantially correct? Is the uncomplimentary historical record of criticism compiled by contemporary observers entirely accurate? Are later scholarly critics fully justified in their calls for professionalization?

These are the questions addressed in this study. One way to begin an evaluation of this much-maligned group of officers of the 1890s is to lay the groundwork by briefly considering what professionalism is all about.

| 2 |

Professionalism Considered

A man that's expict to thrain lobsters to fly in a year is called a loonytic; but a man that thinks men can be tu-rrned into angles be an ilictions is called a rayformer an' remains at large.

Finley Peter Dunne ("Mr. Dooley")
"On the Crusade Against Vice" (1900)

Early efforts at reform of the foreign service were tentative in the extreme and never got very far. In 1864 an act of Congress authorized the recruitment of thirteen consular "pupils," or clerks, who were protected from arbitrary dismissal. The examination of consular officers first came about as a result of a presidential executive order in 1866. Examiners failed two of nine applicants that year, but the Department of State held no further tests until 1873–74. Two executive orders at that time again required formal tests for consular applicants, and examinations were administered for a brief period. These merit-based reforms, however, proved short-lived and the department took no further action along these lines.[1] In 1883, spurred by the assassination of President James A. Garfield two years previously by an unsuccessful office seeker, Congress passed the Civil Service (Pendleton) Act, a measure affecting only lower clerical ranks of the civil service, not those in the foreign service.

The first stirrings of a lasting professionalization process in the foreign service came with an executive order of September 1895 issued by President Grover Cleveland which provided for testing or experience requirements to fill midlevel consular slots.[2] After this limited move toward merit principles in the Consular Service, an initiative that was not binding on succeeding administrations, the government did not take further steps in the direction of reform until 1905. In that year President Theodore Roosevelt issued an order reiterating and extending Cleveland's consular directive and another directive establishing examinations for would-be junior diplomats. Thereafter the pace of reform quickened. Also in 1905 Congress enacted a measure incorporating a new salary schedule for consular officers, one that did away in most cases with the fee system of compensation. Congress omitted from the measure any requirements that consular appointments be made on the basis of examination or that promotions be made on merit; members of Congress believed both provisions impinged on the constitutional prerogatives of the president. Secretary of State Elihu Root, however, had those same requirements included at certain levels in another Roosevelt executive order of mid-1906. Three years later President William Howard Taft continued the reformist thrust by issuing an order on the entry of lower-level diplomats. His directive laid down specific criteria for tests and sanctioned the merit principle in promotions.[3]

These reform measures were not the equal in complexity and scope of the requirements to come in later years, but examiners applied them in a stringent fashion. In 1907 John van Antwerp MacMurray, a Princeton graduate who achieved senior rank later, "squeaked through" a "searching" test and received appointment as a junior diplomat. That same year the Consular Service examining board failed eight of the eighteen junior-level candidates and in immediately following years caused Secretary Root concern that the standards were being applied too rigorously. By mid-1912 the Diplomatic Service had rejected 60 percent of the 104 candidates for junior officer appointment.[4]

Thus in the period after 1900 the government installed the administrative machinery for the beginnings of merit principles and careerism in the lower ranks of the foreign affairs establishment overseas, the diplomatic and consular services. A climax of reform came in 1924 with the thoroughgoing changes of the Rogers Act and the establishment of a combined Foreign Service. Professionalism took hold.

But given that this process of reform may be desired in the foreign service or any other organization, the very concept of professionalism can be complex and the implementation of ideas of professionalization can lead in different directions. How may we define professionalism for our purposes here? Does it always equate with expert performance? Do we automatically contrast professionalism with a lack of skills on the part of an amateur? Who is a professional? How does he earn that designation? Who is not a professional?

Professionalization does not mean simply the establishment of a merit-based personnel system which thereby advances administrative efficiency. It is not only the installation of standards and ordered routines, nor is it necessarily associated with either technical expertise on the one hand or social station in life on the other. Its ramifications are so broad that professionalism, like beauty, almost resides in the eye of the beholder, whether the turn-of-the-century reformer, later historian, or present-day social theorist.

Professionalism actually is best understood as an amalgam of several elements and possible meanings, some of which are straightforward and unremarkable, if not simplistic. First, we commonly understand a professional to be one who performs a service or produces something tangible as a means of making a living, as contrasted with an amateur, who performs for the fun of it and is unpaid. Professionalism also connotes the adept exercise of skill and knowledge; a "professional" job of carpentry, dentistry, musical arrangement, or whatever usually is deemed superior to the efforts of an amateur. Further, in a slightly different sense, the United States Department of Labor holds that the professionals are those whose work requires special training or educational degrees, or who produce work that is "original or creative in character" involving reliance on invention, imagination, and talent.[5]

Other interpretations are even more involved and have been the subject of scholarly inquiry among historians and sociologists, especially the latter, for decades. Scholars frequently treat professions as exalted forms of occupations, those with claims by their practitioners to superior prestige and enhanced earning power, among other attributes. Certain occupations can be called superior to others in the two characteristic requirements of specialized knowledge and esoteric skills—that is, expertise—associated with the provisions of services of human value. These superior occupational classifications are the professions, or what can be called the "successful" occupations.

Central features other than expertise which scholars also often include with the various ideas of professionalism are credentialism and autonomy. The former is the means by which an occupation certifies the expertise of its practitioners; frequently credentialism rests upon a requirement for organized training of some duration and complexity, as in the Department of Labor definition above. Credentials also form the basis for institutional practices which make possible extended safeguarded tenure in some professions, the very essence of careerism. Autonomy refers to the supposition that the knowledge and skills involved in the practice of a given profession are beyond the ability of laymen to judge. The profession therefore claims for itself autonomous internal control, ideally policing and authenticating the credentials of its own members in a setting of occupational monopoly.

There are yet other variations on the theme of professionalism. The status professions include prominently three traditional learned callings dating from medieval times: medicine, law, and the clergy, the latter encompassing university teaching. Other occupational groups have striven to approximate the gentry status of these three oldest (legitimate) professions, especially in England and America. They have done so for reasons of personal prestige and importantly also because the connotation of disinterested dedication attached to such professions validates efforts by practitioners to monopolize the field. One professor of jurisprudence wrote more than fifty years ago that "law is a profession in theory and monopoly in fact." It is "a monopoly not merely by force of skill and brain but established and maintained by law."[6] Professionalization additionally can include an attempt to standardize the services offered and to develop an institutionalized role supported by its practitioners. As one scholar notes, "Characteristic of each of the established professions, and a goal of each aspiring profession, is the 'community of the profession.' "[7]

This latter approach to the concept sees tendencies toward professionalization in America and England over the past century or more as efforts toward recognition and protection, as moves toward the exclusivity of the status-laden traditional professions of medicine, law, and the clergy. "The uniqueness of the recognized professions," comments one historian, "lies in the high social status which they confer upon the particular band of converts who enter them,"—a remark which clearly applies to the field of diplomacy, if not always to consular affairs.[8] Some groups have achieved greater success in this respect over the years than others. Few would argue with the claims to professional recognition of the engineering or even acting occupations, but studies of how far along the professionalization scale other groups, such as social workers, librarians, and medical support personnel, have advanced fill the sociology literature. Businessmen consistently have failed to gain clear-cut entitlement to professional status from scholars, largely because merchants buy and sell heterogeneous bundles of goods and services. And journalists, by the bureaucratic definition of the Department of Labor, do not fit into the professional class except for editorial writers, columnists, and critics.[9]

Professionalism on the European continent developed along different lines from the English and American concept. There it has centered on elitist professional training at the grandes écoles. Prestige accrues from such education, and the primary indentification of graduates is with the employment group or social class, not with organized occupations. The

French and Germans, for example, do not generally attach the same importance as Americans or Englishmen to professional labels, be they doctors, lawyers, or whatever. If privately employed, the former often consider themselves members of the bourgeois class; if salaried public employees, they identify with their hierarchical rank more than with an occupational group. Hence a leading student of the field has called the focus on professionalism, in the various forms set forth in the preceeding paragraphs, the "Anglo-American" or "British disease."[10]

Although sociologists have prepared most studies of professionalism, historians also have published in the field. For historians the concept of professionalism provides a new means by which to interpret the social reform of the past and implicitly the changes needed contemporaneously.[11] They hold that professionals—experts, that is—replaced bungling amateurs in one field after another, including foreign affairs. "Ours is a 'professional' society," writes one scholar. "The generalized knowledge and the community orientation characteristic of professional behavior," he continues, "are indispensable in our society as we know it and as we want it to be."[12]

Robert H. Wiebe argues that a new middle class emerged in the late nineteenth century as America sought to impose order on a rapidly changing social scene. In a nation becoming increasingly urbanized and industrialized, individuals began to form new identifications to replace a disappearing sense of local identity. They were coming to identify their places in society in a framework of skills based on formal training. According to Wiebe, in the critical period of 1895–1905 doctors, lawyers, teachers, and other emerging professional groups sought and achieved cohesiveness in response to rapid economic, technological, and demographic change. These "members of the new middle class found their rewards more and more in the uniqueness of an occupation and its importance in a rising scientific-industrial society."[13]

Historians also have interpreted social change and the growth of professionalism in a setting of developing bureaucratic organizations, as well as socioeconomic class. Scholars of the subject hold that the bureaucracies which assumed effective leadership roles—in particular, for our purposes in this study, in the exercise of governmental authority—grew out of the phenomenal rise of America as an industrial state during the last third of the nineteenth century. Samuel P. Hays describes the conditions that dictated the efforts of business, labor, and farming groups to reach organizational unity. In the name of efficiency, centralizing pressures won out over differentiating tendencies in the society. Richard Hofstadter noted the rise of collectivism as a general trend of reformist thought at this time. Unable any longer to depend on individual self-assertion as a remedy for the various problems of the day, as he wrote, "men turned toward collective action." Wiebe's study of the breakdown of autonomous "island communities" depicts the societal response of bureaucratization as a means to meet an increasingly compelling need.[14]

The study of bureaucracy and its role in modernization reflects the scholarship of Max Weber, the German social theorist. Writing earlier in the twentieth century, he emphasized technical efficiency in the development of bureacratic institutions. Contrasting charismatic or individual, and bureaucratic or institutional rule, Weber called the latter "the most rational known means of carrying out imperative control over human beings."[15] He saw bureaucracies emerging as a result of democratization in Western society, not as a result of the furtherance of privilege.

Much of the more recent scholarship in the field, however, has been directed toward elites as privileged groups, linked usually to considerable wealth. One study finds that there is a measurable class and monetary bias in the makeup of political elites in a democracy. Merit is a determinant for inclusion in elite ranks, but if a background of wealth is missing, meritorious achievement warranting inclusion has to be on a grand scale.[16] Political theorist Gaetano Mosca investigated a middle-class stratum with a claim to intellectual attainment, a "sub-elite" as he termed it, which clearly ranked below the political elite. This group included senior civil servants and diplomats in the government sector, but not the elected political leadership.[17]

Although specialized bureaucratic knowledge was one principal Progressive Era factor in the rise of professionalism, a thread of elitism ran through the fabric of reform efforts in one of America's fin de siècle foreign affairs agencies. A separate, supplementary aspect of reform reflected the elitist outlook present in the Diplomatic Service. Junior diplomats frequently started their terms of service—"careers" is an inappropriate word in this context—on an unpaid basis. Few if any subordinate diplomatic secretaries on the payroll at the turn of the century, moreover, could support themselves abroad solely on their low salaries. These circumstances patently tended to make wealth a prerequisite to the Diplomatic Service. The veteran diplomat Henry White, for example, a Republican who resided much of his life abroad, rose to senior rank in the early 1900s. For years previously his annual salary as a secretary of legation or embassy in Europe never exceeded $2,625. White had, however, about thirty thousand dollars per year in private income and his first wife was of a wealthy Maryland family.[18]

Youthful members of this socioeconomic group largely monopolized the lesser diplomatic positions, even though not all were as rich as White. Those with family money and influence could afford to serve poorly paid apprenticeships in diplomacy. They favored legislation which would serve to enhance their access to these socially desirable diplomatic appointments, especially in European capitals. Essentially amateurs, they nevertheless cautiously furthered efforts to standardize entry requirements, tenure, and promotion—to professionalize, that is. This they did as a means to preserve their grip on Diplomatic Service positions. In this respect they as elitists were in league with those who saw, for very different reasons related to added efficiency, the need for changes in the Consular Service.[19]

Professionals, bureaucrats, and elites thus are discrete concepts even though their treatment by scholars frequently overlaps and their consideration in a reform context is rarely differentiated. Viewed with careful consideration of the complexity of these differing elements, however, professionalism in the sense of careerist ideals is most usefully seen as a process, a paradigm shift over time—a change, that is, in the way that society perceives occupational patterns through the years. "Communities of the competent," appropriately credentialed and importantly with a degree of self-control, emerge from what can be called "traditionalism" in response to increasingly demanding societal pressures. They then proceed developmentally toward an ideal of pure professionalism, a state incorporating several, if not necessarily all, facets of the various definitions set forth above.[20]

Bureaucratization is a reaction to increased complexity in modern life and has an evident overlap with ideas of professionalization. But it is more a function of the need for technocratic expertise; it is closely related to considerations of efficiency, hierarchical structure, and an organizational model. Bureaucratization also has overtones of routinized tasks below the policymaking level. Stephen Skowronek casts the concept in civil service reform terms and sums it up thus: "A civil service career system is one of the hallmarks of the modern state. Its chief characteristics are political neutrality, tenure in office, recruitment by criteria of special training or competitive examination, and uniform rules for the control of promotion, discipline, remuneration, and retirement."[21] The chief idea addressed in this definition not previously raised in the above discussion is that of political neutrality, a requirement that was anathema to political leaders of the late nineteenth century, except perhaps in principle or when their party was out of office.

Elites, a third conceptually separate group, usually simply are. Elite status is conferred by birth, inherited wealth, and social position, or by the accumulation of substantial wealth and possibly the demonstration of meritorious achievement. A key requirement is money; only in rare instances can even an accomplished person enter the ranks of the elite without a considerable fortune. Elite status can be shifted to positions of governmental authority, but that is not always the case. Elites rule in democracies much of the time, although not necessarily because of professional attainments or mastery of the rules-giving functions of bureaucracies. Members assume authority when they so choose because of their exalted positions in society and the freedom conferred by personal wealth.

The various critics of the late nineteenth-century foreign service cited above, both those of the period and of our own time, shared the assumption that the organization should have undergone a process of professionalization. By that these critics usually meant simply developing a service made up of trained careerists, better able to further United States interests abroad in an efficient manner. As one author has it, the "real fight" for reform then was not waged as a reaction to the evils of political patronage, but "was embodied in the drive to increase efficiency and economy in the public service."[22] Foreign affairs intellectuals of the day, such as Lodge and Roosevelt, who envisioned a large world role for the United States saw reform in this light, as a particularly compelling need for the efficient conduct of foreign affairs.

Scholars also cite business interests as among the most vocal in attempting to ensure that consular officers effectively promoted American trade and investment abroad. Tales of ineptitude, malfeasance, and just plain laziness on the part of consular officials sometimes were all too true. A 1904 in-house Department of State inspection report on East Asian consulates, for example, eloquently indicts two posts in China. In the previous two years critics had brought charges against the principal consular officers at Shanghai and Canton, alleging irregularities in fee collection and the issuance of passports, among other improprieties. The charges went unproven, but the incumbents did not remain much longer in office.[23]

Nor was the Diplomatic Service exempt from accusations of poor appointments—far from it, in fact, although no one inspected diplomatic missions at that time. As an example, in 1893 Alexander Watkins Terrell, a former Confederate colonel from Texas, caused amusement among his more sophisticated diplomatic colleagues by having the temerity soon after his arrival at Constantinople to lecture the sultan of the Ottoman Empire on the merits of constitutional government, a singularly inappropriate subject of conversation under the circumstances.[24] Washington took note of the performance of Henry Maxwell Smythe of Virginia, minister resident and consul general in Haiti at the turn of the century, and eased him out of the service for repeated instances of public drunkenness at Port-au-Prince.[25] Other such episodes both in the consular and the diplomatic services will come to light later in this study.

By the early years of the twentieth century the idea of professionalism was afoot in the land for whatever reason and however defined, due in large part to the reform efforts of critics of the patronage system in government. The foreign service was set to enter the mainstream of these reform moves, only slightly delayed in comparison with other professional groups.

In the 1890s, however, no true diplomatic or consular professionals were yet on the scene. America made do, year after year, with a system for staffing posts abroad that was geared to the fortunes and needs of political parties. The foreign service in those days was a compact, if not to say tiny, organization by present-day standards, an organization still with limited sets of duties, again if we compare it with the diplomatic and consular establishment of the post–World War II period. Post complements were small. There were far fewer diplomatic missions than today, more small consular posts, and, to the last legation and consulate, all were staffed by amateurs by definition—well-to-do gentlemen amateurs in some instances and so-called party hacks in others. It was the twilight era of amateurism in American history.

These posts obviously had to be staffed, whatever the system or the state of play in reform efforts. How was the officer complement chosen? How did one obtain an appointment in the nonprofessional foreign service of the days just before the turn of the century? In assessing the validity of the critical evaluations of those appointees and the need for professional reform, the next chapter will provide an account of the selection and appointment procedures of the 1890s.

| 3 |

Staffing the Senior Ranks

*Every little thing in the way of a public office seems to be so stren-
uously sought for that it is very difficult to obtain even the humblest
position.*
　　　　　*Assistant Secretary of State David J. Hill to Andrew D.
　　　　　White, 6 Nov. 1900, Andrew D. White Papers*

One day in November of 1894 J. G. Martin of North Carolina sat
down to compose a letter. As chairman of the county Democratic executive committee, he wrote from Asheville to his senator in Washington,
the veteran politician and former Confederate general Matt Whitaker
Ransom. Martin asked Ransom for help in getting a government job,
more specifically, an assignment in the Consular Service. He cited his
services to the party and noted financial losses of recent months. Martin
failed to set forth any qualifications that he may have had for a consular
appointment, possibly assuming it was not necessary because the senator
knew him personally.

The local party leader showed in his letter that he had done his home-
work by mentioning specific assignments remaining unfilled by deserving
Democrats in President Grover Cleveland's second administration, inaugurated over a year and a half before. The consular posts at Havana,
Manchester, Canton, Osaka, and "a few others" particularly interested
the applicant, with the first two named highest on his wish list. He
concluded his missive with a plea for Ransom's urgent assistance in beat-
ing "the great rush for what is left of Executive patronage . . . before the
few remaining places are filled."[1]

Martin's efforts went unrewarded. The consul general at Havana, Ramon O. Williams, who began as vice consul general in Cuba in 1874,
exceptionally lasted in office until 1896. Williams thus can be counted
as one of the few old-timers in the nineteenth-century American foreign

service. The other posts Martin mentioned went to other aspirants. He nevertheless followed the normal procedure for the times by seeking appointment to a consulate or diplomatic mission on the basis of connections and party affiliation. There was little or no nonsense about examinations, prior experience abroad, language abilities, or other explicit personal criteria on suitability.

Diplomatic envoys and consular representatives came and went in those days, with a few exceptions like Williams at Havana, in synchronization with the changing tides of political fortune. Secretary of State John Hay remarked in the late 1890s that the pressures brought to bear on him for appointments to posts abroad were "almost indescribable." In dealing with the same pressures some years earlier Secretary William M. Evarts threatened to place over his door a sign reading, "Come Ye Disconsulate." Picking up on the phrase, Hay also commented as secretary that "the Major" (President William McKinley) had already promised all the consulates, but importuning senators would "refuse to believe me disconsulate." A young Yale graduate, himself a seeker after a diplomatic post, describes the scramble for appointments in March 1897 when McKinley was inaugurated: "I was one of the countless office-seekers that turned [Washington] into a mad-house. . . . Uncouth men, with Foreign Service lists in their hands, would run down the salary column, stop at an attractive figure, and ask me 'where in hell' the place was."[2]

In the nineteenth century it was a "quadrennial Washington phenomenon, the convergence on the city of would-be officeholders which [resembled] nothing so much as a blight of locusts."[3] The men in this study—there were no women in the ranks at all—held top diplomatic and consular service positions during three administrations in the last decade of the nineteenth century (see appendix B for a list of posts): the Republicans under Benjamin Harrison at the beginnings of the nineties, Grover Cleveland and the Democrats from 1893 to 1897, and the Republicans again with William McKinley's victory in the election of 1896.

Harrison's secretary of state for most of his term was the Plumed Knight, the popular James G. Blaine of Maine. Blaine had been secretary briefly in the Garfield administration a decade earlier, before he was an unsuccessful presidential candidate. When Blaine abruptly resigned as secretary in 1892, John W. Foster of Indiana, a veteran senior diplomat in Republican administrations, took his place and held office until early 1893. Cleveland appointed Walter Q. Gresham, also of Indiana, a longtime nationally prominent Republican who nonetheless supported the Democratic cause in the 1892 elections. After Gresham's sudden death in office in 1895, Richard Olney, the combative attorney general from

John Milton Hay, ambassador to Great Britain, 1897–98. Photo by famed Washington, D.C., portrait photographer Frances Benjamin Johnston, ca. 1898. Hay also held office as secretary of state from 1898 to his death in 1905. (Courtesy Library of Congress.)

Massachusetts, succeeded him. Beginning in 1897 McKinley's secretaries of state in turn were the venerable Ohio senator, John Sherman, William R. Day of Ohio (briefly), and from 1898 former junior diplomat, assistant secretary of state, ambassador, and editor John Hay, whom the president plucked out of the embassy at London for the job.

Patronage appointments to the ranks of the foreign service made through the time-honored spoils system, the system that Martin attempted to use through his senator, were the rule almost without exception. In 1893 the outgoing minister to Peru, John Hicks of Wisconsin, put the point with perhaps inadvertent bluntness in a letter to the president of Peru: "Following the custom which prevails in the United States of organizing its diplomatic representatives in accord with the actual [i.e., current] administration," he announced his recall and the arrival of his successor.[4] In 1890 when the administration named the editor and publisher of the Republican *Press* of Philadelphia as minister to Russia, a journalistic colleague praised the appointment editorially, although writing for a Democratic paper. With humorous hyperbolic abandon this southern editorialist commented, "Of course, it would be better for this country, and for civilization, to have a Democrat lunch every day with the Czar; but since it must be a Republican, why, then, God speed you Charles Emory Smith."[5]

No clear-cut path led to entry into the fin de siècle foreign service. Someone not well known in Washington usually wrote to the secretary of state or to the president or president-elect. Some of those who sought office abroad did so by personal visits to Washington, but most seem to have submitted applications in writing. Contact with an aspirant's congressional delegation definitely helped; a senator was an almost-necessary ally, and aspirants often enlisted the support of state political leaders. Nearly all applicants were associated with the political party in power or coming into office, and they were at pains to feature that association. But during the 1890s they were not usually nationally known political figures. A few examples of successful applicants may be illustrative.

John Robert Graham Pitkin, for instance, a New Orleans lawyer and government official who remained loyal to the Union during the Civil War, submitted sheaves of letters and petitions from supporters both in 1889 and in 1897 to show his loyalty and service to the Republican cause. In 1889 he obtained the legation to Argentina under Harrison, but later settled for the postmastership at New Orleans during the McKinley administration. Many who were appointed to senior posts came well recommended by their congressmen. Wakefield G. Frye of Maine, consul general at Halifax, Nova Scotia, from 1882 to 1885 and again from 1889 to 1893, could claim support for the position in a thick file of petitions and letters from, among others, the state legislature and Maine's influential Senator William P. Frye, a "kinsman." In 1897 William Frank Powell of New Jersey, a black educator, mobilized eight members of the House of Representatives and Senator W. J. Sewell in his successful bid to be named minister to Haiti.[6]

A number of applicants highlighted special qualifications. In 1893, as one example, an Indiana newspaper editor and publisher named Luther Short submitted a hefty set of recommendations to the Department of State from his backers to demonstrate his links with the Democratic party as a journalist, member of the state legislature, and national elector in the victorious campaign of 1892. He was rewarded with the consul generalship at Constantinople, his first choice among seven posts he specified. William T. Townes of Danville, Virginia, became the United States consul general at Rio de Janeiro in 1893 as a result of endorsements by all of the local Virginia and North Carolina tobacco associations; under a new treaty with Brazil, the tobacco industry expected to increase exports to that country and Townes was an acknowledged expert in the field.[7] In 1889 John True Abbott of Keene, New Hampshire, aspired to the diplomatic mission in Colombia on the strength of a previous sojourn of about a year at Medillin. He could claim therefore to be familiar with the language and customs of the country. The initiative was successful; Abbott was United States minister at Bogota throughout the Harrison years.[8]

The record reveals other instances of applicants with out-of-the-ordinary qualifications. In 1893 Edward Spencer Pratt presented several special reasons he should be appointed. First, he was the son of a wealthy banker and previously had been minister and consul general at Tehran. His "considerable social prominence" helped his case, according to the press. Also, as he wrote to President Cleveland, his education in Europe was undertaken "with the distinct object in mind of equipping me for the Diplomatic Service." Further, after talking with the president he wrote in support of his application for an assignment in Turkey that he was an experienced physician who could assist there if an epidemic should break out. Lastly, to bolster his candidacy for the post as envoy to Belgium, he claimed acquaintance with the royal family. It is not clear which of these arguments was most persuasive, but Pratt did become consul general at Singapore.[9]

The magic political wand touched others seeking office abroad. In 1893 Charles Monroe Dickinson, a fifty-one-year-old editor in Binghamton, New York, had just made a year-long tour abroad with his family. "My year in Europe had given me a taste for the attractions of the Old World, and I greatly desired to extend my European travels," he wrote. The *Binghamton Press* picked up the story:

After his return to Binghamton in 1893 he resumed his activities with his newspaper, politics and writing. Shortly afterward George A. Kent and James C. Truman of this city, chatting together on their way to New York by train, agreed that Mr. Dickinson was the type of man needed abroad, and on their return home they broached the matter to Colonel George W. Dunn, the county Republican leader, who approved it enthusiastically. Colonel Dunn went to Thomas C. Platt, the all powerful state leader, who said, "Anything I can do for Mr. Dickinson I will do."

Since the Democrat Cleveland was in the White House at the time, the Republican Dickinson had to wait. In 1897, soon after McKinley entered office, Platt telegraphed to Dickinson that the president would like to see him. Dickinson went to Washington and met with Platt and Congressman George W. Ray of his district. " 'I am urging you as Minister to Spain,' Platt said" in the third-person press account.

> "I want no kid glove post," Mr. Dickinson replied. "There is business—real business—that needs attention abroad, and I have no desire for a ministry and the social functions that would go with it."
> The President was cordial at the interview which followed, but made no promises. Within a short time, however, he informed Platt that he was so favorably impressed with Mr. Dickinson that he could have his choice of any post then open. Cairo, Constantinople, St. Petersburg and others were mentioned.
> Mr. Dickinson's decision was promptly made. "I will take the consul-generalship in Constantinople."[10]

In January 1898 he arrived at post to begin an unusually long eight-year assignment as consul general there and, concurrently for two years in the early 1900s, as diplomatic agent accredited to Bulgaria.

North Carolina's local Democratic leader J. G. Martin, on the other hand, failed like many others in his bid to go abroad as a consular officer in 1894, "if only for the next two years," as he had put it. One possible reason lay in his timing. His letter to Senator Ransom was occasioned by the surprising state elections a few days previously which resulted in a legislature captured from the Democrats by a Populist-Republican coalition. Since state legislatures elected members of the United States Senate then, Ransom, a Democrat whose term was expiring and who was approaching seventy years of age, had his own problems. He was soon to be ousted from office after twenty-three years in Congress. Ransom also could use some gainful employment, and understandably he would be less concerned about Martin's needs than his own.

The North Carolina senator had a considerably stronger claim on the administration than did an obscure county-level politician. Ransom had played a prominent role in the political Compromise of 1877 that ended the era of Reconstruction. He was one of the half dozen leading southern Democrats considered for a place in Cleveland's first cabinet in the 1880s. Congress officially designated him and Senator John Sherman of Ohio in March 1885 to escort the president to the inaugural ceremonies at the Capitol. Although faced a decade later with the loss of his seat in the Senate, he was a political figure of some prominence. Accordingly, the Cleveland administration found a place for him as United States envoy extraordinary and minister plenipotentiary—minister, that is—to Mexico, one of the forty-four nations with which the United States had diplomatic relations in the mid-1890s. Confirmed by his colleagues in the Senate shortly after nomination, Ransom was in Mexico City by April 1895 to take up his new duties.[11]

These two maneuvers to obtain place, the one by Ransom successful and the effort by Martin not, illustrate the way America staffed its diplomatic and consular services in the decades prior to the reforms which began in the early 1900s. While a given individual application and its disposition may be of little historical consequence, instances of the appointive process provide useful clues to staffing procedures and the organizational structure of the foreign service.

Another illustration of how the political process worked is the case of Edward Campbell Little, a young Kansas lawyer active in Republican party affairs on the state level who continued petitioning the executive mansion for the somewhat hollow honor of being named diplomatic agent and consul general at Cairo late in 1892. The previous incumbent at Cairo, John Alexander Anderson, a one-time college roommate of President Harrison's, had died on his way back to the United States in 1892. Little began his campaign for the job that summer. He remained interested even though the Republicans lost the national elections that fall and an almost clean sweep of the administration's appointees could be expected within months. With an eye to his future career, Little nevertheless wanted the eleventh-hour assignment. The president obliged by naming him to the post, one of several of his "midnight" appointments late in his single term in office. Little made the long voyage to Egypt, presented his credentials as American diplomatic representative in April 1893, and returned for good to Kansas four months later. Similarly, Sempronious Hamilton Boyd of Missouri, a lawyer and staunch Republican who had served two terms in Congress in the 1860s, applied for the position of minister to Venezuela when Harrison was inaugurated in 1889. As part of Boyd's argument that he should have the job, he contended in the many letters he and his supporters sent to Washington that many years before he had been selected for the post by Abraham Lincoln, but that Lincoln's assassination prevented his nomination. A quarter of a century later Boyd was still eager for the post. In one of several letters to incoming Secretary of State James G. Blaine, he even offered to decline or resign an appointment to Caracas in advance "as a last resort" if the administration wished.[12] The essential point for him was that an offer be made publicly, even if not a sincere or valid one, because his fellow Missourians were aware that he was angling for the assignment. He did not get Venezuela after all, but his perseverance paid off; he went to Bangkok as minister resident and consul general.

The institutional makeup of the foreign service at this time included one important pre-careerist aspect aside from the patronage character of the appointment process. Diplomatic and consular titles and salaries were attached to the posts; titles and ranks were not granted as personal designations until passage of the Stone-Flood Act of 1915. A fortunate job seeker who managed to obtain one assignment as consul general, say, and then was doubly blessed by being named to another post, did not necessarily receive the same title or salary the second time around; that depended on where he was sent. Because of this administrative detail, would-be diplomats and consular officers often petitioned the executive mansion and the Department of State for specific posts and positions, not for appointment at large into an organization.

The experience of a Mississippi editor named William Brooks Sorsby exemplifies this facet of the system. During the Harrison presidency, Sorsby was consul general at Guayaquil. Out of the Consular Service during the Democratic administration of Cleveland, 1893–97, he returned upon the election of McKinley, but only as consul at San Juan del Norte, Nicaragua, and at less pay. Another officer included in this collective biography is George Herbert Bridgman, who practiced medicine in New Hampshire and New Jersey for many years. He started out in the foreign service as minister to Bolivia under McKinley. Bridgman obtained office later under Theodore Roosevelt, but faired less well; in an unusual move, he accepted a less prestigious position as consul at Kingston, Jamaica, like Sorsby at a smaller salary than before.[13]

Few aspirants for diplomatic or consular office were as fortunate as Little, Boyd, Sorsby, and Bridgman. More usual was the fate of our friend Martin or that of Walden Pell Anderson of New York City. In 1897, early in the McKinley presidency, Anderson received a brush-off letter in response to his attempts to obtain a European assignment: "The President is unable to give as much personal attention as might otherwise be the case to individual applications for office," wrote the president's secretary, J. Addison Porter. "I cannot see that your chance of success would be increased by another personal visit to the Executive Mansion." Porter suggested that the applicant send additional testimonials to the Department of State for further consideration. Anderson was a college graduate; he had a long list of supporters, including members of the New York congressional delegation; he reportedly spoke three foreign languages; the outgoing consul at Brunswick, Germany, recommended him as his replacement; and he was well known in New York society. But for some reason not revealed in the record, the president and the Department of State passed him over. By early summer Anderson gave up and departed Washington for New York after two months in town seeking an assignment abroad.

His case illustrates the point already made, that there was no clear path to office, no uniform set of rules to the game. Even one so adept at securing patronage as Illinois Senator Shelby M. Cullom on occasion failed. In 1892 he tried to obtain from President Harrison an appointment as envoy to Italy for Governor John H. Hamilton of Illinois, citing the latter's legal abilities and integrity—and his need for "a little more salubrious climate" due to a recent illness.[14] Perhaps fortunately for the governor's health, he was spared the rigors of an ocean trip; Cullom's possibly tongue-in-cheek request was not honored in this instance.

The National Archives in Washington, D.C., contains shelf after shelf of carefully ordered Department of State files on these applicants for diplomatic or consular appointments. The documents cover more than a century. Most of the applicants' files consist of letters to the president or secretary of state either from job seekers or from their backers. Some applicants submitted elaborate folios of testimonials and petitions from dozens of supporters. Others limited themselves to a letter or two of inquiry.

Many were called but few were chosen. Not enough posts existed abroad to satisfy the patronage demand, and many applicants, even though of the "right" party and possibly even qualified, evidently had no compelling political claim on the administration for a patronage reward. A systematic sampling of these Applications Files for the period 1885 to 1901 indicates that roughly 21,400 persons inquired about Department of State jobs abroad or had inquiries or recommendations made in their behalf. The approximate subtotals by filing period are: 1885–93 (eight years), 8,300 applicants; 1893–97 (four years), 5,000; 1897–1901 (four years), 8,100. The total number of positions overseas available during those years (see chapter 5) suggests that less than one in five job applicants succeeded.[15]

For those who did succeed, no explicit criteria for appointment are readily apparent from perusal of these files. The authorities chose some few individuals not well known to history on the basis of word-of-mouth reputations, friendships, or unwritten recommendations. An example in this category is Richard Gregory Lay, a Civil War veteran who was consul general at Ottawa from 1889 to 1893. A Department of State application file under his name in the National Archives contains only one item, a telegram from Vice President Levi P. Morton to Secretary Blaine confirming that "Colonel Lay" accepted the assignment and that he was from the District of Columbia.[16] Lay's ties with Morton, Blaine, or the president at the time are not reflected in the file and he was far from being a well-known individual.

Some would-be senior diplomats of the period did not have to bother with letters of application and petitions, given the political criteria for appointment. These were the nationally known figures, or those with close ties with Washington leaders, who were interested for one reason or another in service abroad. Robert Todd Lincoln, the late president's son, filled the prestigious post of minister to Great Britain during the Harrison administration, and presidential offspring Frederick Dent Grant was at Vienna during the same time span. In 1893 Thomas Francis Bayard, a long-service senator from a prominent Delaware family, succeeded Lincoln at London, thus actually taking a demotion from his previous position as secretary of state in the first Cleveland administration (1885–89). John Hay—he of the "dis-consulate" remark—had been a private secretary to President Lincoln and by the 1890s was a well-known New York newspaper editor and author. As we have remarked, he made the reverse transition; after a year as President McKinley's ambassador at London, he returned to Washington in 1898 as secretary of state. (The post was raised from legation to embassy rank in 1893, with Bayard as America's first ambassador.) Truxtun Beale held senior diplomatic assignments from 1891 to 1894 while in his thirties; although not nationally prominent, he happened to be the son-in-law of Secretary of State Blaine. The American minister to Belgium under Cleveland in the nineties, James Stevenson Ewing, was the law partner and relative of Vice President Adlai Ewing Stevenson. In 1897 McKinley appointed his cousin, lifelong friend, and political associate William McKinley Osborne to the desirable post of consul general at London.

Senior foreign service appointees of whatever personal standing entered the 1890s service with but the most cursory examination, if any at all. The McKinley administration initiated standardized application forms and instituted board interviews in some instances for aspiring high-level consular officers. One such nominee who was subjected to scrutiny by the Department of State was John Kilby Pollard, an Ohio state official and former state senator. Provided in advance with a copy of the consular regulations and a pamphlet on the new screening procedures, the fifty-four-year-old Pollard underwent a test in December 1897 in Washington. Two assistant secretaries of state and the consular bureau chief composed the examining board. They noted after meeting with him that the applicant was wanting in knowledge of the consular regulations and unable to speak Spanish, even though evidently he had wintered in Mexico several times, but found nevertheless that "his general intelligence qualifies him for the duties of the office."[17] The office in question was that of consul general at Monterrey. Pollard essentially already had the political appointment in hand, and the examining board's action simply ratified him as the president's choice. He duly received the post and proceeded to Mexico with his wife and daughter.

Turnover in senior staff through the years was extensive, given the nature of the patronage system and changes in administrations. Few officers lasted very long in the senior ranks of the diplomatic and consular services. From among the thousands of applicants for place brought on by three changes in administrations during the nineties, the Washington leadership picked over two hundred men perforce to head up the approximately seventy major posts abroad that were staffed at any one time during this period. The advent of each new president brought widespread changes in diplomatic and consular representation abroad. This was true at all levels, junior and senior. The political system sooner or later touched practically all ranks, and the decade of the nineties was a particularly restive period because of the changes from Republican to Democratic and back to Republican administrations.

As an illustration of how shifts in current staffing came about, in 1899 Consul Julius Gareche Lay at Windsor, Ontario, got a rude shock. He had begun in the service ten years before as a young clerk at Ottawa under his father, Consul General Richard G. Lay, and had survived as a lower-ranking consular officer through both the Harrison and Cleveland administrations and for two years under McKinley. By now he perhaps had reason to expect continuity of service. But in April he read the following in the *Detroit Free Press:* "The Michigan senators went to the White House this morning [April 10] to remind the President that a good many Republican faithful of the state are still out of office. The President received the intimations very sympathetically. . . . As an evidence of good faith, he promised that Stanley W. Turner should have the United States consulship at Windsor, and that the present incumbent, Mr. Lay, should be provided for elsewhere." Little did Lay, like his father a native of the District of Columbia, know that the department had already decided to shift him to the post at Barcelona, as consul general it happens, and at twice his salary at Windsor. By July 1899 he was in Spain and his earlier grounds for complaint were overtaken by promotion to a major consular post.[18]

The aforementioned E. Spencer Pratt is another long-serving officer who was relieved. By 1899 Pratt, the consul general at Singapore since 1893, had a total of eleven years of service in three administrations over the previous thirteen years (he was minister resident and consul general at Tehran from 1886 to 1891). Nevertheless, his days were numbered. Born near Mobile, Alabama, Pratt had spent most of his life abroad and, exceptionally, had not been active in politics. Incoming President Mc-Kinley inquired of the assistant secretary of state: "Judge Day: Is there any reason why a change should be made at Singapore . . . ? If made, Moseley of Ala. is recommended. WMcK." Robert Alexander Moseley, Jr., was a Birmingham editor and holder at one time or another of several political offices, including Republican state committee chairman during the 1896 election. He had backed McKinley for the presidential nomination after earlier wavering between supporting him, Levi P. Morton, and Thomas B. Reed. In early 1898 a letter to the Department of State from a Treasury Department intermediary cleared the way for the Alabama politician, Moseley, over the apolitical Alabaman, Pratt. The treasury official noted that Senator John Morgan of Alabama "has no interest in the retention of E. Spencer Pratt, consul at Singapore." Morgan agreed that the president could "make a change if he wishes to,"[19] and the Department of State made a change. Pratt was out, and Moseley was in as consul general at Singapore.

The axe could fall suddenly, even if not totally unexpectedly. In July 1890 Consul General Jared Lawrence Rathbone wrote to Secretary of State Blaine to acknowledge receipt of the latter's "cable in cypher in which [it is stated] that the President desires that I tender my resignation, &c &c." Rathbone, who was appointed to the position from the business sector in California in 1887, noted to Blaine that he had accordingly cabled "same & beg you now to convey to 'the President' my formal resignation of the office of Consul General of the United States at Paris to take effect September 1st 1890," the date arranged with his successor for the assumption of office.[20] His replacement at Paris as consul general in turn was succeeded after three years at post.

If any lessons about the would-be senior foreign service officer of the nineties finally emerge from this description of a nearly chaotic "system" of appointments, one is that political connections and reputation, including importantly in party politics on the state level, were paramount. Given this prerequisite, an aspiring appointee to any level of position from clerk to chief of mission further could expect to write frequently to the executive mansion, to the Department of State, and to his congressman or senator. A personal interview occasionally was vital, but from the record it appears this was not so as frequently as one might think in that day of small government, nor were previous experience abroad or language abilities often important qualifications. The administration usually made senior appointments to major posts on the basis of prior personal contacts or information submitted for the file and, importantly, explicit congressional support. Endorsements from the business sector also sometimes decided matters (see chapter 4). The White House closely involved itself in the most prestigious Diplomatic Service selections, and bureaucratic underlings did not take responsibility for even the lesser senior appointments. But many of these latter nominations, especially in the Consular Service, seem to have been decided at the level of the secretary of state.

The government changed every four years. In a worldwide pattern, all aspiring officers submitted their applications and supporting materials. Each serving officer then also submitted his resignation, and if he had any notion of staying on, he began marshalling whatever backing he could muster to support his petitions to the Department of State to be retained. Sometimes the process worked for a given individual, either a would-be appointee or a serving officer, but more often it did not. So the appointment merry-go-round continued its regular course. But what manner of men rode it to office? That is the concern of the next chapter.

| 4 |

A Group Portrait

*I do not want [an envoy] produced from the shades of the schools:
I want him educated in practical politics and in the administration
of high offices.*

Alberico Gentili, De Legationibus Librites (1585)

Foreign service officers gained their posts by a process that was, as
critics have long charged, political to the core. Were those, however, who
succeeded in obtaining place generally incompetent, ill-prepared for the
duties thrust upon them, as also has been charged? The answer requires
an extended analytical look at the group under study.

The following pages present certain of the essential characteristics of
the two-hundred-plus individuals who gained senior posts in the decade
of the 1890s. Those traits and attributes help to identify what kind of
people they were. As varied a lot as the 226 members of the study group
were in some respects, they had identifiable attributes of age, public reputation, occupational background, personal wealth, political experience,
race, military service (or lack thereof), and time spent in the foreign
service. Washington appointed each from a specified home state or territory, regardless of place of birth,[1] which information reveals the regional composition of the group. These various attributes, in addition to
places of birth, language abilities where known, and educational attainments will be considered in this chapter.

A survey of these various items of information permits delineation of
a suggestive set of background factors present in many senior officers
of the 1890s foreign service. An outline comes through of the kind of
persons sent abroad to represent the United States as senior officers
in the diplomatic and consular services just before the turn of the twentieth century. Despite the elusive nature of averages when applied to

groups of people, pertinent conclusions can be developed from the background data.[2]

A picture emerges from this information of a professions-oriented, educated white man just over fifty years old as the typical senior-level appointee to the United States foreign service of nearly one hundred years ago. As will be seen in the following pages, in most instances he was born in the United States and was from the Midwest or a northeastern state. Very probably he was college-trained and a lawyer, businessman, or journalist before being named to head a major post. He had an active interest in the great game of politics in nearly every case, as shown by the substantial number of appointees who had held elective office. He was not typically a full-time politician, however, even though often involved in partisan political activities, especially at the state level. Nor was he usually a national political figure. Possibly he had prior military service in a senior rank to go with his years of experience in civil life. Likely he would serve abroad only once and for a period of only some three years before returning to his usual pursuits.

Age, one of the widely varied factors present in the makeup of the appointees, serves as a basic starting point for analysis. Jacob Sleeper, a monied Bostonian educated in Europe, was only twenty-four in 1893 when given the double title of secretary of legation and consul general at Bogota. (Naming him to a consular position as well as diplomatic secretary patently was a budgetary device to avoid the expense of sending two people: his annual salary was only two thousand dollars.) John Barrett, an Oregon journalist, began service as minister resident and consul general at Bangkok in the mid-1890s at the age of twenty-seven, and the already-mentioned Julius G. Lay was the same age when he received his unexpected appointment as consul general at Barcelona. Among the older appointees was the famed abolitionist Frederick Douglass, minister resident and consul general at Port-au-Prince, 1889–91, who was close to seventy at the time, although his year of birth as a slave is uncertain. James Overton Broadhead, minister to Switzerland in middecade, was born in 1819. The ambassador to Germany during the second Cleveland administration, Theodore Runyon, died in harness at Berlin in 1896 after three years at post, aged seventy-three years.[3]

Most senior officers of the era were neither that young nor that old; well over half were in their forties or fifties when appointed. Of the 213 officers whose years of birth are known or can be estimated with reasonable accuracy, the median age at the time named to a major post is just above fifty; 103 were under fifty when appointed, and 110 were fifty years of age or older. Persons in their thirties, forties, or fifties accounted for about 80 percent of these appointees.

The men under consideration varied widely in national standing among their fellow Americans. Some few were well known, but most were not. Millions of Americans knew Frederick Douglass. Whitelaw Reid, the Republican vice presidential candidate in 1892 and *New York Tribune* publisher, was envoy during the nineties to France and later to Britain. Isaac Wayne MacVeagh was a Republican minister to Turkey in the 1870s, United States attorney general in 1881, a friend of Henry Adams, and a prominent Progressive in later years. He attained further fame of a sort by coming out publicly for Cleveland in 1892 (as did Walter Q. Gresham, Cleveland's second-term secretary of state). MacVeagh's reward was appointment as ambassador to Italy, 1893–97.[4] James Burrill Angell and Andrew Dickson White were two of the leading educators of their time. Angell was minister to Turkey at the close of the century, after earlier having served as minister to China, and White was envoy to Russia and twice to Germany.

On the other end of a "fame scale," Ellis Mills, at one time the secretary of state's stenographer, was unknown to the general public; he nevertheless became secretary of legation and consul general at Honolulu, another of the budget-saving postings, in the second Cleveland administration.[5] A little-known former schoolteacher from Vermont, David N. Burke, rose to consul general status at Tangier in middecade. Daniel W. Maratta, whose earlier employment as a United States marshal in the Dakota Territory and a steamboat captain made him something of a figure out of the old West, was consul general at Melbourne from 1893 to 1897; he is otherwise unknown to history.

These officers came from no single mold, but factors can be identified that characterized many of them, including, importantly, the way they made their living before foreign service appointment. (The group includes six persons on whom occupational information is lacking or ambiguous; see table 1.) Nearly one-half of the individuals had legal training, whether or not they pursued active careers in the law before entering the Diplomatic or Consular Service. The legal profession was the primary occupational focus of the largest segment of the 226-member group: 71 officers, or 31.4 percent of the group, were practicing lawyers or jurists.[6] In some instances these careers were combined with other activities such as business interests or, frequently, political endeavors.

All of the subjects of this study cannot readily be categorized as to one single lifelong occupation such as the law, but those on whom reliable biographic information exists nevertheless can be placed in one principal

TABLE 1

**Primary Occupational Backgrounds of Senior
U.S. Diplomatic & Consular Officers, 1890–99**

Occupation	No.	Percent
Law	71	31.4
Business	44	19.5
Journalism	35	15.5
Government	29	12.8
Agriculture	13	5.8
Education	12	5.3
Physicians & clergy	10	4.4
None[a]	6	2.6
Unknown	6	2.6
Totals	226	99.9[b]

SOURCES: Standard biographic references, Dept. of State Applications Files, press reports.
[a]Includes those with only prior foreign service experience at lesser ranks.
[b]Does not add to 100 percent due to rounding.

or most recently practiced significant occupational specialty. The background of Joseph Alexander Leonard, consul at Edinburgh and consul general at Calcutta in the 1880s and at Shanghai from 1889 to 1893, exemplifies the occupational (and also incidentally the geographic) mobility of some nineteenth-century professionals. He earned an M.D. degree at Pennsylvania in 1851 but was admitted to the bar seven years later. He practiced medicine for two years in the 1850s in Michigan and Wisconsin, edited a newspaper in Wisconsin for three years, took up the active practice of law, and then served as a captain in the Union army. After the war Leonard was a state senator and a federal land office official. A man of many parts, Leonard in later years mainly practiced law in Minnesota. He is therefore counted as a lawyer for the purposes of this study. A similar approach is used in deciding other ambiguous cases.

Among the more prominent attorneys who served at major foreign posts in the period was Joseph Hodges Choate, ambassador at London from 1899 to 1905, the foremost American corporation lawyer of his day. George Sherman Batcheller, a judge on the International Tribunal at Cairo and later a court of appeals jurist, served as minister resident and consul general at Lisbon in the early 1890s. John Ewing Risley, a minister to Denmark under Cleveland, was a successful trial lawyer in New York City before and after his diplomatic stint. Bartlett Tripp was chief justice of the South Dakota Supreme Court, and Benjamin F.

Bonham held the same position in Oregon. Tripp became minister to Austria-Hungary; Bonham was consul general at Calcutta from 1885 to 1890.

The business world and journalism are the next two largest categories of prior occupations after the law. Forty-four senior officers (19.5 percent of the total number) came primarily from banking, railroad management, manufacturing, retailing, wholesaling, overseas trade, or other business backgrounds. William Franklin Draper, as one example, presided over his family's Massachusetts textile fortune and was a congressman before serving as ambassador to Italy for three years at the end of the century. T. Jefferson Coolidge was minister to France for a year in the Harrison administration. A grandson of the third president, he set out in 1857 deliberately to amass a fortune. The tall, distinguished-looking Harvard graduate successfully involved himself in the rough and tumble of New England textile manufacturing, along with banking and railroad interests. William Simpson Carroll, first the consul and then consul general at Dresden for the unusually long span of twelve years, 1893–1905, made his fortune by investing wisely in Pennsylvania oil holdings after the Civil War. Hector de Castro was vice president of the Commercial Cable Company before his appointment in 1897 as consul general at Rome. John G. A. Leishman held an even more responsible managerial position; he was president of Carnegie Steel for more than a decade prior to beginning a sixteen-year diplomatic career, first as minister to Berne in 1897.

The number of appointments made from the business sector late in the decade is no great surprise. As a manufacturer wrote to president-elect McKinley at the beginning of 1897, "Now that this country is commencing to do business with the world, business men are requesting if not demanding . . . that thorough and practical businessmen shall be placed in the Consular service." Shortly thereafter, another business figure expressed to a colleague: "As a manufacturer interested in export trade, I trust and believe that the incoming President and his advisers will conside[r] the business qualifications of applicants for Consular positions, as the opinion now prevails that lawyers and other professional men are not as well qualified for such places as those who have seen active service in the commercial world." McKinley was receptive to these arguments. In 1895, as governor of Ohio, he wrote to a trade paper in St. Louis "that in [his] judgment the commercial travelers have peculiar qualifications for the consular service. . . . Business men accustomed to trade . . . are required in our consular service."[7] The president was as good as his word when he entered office two years later. He appointed sixteen business sector representatives to senior diplomatic and consular posts, including several persons who had served earlier in the Harrison administration.

President Harrison, however, two administrations before, had appointed an even larger number of businessmen—more than twenty—to similar positions. The business appointments over the decade were about evenly split between the diplomatic and consular services, not weighted toward the latter as one might expect from the above-cited rhetoric.

The Republican party was the party of business throughout the decade as far as foreign service appointments were concerned. Scrutiny of appointment patterns shows that the contrast in business and nonbusiness appointments is not between McKinley's and earlier administrations, despite his explicit recognition of the importance of businessmen in promoting foreign trade. Rather, the contrast is between Republican and Democratic rule of the executive branch at the end of the nineteenth century. Cleveland named fewer than half a dozen business figures to the senior foreign service ranks during the nineties, and not all of them necessarily were due to commercial qualifications; he selected two of those in question largely to meet the needs of ethnic voting blocs. The Democratic appointees in middecade included more lawyers and persons from agricultural backgrounds than were named in each of the Republican administrations of the era.

Editors, publishers, journalists, and men of letters in the 1890s senior foreign service totalled thirty-five appointees (15.5 percent), the third largest grouping of prior occupational specialties after lawyers and businessmen. This is less than startling in an age of governmental appointments as political rewards. Partisan editors, if influential and on the winning side in national elections, could demand their due from an incoming administration for past support rendered in the black and white of newsprint. On occasion this reward took the form of a foreign service nomination. Named consul general at Montreal in the Republican year of 1897, John Lawrence Bittinger, a Republican editor in Missouri for more than three decades, remained at his Canadian post for five years. Lewis Baker was an editor and publisher for many years in West Virginia and Minnesota before being named in 1893 as chief of diplomatic mission to three Central American countries, based at Managua, Nicaragua. The ethnologist William Churchill, consul general in Samoa from 1896 to 1897, later was an editor of the *New York Sun,* and the wealthy socialite Frederic Courtland Penfield, consul general at Cairo in the mid-nineties and minister to Austria-Hungary fifteen years later, earlier had worked for a few years as a reporter in Connecticut. Both are included in this category.

Next in the list of prior occupations is the general grouping of those from appointive and elective government, including local, state, and national. Twenty-nine envoys and consuls general (12.8 percent of the total) can best be described as semipermanent government employees at the time of their appointments, even though only the rudiments of a career civil service existed as yet. The former congressman and short-term minister to Hawaii, James Henderson Blount of Georgia, fits into this category despite his legal training; he was directly involved in the federal government as a member of Congress for more than two decades before losing an election and being handed a diplomatic assignment.[8] The minister successively to Greece and Spain in the early 1890s, Archibald Loudon Snowden, also read law but spent his career before the foreign service mainly at the United States Mint at Philadelphia, with two years out as mayor of the city. The renowned William Woodville Rockhill was in and out of the Diplomatic Service and the Department of State so often for so many years, beginning in a junior capacity when he was thirty years of age, that his background can best be counted as governmental. John P. Bray exemplifies an officer from appointive positions at the state and local government level. He was a county and state auditor and a postmaster in North Dakota for a decade before starting a long Consular Service career in 1897 as consul general at Melbourne.

Disregarding occupations for the moment, we note that thirty senior officers served in Congress before appointment to an overseas post. Five others were elected to Congress for the first time after service abroad, and one later held a one-year appointment as United States senator. Many of the thirty former congressmen possibly saw such foreign service assignments as a comedown. Gilded Age senators, at any rate, did not especially seek appointive office, not even in the president's cabinet, in the view of David J. Rothman. "Positions on the court or in an embassy were even less attractive," he writes. "Both places usually ended political careers and neither offered compensatory rewards."[9] Fourteen of the 1890s appointees had been governors, including six who also were United States representatives or senators. A net total of thirty-eight senior diplomats and consular officials (16.8 percent of the group under study) thus had prior high-level political experience and reputations in the Congress or governors' mansions or both—about one in six of those appointed. Most are not classified herein as having primarily government backgrounds, however; only those such as James H. Blount who for years had not done much of anything else but serve in the halls of Congress are so categorized. As an additional commentary on the political

William Woodville Rockhill, envoy to Greece, China, Russia, and Turkey at different periods from 1897 to 1913. Photo by Frances Benjamin
Johnston, taken in Washington probably about 1895, when Rockhill was
assistant secretary of state. (Courtesy Library of Congress.)

nature of most appointments, fifty subjects of the study (22.1 percent),
including individuals already counted as congressmen or governors, are
known to have been members of state legislatures. One further appointee
was elected to a state legislature for the first time after service abroad.

The occupational field of education accounted for twelve senior appointees (5.3 percent), including James B. Angell and Andrew D. White, previously mentioned. Laurits Selmer Swenson held a number of assignments abroad off and on during Republican administrations, starting as minister to Denmark in 1897 and not ending until 1934 when he retired as minister to the Netherlands. He was a school principal in Minnesota before taking his first post abroad at the age of thirty-two. Arthur Sherburn Hardy was posted overseas in several senior assignments, also beginning under McKinley. He had been a professor of engineering and mathematics for more than twenty years, most of the time at Dartmouth College. Minister to Haiti William Frank Powell earlier taught with the Freedmen's Bureau and served as a school superintendent in New Jersey.

As demonstrated thus far, the occupational backgrounds of these officers fall largely into the areas of law, business, journalism, government, and education. One remaining grouping represented in appreciable numbers is agriculture—ranchers, farmers, and planters—with thirteen (5.8 percent of the total). Finally, four clergymen and six physicians (for a combined percentage of 4.4) also were to be found among the senior diplomats and consuls at major posts; they comprise one further category of occupations in table 1. As one example of a clergyman-diplomat, William Henry Heard of Pennsylvania, assigned in the double capacity of diplomatic envoy and consul general at Monrovia in the mid-1890s, was an ordained minister for more than two decades. Physicians in the group included the Irish-born Jeremiah Coughlin, an expatriate American who spent most of his life in Colombia. He was secretary of legation and consul general at Bogota, his then-current place of residence, for seventeen months at the end of the Harrison administration.[10] It is unusually difficult to classify a few officers on whom background information has been developed; several younger appointees are considered not to have followed any career prior to entering the foreign service. Finally, information on occupations followed is simply lacking on six individuals.

As to financial standing, many of the businessman-consuls general and lawyer-envoys were well off. In some instances they had to be to accept appointment. William Walter Phelps of New Jersey for instance inherited a large import trade and railroad fortune; he was minister to Austria-Hungary in the early 1880s and to Germany under Harrison. Charlemagne Tower of Pennsylvania was well suited to the foreign service; his "wealth, reputation for learning, and Republican politics made him a logical candidate for diplomatic honors" when McKinley came to office.[11] He went from the presidency of a railroad and the managing directorship of a large iron manufacturing company founded by his father to an eleven-year career as minister or ambassador to three European nations in succession. Ethan Allen Hitchcock made a fortune as an active partner in the trading firm Olyphant and Company of Hong Kong by the time he reached his midthirties. After returning to America he had interests in manufacturing, mining, and railways until named by McKinley as minister to Russia in 1897. The listing of demonstrably rich senior diplomats (especially) and consular officials could be continued at length.

Some senior officers were not so rich, however. Edwin Hurd Conger of Iowa, a former rancher and ex-congressman, served as minister to Brazil twice and to China during the nineties. He resigned as minister to Mexico in 1905 after only a few months, however, pleading his inability to meet the expenses of the post despite the allocation of a $17,500 salary, tops in the Diplomatic Service. Matt W. Ransom, one of Conger's predecessors at Mexico City, had to economize because of pressing money problems at home. "I am determined to save at least $1,000 per month," he wrote to a son in North Carolina early in his two-year tour as minister, this on a monthly salary of $1,500. He was "enduring misery" in a foreign land for the sake of family finances.[12]

The Washington political leadership generally made appointments to senior Diplomatic and Consular Service positions on a nationwide geographic basis over the decade under review. No available evidence, however, suggests that conscious policy decisions dictated the appointment pattern, as was the case with junior career appointments years later in our own time. One exception to the national character of these appointments is the relative paucity of appointees from the Deep South, which clearly shows that former Confederates, by now late in the century mainly Democrats, not surprisingly had difficulty in obtaining jobs under a patronage system in a primarily Republican era. Diplomatic envoys and consuls general were chosen nevertheless from states as widely separated as Maine and California, as Florida and Washington, and from most states and territories in between (see table 2). In the 1890s the Department of State sent overseas a broad geographic representation of Americans, with the one regional exception noted, not a selection of individuals principally from the Northeast or from any other one area of the country.

New York was the leading state of residence for appointees; 25 of the 226 officers in this study hailed from the Empire State, Cleveland's home base as it happens. New York also had the largest number of electoral college votes in the nation at this time (see table 2 for a comparison of appointments, 1890 population, and 1892 electoral votes). Following New York, the states next most heavily represented were Indiana, Harrison's home state, and Pennsylvania, with 14 appointees each. The latter had the second-largest number of 1892 electoral college votes, but Indiana ranked down the line in that regard. Far off (from Washington) California had a dozen senior officers during the decade. The presidents named 10 representatives each to posts abroad from Ohio, McKinley's state of residence, from the District of Columbia (which had no electoral votes), and from politically important Missouri. Most appointees from Missouri had moved there from elsewhere at some stage of their careers. John Lee Peak, minister to Switzerland for eighteen months under Cleveland, for example, was born and educated in Kentucky; in 1879 at the age of thirty-one he moved to Kansas City to take up a law practice. There he remained, except for his tour at Berne, until his death in 1911.

Administrations in Washington made statistically significant numbers of appointments from several other states in the nineties. Illinois and Iowa had 8 each; Minnesota, Michigan, and Massachusetts, 7 each; Wisconsin, Virginia, and North Carolina, 6; and Maine, Tennessee, Oregon, and New Jersey had 5 each. The only state outside the sparsely populated West not favored with a senior appointment during the decade was South Carolina.

On a regional basis, the bulk of the appointees did not come from the Northeast, New York's record notwithstanding. The twelve North Central states as designated by the Census Bureau—most of the Midwest—had 35.4 percent of all appointments, but only 26.4 percent of the 1892 electoral college votes. This area had as well 35.7 percent of the United States' 1890 population of almost sixty-three million. The Census Bureau's North Atlantic states, from New Jersey and Pennsylvania northeastward through New York and New England, got 29.6 percent of the senior appointments through the 1890s, compared with the region's 27.8 percent of the 1890 population. The South Atlantic census area, the Atlantic seaboard from Maryland down to Florida, had 15.5 percent of these political appointments and 14.2 percent of the people. The West, with only 4.8 percent of the population, received 9.7 percent of the senior posts. Viewed from this regional angle, the total of appointments made in comparison with national population figures indicates the approximately proportional representation of most regions other than the South Central census area.

Only the eight South Central states from Kentucky through the middle South to Texas and Oklahoma Territory were slighted. Those largely

TABLE 2

**Census Regions and States of Residence of Senior U.S.
Diplomatic and Consular Officers, 1890–99**

Total Appts. by Region[a]	Region Totals	Region %		
		of total appts.	of 1890 pop.	of 1892 Elec.[b]
N. Central Region: Ind.-14, Ohio-10, Mo.-10 Ill.-8, Iowa-8, Mich.-7 Minn.-7, Wis.-6, Kans.-4 Nebr.-3, N.D.-2, S.D.-1	80	35.4	35.7	26.4
N. Atlantic Region: N.Y.-25, Pa.-14, Mass.-7 Maine-5, N.J.-5, Conn.-3 N.H.-4, Vt.-3, R.I.-1	67	29.6	27.8	26.4
S. Atlantic Region: D.C.-10, Va.-6, N.C.-6 Ga.-5, Md.-3, Fla.-2 Del.-2, W.Va.-1	35	15.5	14.2	12.8
S. Central Region: Tenn.-5, Ky.-4, Ala.-4 Ark.-3, La.-2, Tex.-2 Miss.-2	22	9.7	17.5	19.1
W. Region: Calif.-12, Oreg.-5, Wash.-3 Mont.-1, Ariz.-1	22	9.7	4.8	15.3
Totals	226	99.9[c]	100.0	100.0

SOURCES: *Official Registers; F.S. Lists;* Diplomatic and Consular Lists; *Abstract of Census 1890.*

[a]The following had no appointees: S.C., Okla., Terr., Wyo., N.Mex. Terr., Utah, Nev., Idaho, and Colo.
[b]Electoral College percentages.
[c]Does not add to 100 percent due to rounding.

Democratic states got only 9.7 percent of the senior assignments in the decade of the nineties, compared with their 17.5 percent of the 1890 population and 19.1 percent of the electoral college votes. Southerners could hardly expect appointment through the spoils system under Republican administrations if they retained affiliations with the Democratic party, as most did. Republican administrations were in office six years during the decade in question. One other explanation of the South's fewer appointments is possible, however; blacks made up almost a third of the region's nearly eleven million people, a would-be Republican segment of the population that was in process of being almost completely disenfranchised. If we disregard that group, the South Central region's white—that is, voting—population was closer to being proportionally represented by the political system in the senior foreign service of the era.[13]

The ranks of the senior foreign service included a substantial number of Civil War veterans. Although the military records of all 226 subjects are not available, at least 68 of the officers, or about 30 percent of the total, are known to have served in either blue or gray uniforms. About two-thirds of the veterans were in the Union army. At least 8 appointees served actively in the military at some time other than the 1861–65 era, although no active duty military officers were named to the foreign service. George Earl Maney, a Confederate general turned Republican and a senior diplomat in Latin America from 1881 to 1894, also saw action in the Mexican War, for example. James Ray Hosmer was on General Sheridan's staff during the Civil War and went to Cuba as a captain during the Spanish-American War. He was secretary of legation and consul general at Guatemala from 1887 to the autumn of 1890.

A number of former soldiers held modest ranks during the Civil War. John Kennedy Gowdy of Indiana, consul general at the highly desirable post of Paris from 1897 to 1905, served for three full years as a private in the Union army. Clifton Rodes Breckenridge, son of a vice president and Cleveland's minister to Russia in the midnineties, enlisted as a fifteen-year-old private in the Confederate army before switching over to the navy as a midshipman.

These senior foreign service veteran-appointees to foreign service positions were remarkable, however, in the number who had already held senior rank—as military officers—some thirty years previously. Fifteen of the group achieved at least brevet brigadier general rank by the time the Civil War ended. They and numerous other officers of only slightly less exalted rank clearly were not strangers to responsibility and stressful demands upon their capacities when they entered the diplomatic or consular services. They had already shown an ability to cope with severe pressures; many of them had long since been involved in the ultimate of decision-making, that which directly affects whether men live or die. Fitzhugh Lee was the nephew of Robert E. Lee and a Confederate major general with a distinguished war record. From 1896 to 1898 he filled the position of consul general at Havana. Others renowned for their military records a generation before include Horace Porter, ambassador to France at the same time former-private Gowdy was consul general at Paris.

Porter was a Union army brevet brigadier general, a trusted aide to General Grant; he was decorated with the congressional Medal of Honor for bravery at Chickamauga.[14] Pierce Manning Butler Young, consul general at St. Petersburg in the eighties and minister to Guatemala, 1893–96, had campaigned as a youthful Confederate major general commanding the famed Hampton's Brigade.

At a slightly lower level of rank, Samuel Hawkins Marshall Byers of Iowa emerged from the Northern army as a brevet major after he also was captured and after three escape attempts, the last of which was successful. Later Byers was consul for fifteen years at Zurich and consul general for briefer periods at Rome and St. Gall, the latter during the Harrison presidency. Thomas Theodore Crittenden, consul general at Mexico under Cleveland, served as a Union lieutenant colonel in command of a Missouri calvary regiment.

In most cases the Democrat Cleveland appointed the Confederate veterans who were chosen for the foreign service. Two exceptions have already been mentioned: Fitzhugh Lee was at Havana under both Cleveland and McKinley, and George E. Maney served in a succession of Republican administrations. The Alabama Republican party leader named to Singapore, Robert A. Moseley, Jr., had commanded a Confederate company and was wounded in action. Another exception, Oliver Hart Dockery, a North Carolina Unionist who served briefly in the Confederate army, held office as consul general at Rio de Janeiro in Harrison's term in office. Perry M. DeLeon of Georgia, consul general at Guayaquil, Ecuador, from 1897 to 1902 in Republican administrations, had been a captain in the Confederate army more than thirty years before.

Republican presidents of the 1890s occasionally named other persons residing in the Deep South to diplomatic and consular offices at a senior level. In some instances appointees were carpetbaggers, such as former Congressman Alfred Eliab Buck of Georgia and Robert Franklin Patterson of Tennessee, both originally from Maine. Buck was minister to Japan from 1897 until his death in 1902; Patterson served seven years as consul general at Calcutta, beginning in 1897. But Harrison and McKinley commonly did not select for the senior ranks of the foreign service anyone who had borne arms for the South.

The mention above of educator William F. Powell and clergyman William H. Heard raises the question of the racial composition of the group under consideration. Powell and Heard were two of only eight blacks to fill senior positions during the decade. This total comprises less than 4 percent of the group as a whole. Other than the District of

Columbia's Frederick Douglass and North Carolina's Owen L. W. Smith, all were named from northern states. Only Heard and Smith were born in one of the eleven states of the Confederacy. All went to Monrovia, Port-au-Prince, or Santo Domingo, the usual posts for black senior officers.[15] In 1893 Cleveland tried to appoint blacks to the legation at La Paz and the consulate at Calais, two posts that whites invariably filled, but Congress would not go along and the nominations were withdrawn.[16] Harrison named four blacks to major posts, and McKinley, two; one additional person, Campbell L. Maxwell of Ohio, served twice at Santo Domingo, once as consul in the early 1890s under Harrison and again as consul general (1898–1904) in the McKinley and Roosevelt administrations. One Harrison appointee, Philadelphia editor John Stephens Durham, was chargé d'affaires at Santo Domingo in the early nineties but stationed at Port-au-Prince as the replacement for Frederick Douglass when the latter departed. The University of Pennsylvania-educated Durham stayed on as a sugar planter in the Dominican Republic upon the change in administrations in 1893. "My future must be worked out beyond the borders of the United States," he had written earlier.[17] Two of the appointees to Liberia as minister resident and consul general died in succession at post. Alexander G. Clark, an Iowa businessman-lawyer and editor, met his death from disease there in 1891 at the age of sixty-five, and William D. McCoy, an Indiana schoolteacher who actively sought to replace Clark, died at Monrovia in 1893, only forty years old.[18]

In 1890 one in almost seven persons in the United States as a whole was born in another country.[19] Senior diplomats and consuls, however, totalled fewer nonnative Americans on a proportional basis in the following decade. Eighteen of the 225 appointees on whom information is available, for a ratio of about one in thirteen, emigrated to the United States and went through naturalization procedures. Seven of the naturalized officers came from the British Isles and a half dozen from Germany. The latter group included the veteran envoy Oscar S. Straus, born in Bavaria. Ireland claimed four of those born in Great Britain, including Patrick Egan, Harrison's minister to Chile during troubled days early in the decade (see chapter 6). Carl Bailey Hurst was born in Germany of American parents and thus not subject to naturalization. He held a series of consular assignments, including consul general, over a period of more than thirty years. Romualdo Pacheco, minister to the Central American States at the beginning of the decade, was born in California under Mexican rule, but as a teenager in 1846 he swore allegiance to the United States after the Mexican War.

The ethnic vote was important in several states, and an element of political calculation for that reason figured in some of the relatively few appointments of foreign-born citizens. In March 1889 Senator John C. Spooner of Wisconsin wrote to newly installed Secretary of State Blaine pointing out that 32 percent of his state's voters had German backgrounds. Spooner noted that a Swede had been named to an "important position" in the administration and insisted that something be done for the Germans.[20] The ethnic vote at least partly dictated another choice during the decade, that of Max Judd of St. Louis, Missouri, a Jewish émigré from Austria-Hungary, who incidentally had an international reputation as a chess player. With extensive backing from local Democratic figures and the business community, he obtained the consul generalship at Vienna to succeed Julius Goldschmidt, thus setting off a minor diplomatic incident reminiscent of an earlier controversial appointment to the same post in the first Cleveland administration. The Austro-Hungarian government relucantly accepted him—the Austrian premier claimed that the objection was to his previous nationality, not his religion. Judd eventually received his official exequatur, his authority from the local government to act in a consular capacity, and served at Vienna until 1897.[21]

Officers sent abroad to major posts possessed language abilities on a strictly hit-or-miss basis, given the absence of any foreign service requirements, in-house testing, or training in those days. Precise information is lacking on how many senior officers could effectively communicate in foreign languages, a skill that is sometimes difficult to measure in any event. A number of them were adept, trained, and practiced, but most relevant available biographic information lacks explicit indications of foreign language skills. The group as a whole was not greatly accomplished in languages other than English.[22]

Some officers, such as James Biddle Eustis, did speak foreign languages. The first American envoy to hold the rank of ambassador at Paris, 1893 to 1897, Eustis claimed acquaintance with the French language and culture on the basis of his own Louisiana background. An earlier minister in Paris lamented, "The more I try to converse in French and to study the language, the more difficult it becomes." A few months of study sufficed for the basics, T. Jefferson Coolidge wrote, "but to do it well is so difficult that I think I have never known more than one or two foreigners to succeed." Coolidge perhaps exaggerated; he had studied abroad for several years as a young man and was able himself to make a short speech in French upon his presentation to President Marie François Sadi Carnot. In fact, an unexpectedly large number of officers from the record seem to have been fluent in other languages. Richard Guenther was born in Germany and was consul general at Mexico City and Frankfort during the decade. He had emigrated earlier to Wisconsin as a young man of twenty-one and thus was able to fit into the Frankfort scene without difficulty as far as language was concerned. Felix A. Mathews, a long-service consul general at Tangier who was born in that city, spoke five languages, including Arabic, in addition to English. An ability in classical Greek was useful at Athens then, and Eben Alexander, minister to Greece under Cleveland, was a scholar in that field.[23] Consul General Charles de Kay at Berlin translated German and French literary works. John Judson Barclay, who succeeded Mathews as consul general at Tangier, likewise spoke Arabic, among several other languages. The American-born but virtually lifelong resident of Havana, Consul General Ramon O. Williams, spoke Spanish like an educated native. John Martin Crawford, a physician from Ohio, was consul general at St. Petersburg for four years under Harrison; appropriately enough, he was an accomplished translator of Russian, as well as Finnish and Estonian. The European-educated W. W. Rockhill spoke French fluently and translated oriental languages. Van Leer Polk, a Nashville, Tennessee editor who had travelled extensively abroad and who spoke three European languages, became consul general at Calcutta in the second Cleveland administration. By the time Edmund W. P. Smith was appointed consul general at Bogota in 1890, he had lived in Colombia for thirteen years and was married to a Colombian; he was said, believably, to speak Spanish with ease. William Widgery Thomas, Jr., of Maine spoke and wrote Swedish fluently. He married successively two members of the Swedish nobility and was three times United States minister to Sweden and Norway between 1883 and 1905.

The list could be continued. Nevertheless, most senior officers of the period likely were little more accomplished and practiced in languages when appointed than were the majority of their fellow Americans. This lack undoubtedly hampered many in the performance of their duties; the ability to speak the local language is especially important for consular officers. On the other hand, the previous nationality that went with native-speaker ability could be a social drawback to an officer sent to the country of his origin—Germany, say—and commentators can overstress the need for fluency on the part of diplomats. Diplomats often use the local language daily, but they are well advised not to attempt negotiations or highly sensitive conversations without a qualified interpreter.

The group was generally well educated, if not exceptionally accomplished linguistically. Its overall high level of education is clear from the record even though individual backgrounds ran the gamut from, as examples, that of Consul General Carl B. Hurst, a Harvard man who earned A.M. and Ph.D. degrees at the University of Tubingen, Germany, to that of Minister Lewis Baker at Managua who had no formal education at all (he was taught for a few years at home by his mother). Notwithstanding this wide range, most were well-educated men by the standards of the day. At a time when only about one in five young Americans went to high school, and when an even smaller ratio represented those in institutions of higher learning,[24] a large majority of the senior foreign service officers of the nineties enjoyed the benefits of at least some college education. Definite information in this regard has been obtained on 210 individuals (data are unavailable or unclear on the other sixteen appointees). Of these, 148, or 70.5 percent, attended a college or university. If the base total is expanded to include the entire group of 226, the percentage of known college men, whether or not they graduated, drops only five points.

Many senior officers had attended well-recognized schools, including the institutions that later came to be called the Ivy League and such state universities as Michigan, Iowa, North Carolina, and Kansas. Thirty-six (24.3 percent of all known to have attended college) went to Harvard, Yale, or Columbia. The service academies, West Point and Annapolis, were represented, as were small colleges such as Miami of Ohio, Waterville (later Colby), Tufts, Asbury (later DePauw), and Georgetown of Kentucky. Some senior officers went to what can be termed "log cabin colleges." William Lindsay Scruggs, a controversial figure whose comparatively long diplomatic career included service as minister to Venezuela from 1889 to 1892, studied at Strawberry Plains College in eastern Tennessee in the 1850s. Hezekiah A. Gudger, who was consul general at Panama in the late nineties and early 1900s, graduated from North Carolina's less-than-fabled Weaverville College.

Others attended a college or university but did not finish. Frank Holcomb Mason was one of several who did not complete their courses; he was at Hiram College in Ohio but left for service in the Civil War. After the war, without further formal education, Mason moved from an editorship in Cleveland to a thirty-four-year career in the Consular Service, beginning in 1880.

More than a score of the officers in this group biography studied abroad, either in addition to courses in America or as their principal educational experience.[25] E. Spencer Pratt received an education in France in medicine. Wallace S. Jones of Florida, consul general at Rome from 1893 to 1897, was graduated from the Sorbonne and St. Cyr. W. W. Rockhill also finished at the latter institution. Philadelphia's

Lawrence Townsend failed to finish at the University of Pennsylvania due to illness, but he put in six years of study in Europe before beginning a series of diplomatic assignments in 1893. As a different kind of example, Eugene Seeger was born in Germany and attended primary and secondary schools in several European countries. He emigrated to the United States at the age of seventeen, entered German-language journalism in Chicago, and eventually served for several years as consul general at Rio de Janeiro starting in late 1897. Solomon Hirsch also was born in Germany, where he received his education—none at the university level—before leaving for the United States in 1854. Later he was Harrison's minister to Turkey.

Continuity in office among diplomatic and consular officers of the era was limited but not entirely absent (see table 3). The amount of practical foreign service experience abroad amassed by the study group members varied widely. Included at one extreme is that of Thomas Adamson of Pennsylvania, consul general at Panama from 1890 to 1893, who had been in the Consular Service nearly continuously since 1862. On the other end of the scale, former United States senator and governor Gilbert Ashville Pierce of Minnesota, the American minister at Lisbon, was at post for two months in 1893, his only assignment. Another officer who had an extended career, J. Judson Barclay, served as a consul in the Middle East for seven years as far back as before the Civil War and he took office again as consul general at Tangier in the midnineties. (Barclay's father and grandfather also had Consular Service experience, the latter as consul general in France beginning in 1791.) Frank Charles Partridge of Vermont, by way of contrast, held the Tangier position for only a year, 1897 to 1898, his second of two overseas assignments.

Only a minority of senior officers appointed in the 1890s put in periods of service longer than the term in office of one administration. Of the 226 men in the this survey, 67 (29.7 percent) had three years or less in office from the time of their appointments to their resignations. Another 59 held commissions for just four years. No fewer than 151 (66.8 percent) served in the Consular or Diplomatic Service at only one post abroad. Thirty-two senior officers (14.2 percent) had a total of two assignments or, in two cases, appointments twice at different times to the same posts. The remainder of the group under study, 43 diplomatic envoys and consuls general (19.0 percent), had at least three assignments over their careers.

Looking at the 1890s alone, we note that 23 officers then in charge of major posts, or about one in ten, served for five or more years during that decade. Herbert W. Bowen, consul and later consul general at

TABLE 3

Diplomatic & Consular Posts & Terms of Service, 1890s Senior Officers

| | Assignments abroad | |
No. posts	No. officers	% of total
1	151	66.8
2	32	14.2
3 or more	43	19.0
Subtotal	226	100.0

| | Years commissioned | |
No. years	No. officers	% of total
Less than 1	6	2.7
1–3	61	27.0
4	59	26.1
5–9	45	19.9
10–14	32	14.2
15–20	15	6.6
21–plus	8	3.5
Subtotal	226	100.0

SOURCES: Consular and Diplomatic Lists.

Barcelona (1890–99), and then minister resident at Tehran; the afore-mentioned Julius G. Lay, his successor at Barcelona; and Frank H. Mason, consul general successively at Frankfort and Berlin, from 1889 to 1905—these three are the only officers with senior rank at the end of the decade who held appointments virtually throughout the period 1890 to 1899. Minister Charles Denby at Peking and Carl B. Hurst, who was consul general at Vienna (1895–97), each served about eight years during the 1890s.

Changing the focus of service from the decade of the nineties alone and considering instead service over an extended span of years, we note that the pattern of longevity and experience abroad at first glance does not appear greatly different. A total of 126 individuals among the senior officers in the study group (55.8 percent) served four years or less from appointment to departure from the service in whatever time period (table 3). But an additional 45 appointees (19.9 percent) held office from five to nine years and the remaining 55 officers (24.3 percent) of the group under study were veterans of even longer periods in the service over their extended careers. Fifteen of this latter group were in the fifteen- to twenty-year-veteran category. Eight officers, included in the 1890s group, all but one of whom were consuls general, had periods of service total-ling more than two decades each. Julius Lay was the leader with close to forty years of service at eleven posts, including time as an unpaid con-sular clerk, before he retired in 1937. Among the leaders in the number of assignments to different posts was Arthur Matthias Beaupre, a law-trained elected county official from Illinois. He began as secretary of legation and consul general at Guatemala in 1897 and closed out his career in 1913 after senior diplomatic assignments in Colombia (in two different capacities), Argentina, the Netherlands, and Cuba.

A limited number of officers in senior positions during the last decade of the century thus had long careers abroad. This was in defiance of the usual fate of appointees—service at one post only and for three or four years at most.

To review the information sketched above, the "typical" 1890s United States chief of mission or consul general was a native-born white man, usually college educated, about fifty years old when appointed, and from the Midwest or a northeastern state. His prior profession likely was the law, business, or journalism, although in nearly every instance he fol-lowed politics as an avocation, an important criterion in his selection. In most cases, he served only once and held a commission for four years or less.

Beyond these generalizations the exceptions become numerous. With these common factors in mind, however, four representative individuals, a sample chosen exclusively (and arbitrarily) from among those persons not heretofore mentioned by name in this study, illustrate generally the mold of the 1890s senior officer. Two were chiefs of diplomatic missions and two were consuls general. All were in their fifties when appointed. Two hailed from the Midwest and two from the northeastern United States. One was a publisher, one a lawyer, one a businessman, and one a journalist and editor. Two had college educations. Two had served in the military in their younger days. Only one held a commission for more than four years. The four-man list includes no well-known national figures.

Samuel Merrill was from President Harrison's home state of Indiana and held the office of consul general at Calcutta through three of the four Harrison years. The son and namesake of a prominent publisher and state official, he graduated from Wabash College in 1851. Three years later he received an A.M. from that institution and was an Indianapolis bookseller and publisher from the 1850s onward (his firm evolved into the present-day Bobbs-Merrill publishing company). Merrill served in the Union army during the war, emerging as a brevet colonel; eventually he wrote a history of his regiment. Above the average age for such appointments at fifty-eight in 1890, he was accompanied to Calcutta by his son, Samuel, Jr., who served as his assistant with the title of vice consul general. Merrill, a spare, patriarchal figure with a long white beard, left post in mid-1893 following the inauguration of Cleveland, to be succeeded by Van Leer Polk, a young Tennessee editor. Later he retired in California and lived well into his nineties.

The sojourn in Switzerland of Minister John Davis Washburn reflected a fairly recurrent theme in some patronage appointments—nominations to tours abroad because of personal reasons such as health needs. A Worcester, Massachusetts lawyer and insurance company president, and a close friend of Senator George F. Hoar, the fifty-six-year-old Washburn was unknown to the Senate when nominated in 1889. It soon developed that he was a graduate of Harvard College and Harvard Law School, was descended from early Plymouth Colony settlers, had served in the state legislature, had travelled extensively abroad, and was prominent in Massachusetts Republican party circles. The press said, however, that he was in "very poor health, which is the chief reason why he is sent abroad."[26] Ill health or not, Washburn completed three years at Berne, resigning in 1892, and survived back in Worcester until 1903.

Another veteran of state politics, "prominent in political reform,"[27] Thomas Skelton Harrison of Pennsylvania was a wealthy businessman associated with his family's chemical manufacturing firm. A navy veteran of the Civil War, he did not attend college. Rather, Harrison pursued a successful business career and indulged himself and his wife in occasional travel abroad for more than thirty years before being named consul general and diplomatic agent at Cairo at the age of fifty-nine, soon after McKinley's inauguration in 1897. He already knew Egypt, having received an imperial decoration from the khedive in 1896. After two uneventful years, he resigned his commission in June 1899 while on a trip to the United States. Harrison was replaced by an officer at the lower rank of consul. During retirement, the distinguished-looking Philadelphian produced a handsome book of memoirs, Homely Diary of a Diplomat in the East 1897–1899 (1917). He died in 1919 at the age of eighty-one.

As a final example of a "typical" officer, William Rufus Finch edited and published the Lacrosse, Wisconsin Republican and Leader for thirty years and was a local collector of customs for two. In 1897 the president named him minister to Uruguay and Paraguay, resident at Montevideo. A small, quiet man, fifty years old when he presented his credentials, he remained at post until 1905, a longer-than-usual tour abroad.[28] The rough-hewn Finch, who had a reputation for uncompromising honesty if not downright bluntness of manner, eventually returned to journalism in Wisconsin. He died there in 1913.

All four of the above had unexceptional records at post and, with the exception of Finch, soon returned to their more usual pursuits. None of them was nationally known when appointed, and none made a name for himself while abroad. They were average senior officers with respect to many characteristics exhibited by their colleagues in the service during the decade. While not experienced, accomplished professional diplomats or consular officials, neither were they, according to the record, inept hangers-on or elderly party workers buried in jobs for political liabilities who needed a paycheck while out of domestic office. Virtually all received appointment for political reasons in a patronage age; yet they, like most of their colleagues in this study, were drawn from a segment of society that was well above average as to background of education, professional training, and worldly experience. (See chapter 7 for an evaluation of the group as a whole.)

| 5 |

Living and Working Abroad

*Had diplomacy been a career, nothing would have pleased me more
than to continue in such service of my country.*
Oscar S. Straus, Under Four Administrations:
From Cleveland to Taft (1922)

This chapter presents the institutional basics of the foreign service of
the 1890s. An examination of the posts and their staffing provides information on what it was like to be assigned to the small Diplomatic
Service or the far-flung Consular Service. Questions addressed include
where officers were stationed geographically, how they lived, how they
obtained their quarters, what their duties entailed, and how much they
earned while abroad.

The United States' diplomatic and consular services had their origins
in the Revolutionary-era agents who were sent to Europe to enlist support in the American bid for independence.[1] In 1789, immediately after
independence was gained, the new government had diplomatic missions
abroad only in France and Spain. This representation increased but
slowly as the years passed. Not until 1856 did Congress provide the two
services an overall administrative framework for their operations, including pay scales. By the beginning of the Civil War, diplomatic missions
had increased in number to 33 and consular posts to the surprising total
of 480. All of the diplomatic missions were legations. Nearly 200 of the
numerous consular posts were small part-time agency offices; there were
only 8 of the larger consulates general. Congress formalized diplomatic
salaries in 1875. Consular pay also was fixed, generally at low levels,
with income expected to be supplemented from certain fee receipts or in
some cases through the conduct of business at the post abroad. Washington held the numbers of diplomatic personnel to a minimum throughout

these years, in contrast with the increasing numbers of consular officials, including part-timers. As late as 1880 only a dozen of the diplomatic missions abroad had salaried secretaries of legation in addition to the ministers.

In 1890, the beginning of the transitional period of this study, the United States still maintained only thirty-three legations abroad, staffed by fewer than sixty diplomats of all ranks. (In contrast almost one hundred years later, in 1984, career Foreign Service officers from the Departments of State and Commerce and the United States Information Agency, not including political-appointee chiefs of mission, totalled about five thousand; approximately two-thirds of these were serving abroad at the nation's more than 230 embassies and consulates.) This small number of American diplomats in 1890 compares roughly with that of Belgium a few years later, shortly after the turn of the century. Nine United States military and naval attachés also served abroad at six legations. In 1890 nine diplomatic chiefs of mission concurrently held commissions as consuls general.

Ten years later, despite the fact that the United States' international interests had expanded considerably, it was still pretty much business as usual in the diplomatic establishment. At year's end in 1899, shortly after the war with Spain, the number of diplomatic missions, some accredited to more than one government, stood at thirty-four (see appendix B). This figure includes four legations headed by envoys who also held the title of consul general. Honolulu, with Hawaii now taken over by the United States, was off the list and Quito, Ecuador and San José, Costa Rica, were added. The single mission at Guatemala to the Central American Republics was increased in 1890 to two posts, Guatemala and San José, with multiple accreditation. The size of the overseas diplomatic officer corps of all ranks had risen modestly by this time to nearly seventy persons, plus sixteen attachés. The army or navy provided all but one of the latter. (The separate staff of the Department of State in Washington, incidentally, at the end of the decade stood at only ninety-eight people, including everyone from Secretary Hay to the lowest-paid worker.)[2]

The Diplomatic Service consisted of this small overseas complement. As already noted, the Consular Service was another matter. In contrast with the limited number of diplomats, consular officials abroad of all ranks totalled slightly over one thousand, both in 1890 and at the close of the century. The protection of American citizens, importantly including seamen, and the promotion of commercial interests dictated the existence of no fewer than 323 consular posts around the world in 1890 and a comparable total—318—ten years later. Non-American consular agents, often local businessmen who were nationals of the country of assignment, staffed many of the lesser consular offices on a part-time basis. In many cases, these consulates were one-man outposts at remote, seldom-heard-of locales.[3] Some posts, however, were relatively large establishments in busy commercial or political centers. Consulates general often were located in capital cities along with legations or, later in the 1890s, embassies. The number of these major consular posts, not including combined minister/consul general appointments, varied from twenty-five to thirty-four through the decade as the Department of State changed post designations and assignments.

Washington thus sent senior officers to roughly seventy cities during the decade—to thirty-odd diplomatic missions and a like number of consulates general or combined missions and consulates general. These posts were scattered all over the world, from Apia to Vienna, from St. Petersburg to Tokyo. Only a few major posts were in Africa and Asia, however; the American diplomatic presence—the legations and embassies around the world—was concentrated in Europe and Latin America. Of thirty-three diplomatic missions abroad in the spring of 1890, the United States maintained fourteen in Europe, eleven in Latin America, four in Asia, and two (Constantinople and Tehran) in the Middle East. Monrovia was the only full-fledged diplomatic post on the continent of Africa, and Honolulu the sole mission in the Pacific.[4]

Each of the presidential administrations in office during the nineties made sizable numbers of senior diplomatic and consular officer appointments abroad, even though the list of major posts was not especially long. Given the political requirements for patronage of the period, clearly no one expected these officials to make a career of the foreign service, although many appointees desired just that. Officers came and went; it was a fact of foreign service life. Most left after a few years (see chapter 4). In the quotation that heads this chapter, three-time Minister to Turkey Straus rued this lack of career opportunities. A young vice consul at Liverpool wrote to a friend in the 1880s, "It is no plan of mine to remain in this service all my life. I hope I am fitted for something better; but now that I am in it, I do not want to retire until I am promoted." The officer, Harold Marsh Sewall of Maine, succeeded in obtaining appointment as consul general to Samoa. For the last year of Hawaii's independence, Sewall served as the United States minister to that country. Upon departing Berlin for home after three years as consul general, another officer wrote to a Department of State official, "Thank you very much for your kind words as to my work here. . . . I did what I could have owing to the peculiar state of our service."[5] His reference to the peculiar state of the Consular Service concerns his belief that the rapid turnover precluded being around long enough to make an imprint on the conduct of affairs.

Overseas diplomatic missions as noted were small in those days. Ministers Charles Denby at Peking and John Franklin Swift at Tokyo had the largest diplomatic staffs in 1890, each with two secretaries of legation and an American interpreter. The important legations at London, Paris, and Berlin also had two secretaries in addition to the chief of mission, but no American interpreters. Ministers at other posts such as Buenos Aires, Vienna, Rome, Madrid, and Mexico City got along with only one subordinate diplomat to assist them, and seven chiefs of mission in Europe were without diplomatic officer aides at all.

At decade's end, ten of the comparatively large diplomatic posts now boasted attachés from the military services on their official diplomatic lists, and several more junior diplomats were in legation or embassy secretary positions. In 1899 Ambassador Andrew D. White at Berlin had not only two secretaries of embassy and two military attachés, but a scientific and agricultural attaché as well. At the end of 1899 Ambassador Joseph H. Choate at London also had an official staff of five—three secretaries of embassy and two attachés from the armed services. But that same year the minister accredited to and resident in Guatemala, Whiteside Godfrey Hunter of Kentucky, was also accredited to Honduras, and William Lawrence Merry of California held office as minister to Costa Rica, Nicaragua, and El Salvador, resident in San José. Throughout the 1890s there were several other diplomatic posts of multiple accreditation.

The Consular Service scattered its small offices around the colonial possessions of the major European powers, but senior consular appointees did not head the consulates or consular agencies. Some of the less important posts were in places seldom heard of, then or now. The rationale for existence of those posts was mainly in the system then in practice of certifying invoices for all shipments of goods to the United States. In 1892, for instance, the Department of State maintained consular offices at Clifton, Ontario; Coaticook, Quebec; and St. Stephen, New Brunswick. A consul and a vice consul staffed each and one wonders what two officers found to do. McAdam Junction, New Brunswick, and Rat Portage, Ontario, were locales with lone consular agents, as were Milk River, Jamaica; Ocós, Guatemala; and Cockburn Harbor in the Turks and Caicos Isles, West Indies. Among the many one-man posts were those at such places as Port Stanley, Falkland Islands, and Sagua la Grande, Cuba, neither of which was (or is) a center of commerce or tourism. In 1899 the Consular Service manned fully three dozen consular offices in France alone other than Paris, not counting French possessions overseas. From 1831 to 1908 the United States maintained a consulate at the historically significant but otherwise unimportant island of St. Helena.[6]

With a few exceptions, Washington placed the major consular posts, the consulates general, either in capital cities such as London, Rio de Janeiro, and Bangkok, or in commercial or colonial government centers. Cairo, Montreal, Shanghai, and Havana exemplify the latter. Exceptions to this rule were Apia in the South Pacific, the locus of a controversy with Germany over control of Samoa, and St. Gall in eastern Switzerland, a scenic delight which had no readily apparent claim to major post ranking in the 1890s. Among the important consulates raised to consulate general status years before were those at London and Paris, both elevated in 1869. (The consular office at London dated originally from 1790 and that at Paris from 1794.) The Department of State made the important post at Calcutta, established in 1792, a senior consular office even earlier, in 1855. Other major consulates raised in title and status in subsequent years were Rome in 1871 and Rio de Janeiro and Berlin in 1874.[7]

By 1890 thirty-six American posts were designated as consulates general, including those at which the incumbent also held a diplomatic title; in 1895 the number was thirty-seven; in 1899, thirty-eight. Washington raised the posts at Antwerp, Barcelona, Cape Town, Hong Kong, Monterrey, Santo Domingo, Singapore, and Stockholm to consulates general during the decade of the nineties. Honolulu, which was the site of a consular office as well as a legation, was incorporated in United States territory, and Lisbon, Nuevo Laredo, and Port-au-Prince were reduced in status to consulates. Apia and St. Gall, the atypical senior posts mentioned above, became consulates general in 1887 and 1892, respectively.[8]

Major consular posts varied in the size of their staffs as much as diplomatic missions. Shanghai probably had the largest number of employees, American and local, and was one of those with extensive responsibilities. In 1890 the post's consul general, Joseph A. Leonard, counted four American employees: a vice consul general, a deputy consul general, a marshal, and an interpreter. By 1897 at the same post Consul General Thomas R. Jernigan supervised five American consular officers and administrative staff, two Chinese clerical employees, two part-time Chinese clerks, and a half dozen servants, plus an indeterminate number of casual laborers. Two of the American positions on the Shanghai staff in 1897 were those of a marshal and a jailor; China was one of eleven countries during the 1890s in which the consul general presided over an extraterritorial court for Americans (Jernigan, it happens, was a lawyer). Two years later, at the end of the decade, the staffing pattern had changed little, except that now yet another consul general held that title, John Goodnow, a businessman not trained in the law. The functional titles of two of the subordinate American officers had changed as well. As substantial as this staff was, at least for the times, the British had roughly four times as many consular officials at Shanghai; British extra-territorial court personnel in particular were more numerous than the American.[9]

In 1896 the substantial American consular presence at Havana con-sisted of a consul general, the former businessman Ramon O. Williams, two American officers who were consular clerks as well, one additional American clerk, and two Spanish nationals in lower-ranking clerical po-sitions. At Mexico City, Consul General Thomas T. Crittenden relied on his son William as the only other American employee at the post. Sim-ilarly and contemporaneously, Consul General Victor Vifquain at Pan-ama had only his son as a clerk, with no other American staff members.[10] Other major consular posts around the world varied widely in their staffing patterns.

The responsibilities of personnel at major consular posts differed as well. Trade matters were important at most. Some, like Honolulu and Halifax, dealt primarily with shipping and seamen. At a few posts, such as Apia, political questions were paramount. Consular Bureau Chief Wilbur J. Carr, in testimony before the Foreign Affairs Committee of the House shortly after the turn of the century, noted that the consular of-ficers at London and Paris certified approximately thirty thousand ship-ping invoices per year. This routine responsibility involved the valuation of goods, the administration of oaths, and the receipt of substantial fees. Similar totals probably obtained in the previous decade. Shanghai, on the other hand, collected less in consular fees, according to Carr, but the consul general there supervised several other consular posts. In addition, the consul general's extraterritorial court responsibilities were a focus of attention. Cases arising under this jurisdiction consisted mostly of petty lawbreaking such as drunkenness and disorderly conduct by Americans, but occasionally they included capital crimes. Further, the consul general at Shanghai sat on a board that supervised the international settlements, and he had the usual duty common to all posts of keeping the Depart-ment of State closely informed on commercial and political conditions in the region.[11]

The Mexico City consulate general, as Carr remarked in his 1906 tes-timony, was concerned less with invoices and fee collection than with seeing to the correspondence of Americans inquiring about mining properties and missing persons. It also looked after the interests of "the great number" of visitors to Mexico. At Marseilles the consul general supervised a small staff concerned with the problems of seamen and shipping, plus a "great number" of immigrants, notably including Armenian refugees on their way to the United States.[12]

Few senior Diplomatic or Consular Service officers professed openly to be lightly employed. Senior diplomats of the period on occasion recited in detail the problems with which they had to deal. Minister to Russia Andrew D. White remarked of the years 1892 to 1894 in his autobiography that the diplomatic questions "were many and troublesome." He went on to specify the problem areas as the Bering Sea fisheries, revising two bilateral treaties (one dating back to 1832), extending invitations to the Chicago Exposition, protecting American citizens in Russia, especially Jews, seeing to American life insurance interests, and keeping Washington informed on Russian religious contacts with Alaska. An American minister on another continent at about the same time had somewhat similar responsibilities. Based on a study of the reporting files, Minister to Argentina William Insco Buchanan's biographer concludes that the envoy dealt with four main areas of concern: overseeing trade relations, revising treaty arrangements, protecting American interests during the Spanish-American War, and assisting Argentina in her effort to define certain national boundaries. The young diplomatic envoy to the kingdom of Siam, John Barrett, assiduously promoted American business in the Far East. In one of his many lengthy reports on the subject, the former Oregon editor warned that "Europe is striving to gain the upper hand," and he called, not for the first time in his tour there, for "an appreciation of the . . . great commercial opportunities . . . of Asia."[13]

Another officer of that era described his somewhat different duties abroad. Thomas S. Harrison, one of the "typical" senior officers (chapter 4) and a man with a sense of humor, wrote about his assignment to Cairo from 1897 to 1899:

It is almost a jest at the expense of the Agent and Consul-General of the United States in Egypt to direct him to "describe the character of his official duties" briefly. What with Americans who are taken half-way up the Pyramids and deserted there, Americans whose landladies cannot get rid of them, Americans who want to be presented to the Khedive, Americans who speak only the English language, Americans whose trunks have disappeared, Americans who are collecting postage stamps, the "social" side of the duties, to employ the current euphemism, is in a state of expansion that is as constant as it is indefinite. Then the judicial capacity in which he acts involves the Agent and consul-General in personal disputes of every conceivable kind. The routine duties on the other hand, are almost nominal. Thus, in 1898, [no] invoices were certified to: no American vessels came to Cairo—no seamen were shipped; and no health bills were issued.

The consulate general opened its doors from ten to four o'clock, hours which Harrison noted did not reflect the substantial amount of time spent on representational activities. In this connection his one objection to life in Cairo was the late hours which "people in society" kept. "They never seem to know when it is time to go to bed. . . ." Everyone snapped back the next day, however. "Perhaps there is something in the air," wrote the diplomatic agent and consul general.[14]

The experiences of senior officers, both consular and diplomatic, varied from post to post. Not all consular officials dealt primarily with commercial questions, any more than all chiefs of diplomatic mission coped mainly with political issues. Consul General Samuel Merrill at Calcutta loosely supervised six consular agencies spread from Rangoon to Madras and reported on such subjects as the use of cobra poison in treating cholera and the cultivation of castor beans. Calcutta, although a seaport, had little American-flag shipping and thus no problems with seamen.[15] Consul General Darius Ingraham at Halifax, on the other hand, dealt almost exclusively with shipping and seamen questions, some of them complex.[16] Consul General James Mulligan's tour at Apia started in 1894 with a bang; he arrived in the middle of a local uprising against the king. During the following year and a half he participated in the deliberations of a United States-British-German consular board and bombarded Washington with long political analyses sometimes so detailed in their treatment of the Samoan scene that senior officials in Washington did not have time to read them (a frequent occurrence in modern diplomacy).[17]

Minister John D. Washburn in Switzerland also took part in three-power negotiations, over a Portuguese railroad concession in his case. Unlike Mulligan with his lengthy despatches, however, Washburn did not believe in overreporting. "It has been my aim . . . to avoid burdening the Department or this Legation with the reproduction, in varied form, of familiar information," he wrote in 1890, "while keeping a constant eye upon the course of events."[18] His diplomatic colleague at Montevideo, William Finch, dealt most importantly with reporting on the unstable local political scene,[19] while the officer heading the consulate general at the large and important post of London, John C. New, spent much of his time on commercial matters.[20]

An official often could mold the job at a major post to his own interests, a practice that is still possible to a large extent in the modern Foreign Service. The interests of Consul General Charles M. Dickinson at Constantinople highlight this fact and also the importance of commercial affairs at many consular posts. As he wrote later, "My primary purpose in going to Constantinople was to get the Oriental atmosphere in order to write a book I had in mind." He soon became absorbed with increasing American trade with Turkey, however. "Our gross sales to that country had amounted to only about $140,000, and all our shipments were by the way of Germany or England." The costs, delays, and breakage made exports from the United States "almost impossible." Dickinson gathered information on Turkish shipments to America from the nineteen consular officials under his supervision and in time managed to interest more than one hundred United States manufacturers and exporters, especially flour-milling firms, in the Turkish market. Complications hindered the consul general's efforts; British and German shippers drastically cut their cargo rates, local millers and flour dealers were irate, and Turkish officialdom undertook through means of dubious legality to exclude American products. Nevertheless, Dickinson remained active and relatively successful in promoting the United States' commercial interests during his eight years at post.[21]

The subject of pay further details the life abroad of senior officers in the 1890s. The annual salaries specified for chiefs of diplomatic mission during this period ranged from $17,500 at the largest diplomatic posts such as London, Paris, and Berlin, to $4,000 and $5,000 respectively at Monrovia and Port-au-Prince (see appendix C for pay scales at selected posts). Monrovia was one of several small legations at which the chief of mission was also designated as a consul general during the decade. The American minister at Lima, as an example of one of the middle-sized missions, received $10,000 per year; his counterparts at Santiago and Peking drew $12,000, at Copenhagen and Constantinople, $7,500. Congress and the Department of State established these base salaries by specific posts and positions, and supplemented them by relatively modest administrative contingency funds that varied from mission to mission. The maximum rate of pay did not change for nearly a century, however. From one decade to the next the minister or ambassador to Russia, for instance, knew that he would draw $17,500 per year in salary, no more and no less.[22]

The pay of principal officers at major consular posts was not so relatively straightforward a matter. In the 1890s the Department of State listed most consular posts—and all consulates general—under an administrative category called "Schedule B." The incumbents were salaried at different specified levels and were not permitted to engage in business locally. Some sixty-odd consuls and consular agents at smaller posts were allowed to do so, however. At the beginning of the decade the consuls general at London, Havana, and Paris, three of the top-rated consular assignments, drew $6,000 in salary annually. Their consular colleagues at Melbourne and Berlin earned $5,000 and $4,000 respectively. The officer with the dual designation of secretary of legation and consul general at Bogota got by on $2,000 a year, a salary for this primarily junior diplomatic position that was lower than that of many consuls.

The rules and regulations permitted consuls general and consuls to add to their salaries certain prescribed fee receipts, mainly from notarial services. By the 1890s limits were set on the charges permitted for those services. From these funds the Department of State specifically authorized principal consular officers to hire additional clerical help. Supervisory consular officials also could retain up to $1,000 per year from the fees collected by subordinate officers at their constituent posts. These higher-ranking officers, however, forwarded "official" fees, which principally were for documentary services required by statute, as contrasted with notarials, to the Treasury Department. Official receipts constituted the bulk of reported funds taken in by consular posts (see appendix C).[23]

The base pay at some posts, both diplomatic and consular, was generous in an age when the vice president of the United States made $12,000 per year, members of Congress earned $7,500, government employees of all ranks gained on the average less than $600, and skilled industrial workers in the private sector received perhaps $500. But these annual rates were the pay scales for heads of mission and principal consular officers of major posts, not the pay of lesser figures or an average for all ranks. Further, diplomatic and consular officers in those days normally paid for their own and their families' travel expenses to and from the posts, for the rental of appropriate living quarters abroad, for entertainment as dictated by the needs of the post, and in the cases of senior officers sometimes for clerical support to supplement the small official staffs of the day.

American diplomatic envoys and consuls general rarely fared as well financially as their European counterparts, and lower-ranking officers were even less well off. As the consul general at Shanghai reported early in the decade, his deputy made only $1,200 per year, compared with the pay of $2,500 and up accorded to incumbents of similar positions at other nations' consulates. Consul General Oliver Hart Dockery at Rio de Janeiro complained by letter to Secretary Blaine at about the same time that he made only $6,000 annually, whereas his British colleague drew $14,000 per year. In 1896 the minister resident and consul general at Bangkok pushed for an increase in pay at the post from $6,000 per annum to $7,500, pointing out that his British, German, and French counterparts made twice as much as he.[24]

The figures reported by the American minister at Bangkok were not far off as an average. At Paris in 1892 the German ambassador received 150,000 marks, not including allowances, or about $35,000 per year, as compared with the American minister's $17,500. At the same post in 1914, a year close enough to the nineties to mark a comparison, the British ambassador to France earned the princely sum of 11,500 pounds sterling, or $56,000 equivalent.[25] At a smaller post, Copenhagen, the figures in the same years were $8,500 for the German minister and $6,500 for the American. The British envoy to Japan in 1914 made $24,350 in salary, while the American by contrast drew $12,000. The highest German consul general salaries of the era were $11,300 and $9,400 at New York and London, respectively, far above the salaries at major American consular posts.[26] Nowhere were the salary scales weighted in favor of the representative from the United States.

Consular pay is complicated by another factor, however. The established salary levels by post and position do not always tell the whole story of the 1890s Consular Service, disparities between the consular pay scales of the United States and other nations notwithstanding. American posts in Europe headed by consuls, as well as those headed by consuls general, sometimes were lucrative in those precareerist days because of the fees that the principal officer could retain. In 1887 rumors had it that the consul generalship at Paris was worth an astonishing $50,000 yearly, including fee receipts, although a high-ranking Department of State official claimed the figure was inflated by a factor of more than four. In 1895 the chairman of the House Committee on Foreign Affairs noted that "only a few posts in the world" had notarial fees amounting "to a considerable sum, say $2,500 and upward." He mentioned London in this connection, as well as Paris with $15,000 annually and Berlin with $3,000. But at many posts, he said, the amounts involved were insignificant.[27]

Principal officers of consulates in England in particular, however, made a practice of contracting with British commission agents to administer the oaths that accompanied shipping invoices. Fees from the schedule of

payments went to the consuls, who paid a smaller fixed sum to the commissioners and pocketed the balance as a supplement to their authorized
salaries. The British contractors who administered the invoice oaths re-
alized up to $1,000 a year for their trouble.[28]

These invoice fee receipts in England were substantial. In 1895 at the
busy port of Liverpool, they amounted to a sum of from $7,000 to
$8,000; at Manchester and Bradford, more than $5,000. All told, including their salaries, the consulships at the latter two posts were estimated to be worth $10,000 per year, even after other expenses such as
hiring commissioners to help in the administration of the invoices. A
Consular Service inspection in 1896 revealed that Consul General
Patrick A. Collins himself paid the salaries of an officer and three or
four clerks on his London staff. Yet the post brought him an estimated
net annual income of at least $25,000, including invoice fees and the
$6,000 salary.[29] (The estimate seems high; see appendix C.) The in-
spector found this practice, as long-standing as it was in the British Isles,
to be in violation of regulations. In 1906 Congress passed a law which
required that all fees, with one set of exceptions, be remitted to the
Treasury Department. The exceptional case was that of consular agents
at small posts who could keep one-half of their fee receipts up to $1,000
per year.[30]

Representational entertainment expenses at some posts were high and
were not reimbursed. The diplomatic mission at Paris is a prime example.
During the period under review, the wealthy minister to France, Whitelaw Reid, who had amassed a fortune through publishing and an advan-
tageous marriage, gained renown as a host. He gave one ball in 1890 for
twelve hundred guests and another in 1891 for fourteen hundred. The
traditional Fourth of July reception at the envoy's Paris residence averaged
more than a thousand guests. His salary of $17,500 did not go very far
in covering such expenses, added as they were to the cost of maintaining
a large house and a staff of servants. As Reid remarked, however, in
words equally applicable to today's senior diplomats, "So much of a Minister's success depends upon cultivating cordial relations with the officers
of the Government to which he is accredited, that I had to be extremely
particular about accepting as many . . . invitations as possible, and to
return the hospitality we enjoyed."[31]

London is another example of a costly post. Ambassador John Hay
held his Fourth of July reception in 1898 on a day of glorious weather
such as can be seen only in England on one of those rare summer periods
of great beauty. Some fifteen hundred guests jammed the residence on
Carlton House Terrace. The rooms were decorated with exotic blossoms,

the terrace was covered with bunting and flags, a Hungarian band played, and many Americans overflowed the residence and sat outside on the grass of the Mall. "Champagne flowed freely" while the ambassador and his diplomatic staff and their wives greeted and circulated among the guests in time-honored diplomatic fashion.[32]

Ambassador William F. Draper at Rome in early 1900 invited to dinner a diplomatic colleague on his way back to the United States from an assignment abroad. "The Ambassador and Mrs. Draper entertain in magnificent style," wrote the guest in his diary. "We have very little diplomatic business with the Quirinal [Palace], the main functions are social and these are elegantly discharged by Mr. and Mrs. Draper. He told me he spent—about—75 thousand dollars a year—his official salary is 12 thousand." Such social events large and small, repeated many times over, did not come cheap; representation was a costly duty at many posts and was a recognized fact of life. One businessman, in writing to President Harrison in 1889 to recommend an aspirant for diplomatic appointment, thought it useful to point out the would-be envoy's heavy involvement in the 1888 campaign, his speaking ability, and his party loyalty. He concluded his missive with the following relevant observation: "I need scarcely add that his . . . possession of a liberal share of this world's goods would enable him to creditably represent our Government at any foreign court to which he might be accredited."[33]

Pay scales bore at least indirectly on two other aspects of foreign service life in the nineties—housing and offices. The heads of missions and principal consular officers often arranged both their official and personal quarters using any available means or methods, frequently starting from scratch upon arrival at post. Office space was then neither in buildings owned by the United States government nor usually under long-term lease, as has been the case in more recent years. The Department of State began acquiring property for the Foreign Service only in 1926, and the bulk of funds originally authorized was not expended until after the Second World War.[34]

American tourists and businessmen of our time have long been accustomed to finding the American embassy in London on Grosvenor Square, the consulate general in Paris on avenue Gabriel just off the Place de la Concorde, the embassy in Cairo in the Garden City district, and the consulate general in Sao Paulo on the Avenida Paulista. In the 1890s the location of the mission or consulate was not always such a known factor in a traveller's plans, nor did diplomats and consuls have living quarters provided by the government, as so often is done nowadays even for junior officers. In 1905 envoy Andrew D. White wrote about his earlier tour as minister to Russia: "The troubles of an American representative at St. Petersburg are many, and they generally begin with the search for an apartment. It is very difficult indeed in that capital to find a properly furnished suite of rooms for a minister, and since the American representative has been made an ambassador, this difficulty is greater than ever." White noted that by "especial luck and large outlay" he was able to resolve the problem, but made the point that many other American envoys were not so fortunate. "Whereas nearly every other power owned or held on long lease a house or apartment for its representative . . . the American representative had lived wherever circumstances compelled him."[35]

What a contrast between the material surroundings of Minister White and the French ambassador at St. Petersburg! White's French colleague presided over an establishment which faced the Neva River and was described as "a large square building, without charm, but spacious . . . and perfectly suited to its use, that is, for representation." A profusion of fine tapestries and magnificent paintings filled the rooms of the embassy, as they did at all large French diplomatic posts. The unimposing American legation clearly was held in lesser esteem than the missions of many of the more than twenty other powers represented at St. Petersburg.[36]

Ambassador to Britain Joseph Choate, like White, was fortunate. After residing upon arrival at the elegant Claridges Hotel in London's West End, he obtained a "first-rate home," a property of Lord Curzon's on Carlton House Terrace in Whitehall adjacent to the property previously leased by the just-departed Ambassador Hay. It was an ideal location for the ambassador, not far from the unfortunately dingy embassy offices—the chancery, that is—at 123 Victoria Street, S.W., in Westminster.[37] But Choate was a wealthy man and hardly had to balk at the cost of a suitable residence.

One of his predecessors in London, the not-so-rich Thomas F. Bayard, lived in a small house near Prince's Gate in Knightsbridge. Minister Straus in Turkey late in the nineties situated himself pleasantly—at his own expense—during the summer months at the village of Therapia, ten miles up the Bosporus from Constantinople, as did Consul General Luther Short earlier in the decade. (Envoys from other nations had summer quarters provided, a perquisite of some importance in the heat.) In the fall Straus returned to the Grande Rue de Pera in the Turkish capital's European quarter. There his mission occupied a one-flight walk-up apartment in an ordinary residential building. There the minister had as an office "a beautiful room in front, overlooking the Grand Rue."[38] During the Harrison administration, Minister Whitelaw Reid found "palatial housing" in Paris at 35 avenue Hoche, near the Place d'Etoile and the chancery. This was the scene of his elaborate entertaining noted above. The chancery moved during the decade from quarters on rue Galilée, which visitors described as shabby, to better facilities at 8 avenue Kleber, adjacent to the Etoile. The Paris consulate general remained at 36 avenue de l'Opéra, close to the Palais Royale.[39]

Senior consular officers also managed to get settled appropriately as American representatives, if in less luxurious accommodations than diplomatic chiefs of mission to major European capitals. In the mid-nineties, Consul General Crittenden at Mexico City rented a building at 5 rua San Diego, facing the Alameda, a few doors from the legation. He used two large rooms on the second floor and a storeroom for consulate general quarters, and the Crittenden family occupied the other rooms at that address. He charged the Department of State one-half of the total rental cost. Late in 1896 the consulate general at Panama was located at 41 Plaza San Francisco, in one of the better sections of the city. Consul General Vifquain, too, rented the entire building, using two spacious front rooms on the ground floor as offices and living with his family on the second floor. Following the usual practice at the time, he claimed a part of his rental expense from the government as an official operating cost.[40]

The Department of State took no exception to principal officers living in the same buildings that housed the consular offices; the department cautioned merely that in such instances "consuls are expected to pay at least one-third of the rent." Not all did; in 1896 Vifquain at Panama ran into trouble with an inspector on this score.[41]

Consul General Williams maintained the busy Havana office at 92 rua Aguair, considered a good location. Four large rooms on the second floor were well suited to business use, although supplied with old and inadequate furniture. The property rented for $1,200 per year, including the services of a janitor. The even larger Shanghai consulate general at the end of the century occupied on lease all five floors of a building located in the heart of the business quarter. The ground floor of the Shanghai office incorporated the consular jail, while the second floor contained a post office and shipping section. Consul General Goodnow used the third floor as office space, the fourth floor as his living area, and the fifth floor wholly as quarters for casual laborers.[42] Minister Resident Hamilton King, who was as well consul general at Bangkok from 1898 to 1903, and then minister only until his death at post in 1912, had his legation on the banks of the Chao Phya River, between the British and French missions. The large, two-story building, described by contemporaries as ramshackle, was set in a walled compound filled with trees and tropical shrubbery. The King family lived on its second story, with a balcony extending around three sides. The legation moored its houseboat close by at a riverfront landing. [43]

On the European consular scene, the London consulate general in 1894 was well located in the city at 12 St. Helen's Place, Bishopgate, and presentable in appearance. The offices were said, however, to be much too small for the number of Consul General Patrick A. Collins's clerks and the constant flow of visitors. In 1896 the Cleveland appointee Charles de Kay located the Berlin consulate "in very handsome rooms in the Equitable Life Insurance Building [on Friedreich Strasse]—probably the best location" in the city. Consul General William Carroll had his Dresden facility at 33 Luttichau Strasse, in excellent quarters and good condition. In 1896 an inspector found Consul General Frank H. Mason's Frankfort offices at 78 Niedenau in very good shape. Some years earlier, in 1890, the consulate general at Rome, headed by Rhode Island manufacturer and former governor Augustus Osborn Bourn, shared a central location at 13 via Nazionale with the legation of Minister Albert Gallatin Porter, a wealthy Indiana lawyer-politician. [44]

Often a first time 1890s American diplomatic envoy or consul general was new to government and thus unfamiliar with bureaucratic levers that could be pulled. He might well be surprised upon arrival by the down-at-the-heels state of his office, even in some of the most important capitals of Europe—witness the poor facilities at London and the move that was occasioned at Paris. It is difficult to generalize from the record as to where the most delapidated offices were located as some were present in all regions. But the descriptive material available suggests that diplomatic missions generally suffered in appearance in comparison with consular offices, and rarely were there funds to refurbish threadbare official quarters. The United States government did not devote official receipts to the foreign affairs establishment in substantial amounts. The Department of State's budget in 1890 totalled only $1.8 million, up just a half-million dollars since the pre–Civil War year of 1860. [45]

In May 1894, when the newly assigned American envoy to Argentina debarked at Buenos Aires to take over from the departing John R. G. Pitkin, he found what he considered to be a real mess. Minister Buchanan, a former businessman and exhibits manager from Iowa who was backed for the post by his home state agricultural interests, found to his dismay that his chancery consisted of two small, unheated rooms with a minimum of furnishings. The mission had no typewriter (a common lack in those days), no letterpress for copying correspondence, and indeed no letter files of any sort. Buchanan set to work to improve the office's system, calling into play his own managerial experience, and after three months moved to larger quarters. All of this he undertook while also searching for living accommodations for his family; eventually he rented temporarily the German consul general's residence for that purpose.[46]

No less dismayed was Minister Bartlett Tripp at Vienna. Tripp arrived at the capital of the Austro-Hungarian Empire in June 1893 to assume the post from Colonel Frederick D. Grant, son of the late president. The empress received him informally first, and then Tripp presented his credentials. Less than three weeks later, in one of his first despatches of any consequence to Secretary of State Walter Q. Gresham, he wrote:

> I desire to call the attention of the Department to the present condition of the apartments occupied by this Legation; the condition of the rooms and their furnishings are shabby in the extreme. The furniture is not only scanty, but old, worn, and valueless. I am ashamed [to receive] American visitors in such apartments and I am sure the feeling is reciprocal on their part. *While I do not expect apartments corresponding in style and equipment with those of European Embassies and Legations,* I do desire to have the Legation furnished in a plain substantial manner somewhat in keeping with the dignity and rank of America among the nations of the world and sufficiently so at least for the comfort and convenience of its officers and those having business to transact therewith.[47]

New envoys and consuls general of the period frequently lamented that quarters and furnishings were not in keeping with the dignity and rank of America among nations, much less up to the standards of the major European powers.

Another concern impelled the new American minister to Chile to seek different housing for his legation in 1893. Former governor James Davis Porter of Tennessee succeeded Patrick Egan at Santiago early in July. Before the month was out he informed Washington, "I found the Legation located at an undesirable place and enjoying a notoriety that did not contribute to its influence. I have therefore moved it to more fitting quarters at no. 204, A, on the Alameda." The vacated offices may well have been poorly located—the monthly rent was only fifty dollars—but likely it was the political ill fame of the location cited by Porter that caused the change. Egan had been involved in several controversies with the Chilean government over extending asylum at the legation to opposition political figures from a previous regime. Minister Porter understandably wanted to make a clean start on his tour in the capital as American diplomatic envoy and evidently decided that one way to do that was to change his official address.[48]

In 1897 Minister Granville Stuart at Montevideo reported that the legation, located in the central part of the city at 176 Calle Zabala, suffered in comparison with the more spacious nearby British mission. He praised his legation's "comfort, convenience, and healthfulness," but held it to be "scarcely large enough for entertaining in a style proper for the representation of 75,000,000 Americans." His successor, William R. Finch, shortly thereafter made a change, whether or not for the better. A month after taking charge, he moved the legation quarters in Montevideo to a less central location, at 112 Asamblea, with a lower rent. He deemed the new site "not inconvenient," given the small amount of business transacted with local officials.[49]

Envoys and consuls general encountered all sorts of difficulties and problems in living abroad during the nineties. There were the unhealthy locales such as Monrovia, the remote posts such as Tehran, and at times the political trouble spots such as Havana and Santiago. The climate could be an important factor in an otherwise agreeable situation: As Minister White wrote from St. Petersburg in mid-1894, "I cannot think of anything earthly which would tempt me to pass another winter here." Even London gave cause for complaint. In early 1896 Minister Thomas F. Bayard wrote to his colleague in Rome complaining of a long-standing bout with influenza: "I am glad you . . . have had the sunshine of Italy instead of the fogs of London this winter."[50]

Nevertheless, many senior officers passed their tours of duty agreeably at pleasant posts. Several factors account for this. Diplomatic and consular representation was concentrated in Western Europe and Latin America, not in the yet-to-emerge Third World countries of Africa and Asia, and relatively few truly serious crisis situations arose during the decade. Official life was slower in those days. Most officers were spared the extensive, time-consuming demands for information that became routine with improved communications. Indeed, to the contrary, sometimes officers in the field found it difficult to maintain contact with Washington. As one minister resident in Latin America complained in 1895 to a Department of State official, "I have written several communications during the last year to which I have no reply." In 1899 an envoy in the Middle East wrote to the secretary of state to thank him for a personal letter: "At this distant post where a minister is frequently compelled to assume grave responsibilities by prompt action, such messages . . . are especially encouraging." [51] Further, at most posts they had none of the visits by peripatetic Washington officials, importantly including congressmen, which became so frequent in later years with improved international transportation.

Despatches forwarded to Washington by ship or train were by far a more usual means of sending messages than cables at a time when communications were less well developed than today. A post measured its reporting load in despatches, not the number of cables sent, as is the practice in the modern Foreign Service. The telephone, although in existence from the 1870s, was practically unheard of as a communications medium. Nor did American diplomatic missions and consular offices then have their own telegraphic facilities, as usually is the case today at major posts.

The decade of the nineties thus generally was a blessedly quiet and calm era for most envoys and consuls general when compared with many periods of the strife-torn twentieth century. Perhaps the experience of one senior officer will illustrate how foreign service life could be enjoyed, even with the occasional difficulty. Eben Alexander was a professor of Greek at the University of North Carolina who spent the Cleveland years in the mid-nineties as chief of mission at the Athens legation. (The consul on his staff was George Horton of Chicago, a scholar of Greek as well.) As he wrote home in 1894, "If all continues to go as well with us as has been the case thus far, we shall probably stay here the whole four years. . . . Not many puzzling questions come up, though there is enough to give me something to do." He noted that his wife and children liked living in Athens "very much." Even household arrangements and personal finances compared favorably with his situation back at Chapel Hill. "We have rented a good house . . . [and] are still getting on well in money matters." "My salary really amounts to more than $6,500, as the government pays our rent out of the contingent funds."[52]

All continued to go well for the Alexanders. In 1895 he wrote that the family had taken up bicycling, often to Phaleron for a swim. In the summer months Minister Alexander and family travelled to France on extended holiday. In 1896 he assumed a leading role in the revival of the Olympic Games at Athens. It was not a bad life at all for the four years 1893 to 1897. Alexander dwelt little on his official duties in his correspondence, an indication that the American envoy to Greece at that time did not find the job particularly taxing. This judgment on the demands of the position, or lack thereof, is supported by the opinion of his successor: The Orientalist W.W. Rockhill found Athens "deadly dull."[53]

Several overall impressions on operations abroad emerge from this review of foreign service life and the official functions of senior officers in the 1890s. Even though the decade saw far-reaching changes on the world scene for America, it was a comparatively quiescent time for most diplomatic and consular officials abroad. Further, the diplomatic establishment overseas was small; the United States got by with fewer than three dozen diplomatic missions, staffed by a limited number of officers worldwide, many of whom were dependent on personal wealth to carry out their expected duties. Senior consular officers at major posts, as contrasted with lower-ranking, often part-time consular officials, were no more numerous. Some few officers at consular posts did well financially with their unsanctioned fee practices, but most were modestly paid.

Calm times for most notwithstanding, these envoys and consuls general dealt with a wide variety of problems and workaday concerns and carried differing sets of responsibilities at different posts. Generally, the legations and embassies coped with issues that were basically similar but which differed in detail from one post to another in substantive content. Few problems were other than routine in nature. One scholar of the period has termed the "staples of American diplomacy the release of naturalized American citizens from foreign military service and sealing rights."[54]

Diplomats and consular officers were not then and are not now responsible for the formulation of foreign policy. They contribute indirectly in this regard through reporting on the local political or economic scene, making representations to the host government on instructions, and gauging reactions, official and unofficial. Diplomatic missions, and on rare occasions consular posts, may make policy-related recommendations, and in trouble-ridden areas sometimes were (and are) expected to do so. But that was not their principal function. Top officials in Washington, largely noncareerists then and now, were primarily responsible for setting policy directions that accorded with presidential wishes. They were charged as well with explaining and defending before the Congress questions that arose on such policies. Diplomats abroad, whether mostly careerists as nowadays or nonprofessionals as at the turn of the century, normally had a different role: they carried out policies once they were determined in Washington.[55]

As to the Consular Service, it misses the mark to assert that its primary goal at every post in the 1890s was to push American exports—or to issue consular invoices, or to take care of seamen, or to accomplish any other single purpose. In actuality, the prime concerns differed from post to post, and the interests of the principal officer sometimes ruled, given the relatively few demands placed on this small foreign service by a miniscule Department of State. Some officers concerned themselves mainly with export promotion, others with political affairs or shipping questions or problems related to the protection of Americans' interests abroad.

The foreign service's administrative operation in the 1890s can be called "informal" and "personalized" at best, and "chaotic" or "slapdash" at worst. This study is not an investigation of the Department of State and the evolution of its administrative framework; that work has been done (see note 3 of chapter 2). But the department took an almost haphazard approach to foreign service selection, appointment, assignment, travel, pay, housing, and office space, all of which indicated the need for administrative changes, as was recognized by reformers of the day. Washington chose individuals for assignment almost always for political patronage reasons and sent them abroad with little or no briefing, much less any training, to countries about which they sometimes knew little, to carry out duties that frequently were ill-defined. Often appointees could not speak the local language. Most were not well paid. Some operated out of shabby offices and occupied rundown living quarters. One can barely recognize that small foreign service as the organizational predecessor of the United States' large foreign affairs bureaucracy which has been abroad in recent decades. Improvements in the 1890s administrative organization—"professionalization" if you will—clearly were needed.

It is not so clear thus far in this study, however, that the quality of the people who held the senior positions of the poorly organized 1890s foreign service system equally needed to be improved. Certain of the chiefs of mission and consuls general made no mark of any consequence on the nation's conduct of foreign affairs, if for no other reason than that they served such brief periods overseas. A surprising number, however, seem to have settled in to their unfamiliar posts quickly and begun efficiently to discharge their duties, including initiating a flow of reports back to Washington on numerous problems and issues. And some of these nineties officers did make a name for themselves over the years as effective diplomats.

The most that can be said at this point about these 1890s political appointees in our reconstruction of life abroad is that many were remarkable neither for very good nor for very bad performances, possibly in significant part than because many of them were not severely or frequently tested by fast-breaking, dramatic events during the decade. Perhaps the nation was well served, despite the chaotic state of its foreign

service administrative system, by the fact that only a few grave international crises had to be faced in the 1890s, at least not until toward the
close of the decade. The life-and-death demands of international relations familiar to us today did not crowd in on the foreign service until
later.

| 6 |

Diplomatic and Consular Episodes

A diplomat is useful, not only for what he does, but for what he is.
Daniele Varé, Laughing Diplomat (1938)

This chapter imparts a further sense of the questions occupying the foreign service during the nineties. Envoys and senior consular officials sent messages to Washington on developments in their host countries then, in the manner that they do now. On occasion they negotiated with local authorities, usually under instructions from the Department of State. They saw to the protection of American interests generally and also with respect to individual citizens in need of assistance. They "showed the flag" by their presence, a basic responsibility still with American diplomats and consuls even in the complicated present-day world. [1]

Among the issues and concerns of the 1890s that involved senior officers of the day were occasional disturbances in the United States' backyard, Latin America. American representatives extensively reported those events, and policy toward the area was fairly clearly defined, if not always openly articulated. Elsewhere in the world, senior officers at their small (by later standards) diplomatic missions and consular offices normally spent most of their time—aside from attending to ceremonial functions—on routine reporting, commercial or shipping matters, or what is called in modern-day consular terminology "welfare and whereabouts," activities related to the protection and representation of Americans overseas. In many instances these last responsibilities involved looking after missionaries and dual nationals. Only rarely did a crisis arise for any given senior officer, other than in the Caribbean and its periphery, that had a significant bearing on policy questions.

The limited survey which follows samples briefly the reporting from several posts and officers in four geographic regions, along with some of the problems which arose affecting posts in two areas (an example is the Cuban question). It is not intended as a summary of the United States' foreign relations or a look at most of the 226 officers in the study group. Rather, the brief episodic treatment is designed to provide an overview of how posts were administered and problems addressed. Some officers involved did well, others did not. Although the next chapter will take up how competently the officers as a group handled their duties, explicit opinions on a number of individuals are provided in this section.

LATIN AMERICA

Latin America was the area of greatest interest to the United States in the late nineteenth century. At the beginning of the 1890s policy in the region encompassed both political-strategic and commercial questions. During the previous twenty-five years, the United States became more active in Latin America than in any other part of the world. American influence was paramount; the United States intervened in disputes, made attempts at annexation, and promoted Pan Americanism. Early in the decade, the Harrison administration stated its primary purpose in Latin America as strengthening political and commercial relations. Later, especially following the financial Panic of 1893 and the depression that followed, trade matters became even more important. Walter LaFeber calls the two facets of United States policy toward its neighbors to the south at this time the "strategic" and the "economic formulation" of America's "new empire."[2]

Central America was one integral part of that policy focus, even without as yet an isthmian canal. This survey starts there with a story of failure. Lansing Bond Mizner, minister to three Central America countries from 1889, was a grandfatherly-looking, wealthy California lawyer and politician admitted to practice before the United States Supreme Court. Sixty-three in 1889, a Mexican War veteran, and a graduate of Shurtleff College in Illinois, he had been a junior clerk at the American legation in Bogota back in the 1840s and spoke fluent Spanish.[3]

In July 1890 Guatemala and El Salvador went to war, indirectly as a consequence of a revolution in the latter country. Mizner reported fully on the hostilities, once in a rare telegram, and on attempts to mediate the conflict.[4] Following instructions from Washington, he played an effective role in these negotiations. But his involvement in peace efforts was overshadowed by another problem that arose in late August. An exiled Guatemalan general and insurrectionist named Barrundia sailed on an American-flag ship from Mexico. He intended to land in El Salvador. When the ship made a scheduled call at a Guatemalan port en route to Salvador, Guatemalan authorities not surprisingly wanted to seize Barrundia. Their way was paved by Minister Mizner. He provided the American ship's captain with a signed letter stating that Guatemala had the right "under the law of nations" to arrest the rebel general. Citing in his brief letter Guatemala's current state of war and Barrundia's reported hostility to the government, he instructed the ship's captain "to deliver him to the authorities of Guatemala upon their demand."[5] When the police went aboard, Barrundia was killed while resisting arrest.

Mizner made a serious error of judgment in issuing the letter, whatever the legal basis for his decision and regardless of whether he was concerned for the safety of the vessel and its passengers, as he later asserted. His action had fatal consequences and led to his repudiation and recall. A precedent for Mizner's decision on Barrundia was an 1885 instruction under similar circumstances from Secretary of State Thomas F. Bayard to a ship's master in a Nicaraguan port. The Department of State interpreted the legal principles involved in the Barrundia case differently, however. As Washington pointed out to Mizner by telegram immediately after he reported the incident, the rebel leader had placed himself within reach of Guatemalan authorities "at his own peril," and it was for those authorities "to assume jurisdiction at their own risk and responsibility." By direction of the president, the department formally disavowed his action and instructed him to leave the post, a most unusual action. It was his only significant mistake as an envoy, but it was enough. Washington speedily named his replacement, Romualdo Pacheco, also of California. Mizner departed under a cloud at the end of the year despite success as a peacemaker.[6]

Was an untrained, aging politician thrown by chance into a fast-moving situation with which he was unable to cope? A seemingly minor issue blew up in his face while he was dealing with larger problems of war and peace. Almost as an afterthought he acted in an unfortunate and poorly thought-out manner. Yet, was his error because of his amateur status? Would a careerist have avoided the error under the same conditions? Possibly. But one senses that extraordinary demands for the times impinged on the judgment of a seemingly well-qualified senior officer who had been at post more than a year; his personal judgment was at question, not his credentials.

Fast-breaking events severely tested few other senior officers assigned in the hemisphere; the mundane was the order of the day at most posts. The experience of a consul general in Guatemala's neighbor to the north, Mexico, typifies the times and illustrates the duties of consuls general in this era. Thomas T. Crittenden was the consul general in Mexico in the midnineties. Aside from the usual run of commercial and welfare duties, his position brought with it the need for an extensive correspondence with Americans in the United States, from high officials in Washington, D.C., to inquiring private citizens in Washington State.[7] The distinguished-looking former Missouri governor and congressman wrote on a wide variety of topics. To many correspondents he replied with information and advice on economic and commercial questions. He passed judgment on the government of President Porfirio Díaz ("a strong conservative and progressive administration"); on occasion he warned the Department of State that France, Germany, and Great Britain were vying with the United States for trade with Mexico, and he suggested specific investment projects.[8]

Although industrious, Crittenden had his limits on patience. Upon receipt of one twenty-three-point scattershot questionnaire on various phases of the Mexican economy, he replied acidly that he was "no encyclopedia" and that research of that sort was not his business. He referred the query to Mexican informants for reply.[9] Withal, despite his lack of experience in the field, in the judgment of one historian, he was "a competent observer of Mexico."[10]

In 1891, when already strained United States-Chilean relations worsened, Washington's "man in Chile" was Patrick Egan, a prominent former Irish nationalist.[11] Egan had immigrated to Nebraska less than ten years before and was naturalized only in 1888. A successful grain merchant, he was a Harrison supporter and a friend of James G. Blaine. When Harrison entered office, he awarded the Santiago legation to the slightly built, mustachioed Egan, whose unusual background included active involvement in Irish home rule questions with Charles Stewart Parnell, election twice to the British Parliament, and trial in England for sedition.[12]

His contemporaries and some later historians have criticized Egan for his handling of United States' interests in Chile, especially for what is seen as his overidentification with a pro-American government during a period of civil war, and to a lesser degree his inaccurate reporting of deadly riots involving American sailors from the USS *Baltimore*, a warship on a port visit to Valparaiso.[13] Not surprisingly he dealt sympathetically with President Balmaceda while he was in office, especially given the latter's tilt toward American business interests. When the congressional insurgents drove Balmaceda from office that winter of 1891 (summer in the northern hemisphere), however, Egan reported this fact and asked of Washington whether the new government should not be recognized, noting that conditions were tranquil. Only days later, on instructions, he extended recognition. Shortly thereafter, the *Washington Post* nonetheless criticized his lack of neutrality toward opposing factions in the civil war, and the *New York Tribune* demanded his recall.[14]

These complications were but a prelude to the *Baltimore* riots in October during which Egan now dealt with the new government headed by a navy captain. Egan's extensive reporting on the incident, after a brief initial underestimation of its significance, bears no readily apparent signs of misrepresentation or lack of appreciation of the issues involved. He necessarily dealt more and more with the explosive anti-American incident during which two American sailors died, even though much occupied also with the problem of political asylum in his and other foreign missions. The two nations for a brief moment almost went to war over the *Baltimore* affair. Both Washington and Santiago adopted hard lines, but by early 1892 the new Chilean government dropped its stance and paid an indemnity. President Harrison reported to the Congress at the end of the year that the matter was settled.[15]

A neophyte as a diplomatic envoy, Egan was no stranger to important issues, however, nor did he lack in ability. A standard biographic source refers to him somewhat fulsomely as being of "unusual ability" and "singularly upright . . . tactful, discreet, courageous." One historian comments that at the height of the developing crisis in Chile, "Egan's dignified bearing . . . aroused the admiration of even the British minister."[16] Unlike the unfortunate Lansing Mizner in Guatemala, he coped with the demands of the post and maintained enough credit in Washington to last the full course of four years in Chile.

Continuing the Latin American survey, two crises of 1895 involved matters of policy. Both set the United States against Great Britain and raised questions of the Monroe Doctrine. In April the minister to Costa Rica, Nicaragua, and El Salvador, Lewis Baker, sent a short cable from Managua to Washington: the British had landed—at the port city of Corinto in Nicaragua. Although the British marines departed without further incident a week later, the landing climaxed a vexing episode that had long been building. The previous year in June Baker had reported "fresh disturbances" and (erroneously) a revolution. Finally, an uprising in July 1894 occasioned the landing of United States Marines for a short period to prevent further violence. A provisional government with participation by local foreign residents proved short-lived. In mid-August the Nicaraguan army reasserted its control. The government thereupon deported two Americans and twelve British subjects, accusing them of complicity in the uprising. By this time in this relatively fast-moving scenario, Minister Baker was under fire from the Department of State and felt compelled to apologize for not keeping it better posted on developments.[17]

Ambassador Thomas F. Bayard in London meanwhile reported British demands for a cash indemnity from Nicaragua and the foreign secretary's assurances that Britain had no designs on Nicaraguan territory. Managua did not meet London's demands, however. For one thing, the government was without funds, as Minister Baker had reported in a lengthy despatch a few months previously. In April 1895, just before the expiration of the deadline, Baker reported by cable Managua's request for American intercession with Great Britain. Shortly thereafter he was so indiscreet as to tell the Nicaraguan foreign minister in a letter that he deplored the "brusque manner" of the British government. Eventually, three British warships appeared off Corinto, the port on the Pacific nearest to Managua, and sent a landing force ashore on 27 April, the landing noted above that Baker reported. Bayard in London on instructions expressed "the hope that the British Government will give opportunity to Nicaragua to settle demands on the condition of withdrawal of forces from Corinto."[18] Managua finally met those demands, and British forces thereupon withdrew from Corinto in May 1895. Their departure closed the Corinto incident and set the stage for the better-known Venezuelan boundary dispute of the same year.

The United States and Britain contested large policy issues in the Corinto affair, mainly over isthmian canal prospects and Monroe Doctrine tenets, and Washington leaders believed themselves to be ill-served by their envoys. Baker at Managua, a former editor from Minnesota and state Democratic party leader in his early sixties, reported sporadically on a confused and difficult situation. One sympathizes with his problem, however, and he sent several useful and timely reports. Walter LaFeber finds no occasion to criticize him in the furtherance of Secretary Gresham's "smooth and subtle" policy of advancing the United States' interest vis-à-vis both Britain and Nicaragua. But Baker's contemporary, Walter Gresham, did. The usually relaxed, informal secretary characterized him as "vain, weak" and an "unfortunate" appointment.[19]

Washington reposed little more confidence in former Secretary of State and Senator Bayard at London, a noted Anglophile who was by then nearly seventy. The Department of State used him primarily to deliver official messages to the British on both Corinto and the subsequent Venezuelan boundary dispute, but the department's leadership did not rely heavily on his reports on reactions.

In August 1895 the Venezuelan boundary dispute began to unfold when the newly installed, combative Secretary of State Richard Olney (Gresham had died in office) sent his famous message to London virtually demanding submission of the Venezuelan question to binding arbitration. This familiar tale need not be repeated here, especially because Washington and London dealt with the Anglo-American crisis almost exclusively at the highest foreign ministry levels after the early stages. Ambassador Bayard initially was reluctant to force the issue by presenting Olney's startling demarche in all its starkness, and when Lord Salisbury finally delivered his haughty two-part reply almost four months later,[20] Bayard inexplicably forwarded it by pouch, deciding against a cable on its contents. It is little wonder that Secretary Olney thought ill of Bayard's abilities, despite the latter's experience.[21] Still less did Washington seek the counsel of the American envoy in Venezuela on important decisions at this time. Earlier in 1895 President Cleveland had sought someone for Caracas "of a much higher grade than is usually thought good enough for such a situation."[22] He eventually got Allen Thomas of Florida, a former planter, general, university professor, and United States Mint official in his mid-sixties who had just spent a year as consul at nearby La Guaira. Thomas remained unconsulted by Olney or the president as the showdown with Britain ground to an ultimately peaceful solution in early 1896.

American diplomats of the 1890s occasionally had the opportunity to observe or participate personally in momentous events. One such occasion, while not significant in a policy sense, resulted in the kind of graphic foreign service reporting that is seen only rarely in the archives. Granville Stuart, minister to Uruguay and Paraguay, was a Montana pioneer cattle raiser and gold miner conversant in two American Indian languages.[23] Over six feet tall and resembling Robert E. Lee, the courtly Stuart was nearly fifty years old when he took up his mission July 1894. That year the Uruguayans elected a second civilian president in a row after a long period of coups d' état and rule by the military. Stuart passed the next three years calmly at Montevideo even though political strife continued in the country. In August 1897 he found himself squarely in the middle of a dramatic occurrence.

A te deum mass was held to celebrate Uruguayan independence day. When it concluded, the Diplomatic Corps and high Uruguayan officials began to walk in procession to a central site in Montevideo to review a parade. President Borda unexpectedly abandoned his carriage and cavalry escort to step to the head of the group. Borda's action was surprising because of the "feeling of [political] uneasiness" in the city, in Stuart's words. As dean of the Diplomatic Corps, the American envoy took a position directly behind the president. "We had walked about a hundred yards when a man sprang from the . . . sidewalk diagonally in front of the President distant . . . six or eight feet, and as he sprang he extended his arm and fired a shot at the President. The swiftness of his action rendered any interference impossible." Borda remained upright and almost motionless. "[I] thought the shot had missed him," wrote Stuart in his despatch to his superiors, "and turned my attention to the assassin who was struggling with several men. . . . [W]hen I again looked at the President he was falling and being caught by those next to him." As recounted in some detail by Stuart, great confusion ensued. Members of the party carried the president into a nearby police station where he died with Minister Stuart standing close by. "He only lived about eight minutes after he was shot and only spoke once, saying, 'They have killed me.' "[24] Later officers marched the troops off to barracks, and the police cleared the area. Two days after the president's death, on instructions from Washington, he called on the new acting president to express condolences; afterward he reported on the state of affairs in the new government. The acting president pacified the country within a month's time, and things returned to normal.

This episode marked the high point of the Montanan's diplomatic career as a one-time political appointee. The policy implications of his tour at Montevideo were slight; the United States' relations with Paraguay and Uruguay were limited. But Stuart ably and clearly reported the rush of events surrounding the president's death and competently represented his country in its aftermath. An envoy could make a worse record for himself.[25]

This survey of the Latin American region in the nineties concludes with the Cuban crisis at the end of that period and a quick review of the roles of two senior officers on the spot, Consul General Fitzhugh Lee at Havana and Minister Stewart Lyndon Woodford at Madrid. President Cleveland appointed Lee to replace the veteran consular officer Ramon O. Williams partly because the latter had become "obnoxious to the Spanish authorities in Havana." Despite his age (he was born in 1827), Williams had shown himself to be vigorous and persistent in pursuing

Fitzhugh Lee, consul general at Havana, 1896–98. Photo by Frances Benjamin Johnston undated, probably taken at the Department of State, ca. 1896. Lee, a famed Confederate general, later was military governor of Havana for a brief period. (Courtesy Library of Congress.)

the numerous welfare and protection cases that arose from the increased turbulence in Cuba from early 1895 onward. Further, the authorities suspected his brother-in-law, resident in the United States, of trade withthe insurgents. By mid-1896 Williams had left, and Lee sent his first despatch from Havana.[26]

The new consul general was a rotund, heroically mustachioed former governor of Virginia and ex-Confederate general. Unlike Williams, he spoke no Spanish. The press adjudged him well qualified otherwise, however, and he had the confidence of President Cleveland. From mid-1896 throughout 1897 he reported extensively on a wide range of subjects, and in January 1898 he summed up the increasingly complex state of political affairs in Cuba. Lee believed that autonomy, a compromise be tween continued colonial status and independence, had little chance of success. Neither the Spanish in Cuba nor the insurgents wanted such a compromise; the latter wanted an independent republic, whereas the educated business elite wanted annexation by the United States.[27]

By that time the "firebrand" Lee too had become unacceptable to the Spanish. Madrid objected to his "active and open sympathy" for the Cuban rebels. In the view of one historian, "from the moment he arrived at Havana in April 1896 he worked for intervention by the U.S. in the [civil] war." The Department of State on 4 March defended him, and Spain dropped the issue.[28] His acceptability or lack thereof became academic a few weeks later with the outbreak of the Spanish-American War.

"The most important problem with which this Government is now called upon to deal pertaining to its foreign relations," announced President McKinley in his 1897 year-end message to Congress, "concerns its duty toward Spain and the Cuban insurrection."[29] The roles of the United States ministers to Spain now came to the fore. Hannis Taylor of Alabama held the position from 1893 to the fall of 1897. North Carolina-born and educated, he was a practicing attorney and legal scholar in his mid-forties.[30] He reported by cable the politically crucial assassination of Prime Minister Cánovas del Castillo in August 1898, but soon thereafter Stewart L. Woodford took over as minister.

Woodford was another general, a Civil War brevet brigadier from New York who was habitually addressed by his military rank, a characteristic of his generation (often the rank was elevated from the grade actually held, and in some instances it was wholly honorific). He presented his credentials in September 1897. In his early sixties, Woodford had previously served as a one-term congressman, as lieutenant governor of New York, and as United States district attorney. He was by no means McKinley's first choice as envoy to Spain; it took the president months to find a Republican replacement for the outgoing Democrat, Taylor. Possibly Woodford's appointment eventuated from a suggestion by a supporter that he would make a good ambassador to France.[31]

Generals Woodford and Lee sent two of the most striking foreign service messages during 1898, both telegrams. Lee first. Soon after his arrival, the former general had recommended that a warship be kept at Key West as a "precautionary measure."[32] This was not done, but eighteen months later, on 24 January, the Department of State informed him that the USS *Maine* was being sent to Havana because of disturbances in the city. Lee cabled back at once advising, contrary to his earlier recommendation, a delay of six or seven days to let things cool down, but the *Maine* arrived the next morning. Early the following month, Navy

Secretary Hilary A. Herbert wanted the ship withdrawn, but Lee now recommended that it stay in its "position of peaceful control of [the] situation."[33]

At 9:40 P.M. on 16 February the ship blew up. Consul General Lee reported the catastrophe in a cable of fewer than one hundred words sent three hours later.[34] The sinking of the battleship was the catalyst for much of what followed.

The focus then shifted to Woodford at Madrid. Despite the envoy's efforts at delay, McKinley took the nation—or the nation took McKinley (historians disagree)—into war. Minister Woodward's famous cable of 10 April counseled restraint: "I hope that nothing will now be done to humiliate Spain, as I am satisfied that the present Government is going . . . as fast and as far as it can."[35]

The Spanish government did not go fast enough or far enough. Following a message from McKinley, Congress passed a joint resolution on Cuba which posed demands that were unacceptable to Spain. Madrid broke relations on 20 April, and on the 25th McKinley signed a declaration of war. During that interim, Lee returned to Richmond, there to await his commission in the army, the only question being whether he would be a brigadier or a major general. Minister Woodford left Madrid by train on 21 April. Early the following day, after the train was stoned on its way to France, he had one last dramatic encounter on Spanish soil. At Valladolid, Woodford personally barred the door to his train compartment to prevent Spanish police from arresting his private secretary, a British subject. The minister prevailed; the police backed off, and Woodford's small party arrived safely at Paris that evening.[36]

Woodford had been at Madrid only a relatively short time and his efforts went for naught in the end. But he worked diligently to stave off the worst in the deteriorating relations. "[He] was an enemy of war and a skillful diplomat," in the view of historian Page Smith.[37] Consul General Lee at Havana had a reputation as an activist and rebel sympathizer. But he reported perceptively and diligently on the Cuban scene and was effective in filling his consular protection responsibilities in an unsettled period. Further, he had a cautionary streak, an essential element of the diplomat—witness his recommendation that the *Maine* not be sent when it was.

EAST ASIA AND THE PACIFIC

American representatives abroad did not usually participate in momentous events such as wars, revolutions, and the landing of British marines.

One overseas episode in the Pacific, an arena for American and European competition, demonstrates, however, the active role that United
States diplomats on occasion could play in determining the course of
events. Republican policymakers, who were in office most of the decade,
saw the region, along with the Caribbean, as suited to the implementation of Captain Alfred T. Mahan's recently published ideas on control of
the seas and great power status.[38] The supposedly vast China market
caught the attention of business interests, and by the end of the 1890s
the rise of Japan as a power and the threatened dismemberment of China
resulted in Secretary Hay's two Open Door notes of 1899 and 1900.
Further, bilateral issues arising from racial prejudices irritated America's
relations with both China and Japan.

The most pressing foreign policy problem for Washington in early
1893, however, was what to do about the Hawaiian Islands. "It is hardly
necessary for me to state," announced the reelected Cleveland at the end
of the year, "that the questions arising from our relations with Hawaii
have caused serious embarrassment."[39] The president's discomfort resulted
from a well-known tale in American diplomatic history; the islands came
close to being annexed by the Harrison administration, but when the
new Democratic president, Cleveland, came to office, he backed off.

Washington's interest in the islands nevertheless dated to the early
years of the century. Both Republican and Democratic administrations
through the years saw the islands as an important adjunct to American
national interests. By 1875 the United States had concluded a commercial reciprocity treaty with Hawaii which also obligated the island kingdom not to transfer territory to another foreign power. In 1881
Republican Secretary of State Blaine termed Hawaii "an outlying district of the State of California." In the mid-1880s expansionist Democratic Senator John Tyler Morgan called Hawaii both the "American
Hong Kong" for its usefulness in the China trade and the "American
Gibraltar" for its strategic value. In 1887 Democratic Secretary of State
Bayard wrote about the islands: "By reason of their geographical position
and comparative propinquity to our own territory they possess an interest
and importance to us far exceeding that with which they can be regarded by any other power. . . . The vast line of our national territory
on the Pacific coast, and its neighborhood to the Hawaiian group, indicate the recognized predominance [of American interests]."[40] This was
the framework in which American diplomats of the nineties worked
when assigned to the kingdom.

Cleveland's "serious embarrassment" stemmed in large part from the
actions of one senior diplomat, John Leavitt Stevens, minister to Hawaii

from 1889 to the advent of the new administration in 1893. He was an activist with a significant impact on events. Annexation of Hawaii failed as a policy in 1893 and was not brought to fruition for another five years, but not through any lack of initiative or effort on his part.

Almost seventy years old when appointed, Stevens was a white-bearded New England divine and former abolitionist editor. This was not his first diplomatic post nor was it his first exposure to questions of political importance. In the 1850s he had been a partner with Secretary of State Blaine in the ownership of a Maine newspaper. He had been a delegate to the Republican national conventions of 1860 and 1876 and a member of the Maine legislature from 1865 to 1870. He had served previously as minister to Uruguay and Paraguay for three years in the 1870s and to Sweden and Norway from 1877 to 1883. Among his accomplishments were the authorship of a biography of King Gustavus Adolphus and a reputed command of French. Historians note that the new envoy to Hawaii was an ardent annexationist from the beginning of his assignment. Secretary Blaine, his former partner in journalism, left him largely without instructions because they thought along the same activist lines, according to some accounts.[41]

The despatches he sent from Honolulu beginning in the fall of 1889 do not indicate such annexationist zeal, however. In his reporting and recommendations he clearly refrained at first from advocating a takeover by the United States. He warned of opposition by British and French interests and cited the usefulness of commercial treaty arrangements for the entry of island sugar into the mainland market as a means "to Americanize these islands and to bind them to the United States." And in those first months in office, Stevens found occasion to suggest that warships be sent to Honolulu to guard against possible disturbances. But he analyzed the forthcoming elections in the context of what was best, in his words, for "the friends of Hawaiian independence." He thought a victory by reform business elements, mostly the offspring of American missionaries, best served American interests.[42]

By March 1890 Stevens felt qualified to send policy recommendations to Washington. He noted the need to develop commercial interests in the Pacific, warned of competition from other nations, and expressed concern about a potentially unstable political situation due to a diverse population. He further recommended that the United States lay an ocean cable from California, improve the anchorage at Pearl Harbor, support "Americans and other intelligent citizens" in reform efforts, and finally, assist those same elements commercially through proposed modifications to the reciprocal trade treaty.[43] The American minister thus followed what had been the sense of Washington's policy toward the islands for many years, but he stopped well short of advocating that the islands be annexed.

For the next two years Stevens's despatches took a similar tone, even though at times he insisted on the need for an American warship at Honolulu. Not until early 1892 did the American minister explicitly call for annexation. His expressed reason was the political volatility of islands-wide legislative elections, not strategic considerations. "The present political situation is feverish, and I see no prospect of its being permanently otherwise until the Islands become part of the American Union, or a possession of Great Britain."[44]

In March 1892 Stevens asked for instructions in the event of an "orderly and peaceful" revolution in Hawaii, obviously meaning a revolution by the pro-American missionary and business elements. The minister wanted to know whether the United States would intervene to restore a government or only to protect American lives, but he clearly implied that pro-American factions should be supported. In that message he remarked that the sentiment for annexation was increasing among all classes of Hawaiians. No documentary evidence exists that Washington ever answered his request for guidance on what to do about an "orderly and peaceful" coup.[45]

As the question of Hawaii's political fate came to a head, the minister set forth two possible courses of action for the United States: "either bold and vigorous measures for annexation, or a 'Customs Union.' " The minister recommended annexation rather than protectorate status as being better for the islands, cheaper, and the course of action that would be less embarrassing in the end for the United States.[46]

In mid-January 1893 business elements dethroned Queen Liliuokalani after she promulgated a new constitution favorable to native Hawaiian political groups. With the crucially important cooperation of Minister Stevens, the pro-American and proannexation "best citizens," as he phrased it, took power. Stevens provided muscle as his chief contribution to the success of the revolt against the queen—military power to back the insurgents. The American minister arranged to have marines and sailors from an American cruiser in the harbor landed at Honolulu, reporting to Washington that they were sent ashore to protect American lives and property. "This [takeover] being an accomplished fact, I promptly recognized the Provisional Government as the *de facto* Government," he further cabled. "The English minister, the Portuguese chargé d'affaires, the French and the Japanese Commissioners promptly did the same."[47] Stevens was convinced, as was the Harrison administration, that annexation should be the next step. In a noted turn of phrase, he wrote, "The Hawaiian pear is now fully ripe, and this is the golden hour for the United States to pluck it."[48] On the first of February on his own authority he raised the American flag over the islands.

The lame-duck Republican administration applauded the energetic septuagenarian's action in recognizing the provisional Hawaiian government. But his extension of protection to the islands under the flag did not meet with approval. Washington more or less reprimanded him for overstepping his authority. The Department of State advised Stevens that he must continue to treat Hawaii as an independent nation. Three weeks later, however, the department accepted privately as "reasonably correct" an explanation by Stevens that a fear of British pressure brought on his raising of the flag.[49]

In the end, as already noted an annexation treaty was not acted upon. The new Democratic administration withdrew it from consideration, and Stevens, the principal architect of Hawaiian annexation, resigned his post at Honolulu. By mid-June he was back at home in Augusta, Maine, his days as an active participant in policy questions over. Two years later he died.

John L. Stevens has incurred his share of criticism. He was not, however, a diplomatic cannon loose on a rolling deck. An experienced diplomat, he reported, analyzed, and acted upon a line of United States policy in Hawaii which had been evident for decades, the policy of at a minimum bringing the islands under American influence. Neither diplomatic knave nor saint, he should not be faulted even for poor judgment. Rather, he showed what turned out to be an excess of zeal in the right place at the wrong time. If Harrison had been reelected in the fall of 1892, Stevens's zeal likely would not have been mistimed.

Charles Denby, minister to China, also held office under circumstances where individual initiative mattered. As indicated above, Washington policymakers viewed China as a likely area for American trade promotion. According to a Department of State White Paper, the cornerstones of United States policy toward China were treaties and equality of commercial opportunity.[50] By the end of the century, with the pressure of foreign competition, Secretary Hay issued the Open Door notes to buttress the United States' policy. It was not always clear, however, either to business leaders or to Washington just what actions should be taken to preserve American market access in the face of other powers' initiatives. Despite the rhetoric, American interests actually were never substantial enough to challenge another power's actions.[51] Related to commercial interests was another important facet of Sino-American relations, the increasing official support for the often-harassed and also demanding American missionaries. "The 1890s brought a major and lasting shift in policy favorable to the mission movement," writes one scholar.[52]

The American diplomat entrusted with implementing these lines of policy was Denby, a tall, slim railroad lawyer from Indiana. Although Virginia-born and educated he served in the Union army as a lieutenant colonel and was wounded in the Civil War. Sixty years old when the decade began, Denby was at Peking an unusually long time, thirteen years, from 1885 to 1898. His lengthy service was due partly to the refusal in 1891 of the Chinese court to receive as minister any senator supporting Chinese exclusion. The Democrat Denby stayed on in Republican administrations.

Denby's most frequently encountered problem as minister to China was representing the interests of the hundreds of American missionaries. Often the missions were involved in riots, destruction of property, and personal injury or death to personnel. Numerous lengthy, detailed reports from Denby recount these incidents. Throughout, the minister exhibited impatience with Chinese officials and also for a time, early in the 1890s, with the missionaries. He thought little of the potential for change in China. Writing about the "cult" of ancestor worship, he asserted that it "must be overthrown before the principles of Christianity can become effective," but he thought that it might well take "hundreds or thousands of years to work this revolution." On one missionary protection issue that year, he wrote resignedly, "I shall not abandon the case though it seems useless to press it at present."[53]

By middecade, Colonel Denby had changed his mind about the missionaries. As noted by Michael H. Hunt, Washington's attitude toward them changed as well. The heading of an 1895 Denby despatch on protecting missions encapsulates the reason for this new, more positive approach: "Chinese are benefited. Civilization is spread. Foreign commerce is increased." Denby wrote that the missionaries were a civilizing force, and trade and commerce follow civilization. His view reflected the old idea that China would provide a vast market for American exports. He sought to promote those business interests, but the number and content of the legation's despatches over the years indicate that he spent more time on missionary issues and political reporting.[54]

Denby's time in China ran out eventually, even though backers submitted scores of petitions that he be allowed to stay on.[55] In 1897 President McKinley first named Charles Page Bryan to replace him. Then, because some thought Bryan insufficiently experienced for such an important post, the president sent him to Brazil and the minister to Brazil, Edwin H. Conger, to China. Denby was named to the Philippine Commission until the following year. Later he published a two-volume study and numerous articles on China.

Historians sometimes fault Denby for his imperious attitude toward Chinese officials and for excessive identification with missionary interests. But he should not be judged on present-day standards of sensitivity in dealing with less developed nations. He pursued and partly formulated America's China policy in an era when the great European powers and the rising sun of Japan were intent on staking out claims in a tottering Chinese empire. His numerous, informative reports[56] and his persistent efforts to advance American interests, along with his long experience in China and knowledge of the local scene, mark him as one of the more able American envoys of the late nineteenth century.

EUROPE

The student of diplomatic history has difficulty identifying specific United States policy formulations that pertained to Europe as a region at the turn of the century. As Robert L. Beisner observes of the period under review, "Some regions of the world inspired more consistent and coherent policies than others." He mentions Latin America and China as qualifying in this sense, but not Europe. Routine statements by Washington on maintaining cordial relations abounded, along with general injunctions about safeguarding American citizens' interests, including reciprocal trading privileges granted through most-favored-nation status. These last concerns highlighted the importance of existing (not potential, as in China) trade and investment interests on a country-by-country basis. In addition, the dogma of Anglo-Saxon superiority which was reaching its apogee of influence at this time provided bonds of interest with at least England, if not always with other European nations.[57] Mutual European-American interests in the less-developed world on occasion reinforced such bonds, but in several instances these ties were strained by rivalries, especially in the Western Hemisphere. Threats to the nascent Anglo-American amity grew out of controversies during the 1890s over Nicaraguan debts and the Venezuelan boundary, recounted above, and over commercial fishing rights and seal hunting. American envoys in Britain and Spain coped with certain Latin American crises which affected those countries, but the unfocussed reporting of most posts in Europe indicates this lack of policy cohesiveness.

At Athens, A. Loudon Snowden served as minister to Greece, Romania, and Serbia early in 1890s. A former director of the United States Mint at Philadelphia, in 1890 he was a stocky fifty-three-year-old graduate of Philadelphia's Jefferson College who resembled Grover Cleveland. A combat veteran of the Civil War, he studied law and was an authority on coinage. Later (1892–94) Snowden was the minister to Spain, but in Greece about the most exciting issue that he encountered was the plight of a naturalized American citizen who was dragooned into the army while on a visit to his native island of Corfu. Minister Snowden got him released from the military after making several high-level representations to the authorities upon instructions from Washington. As he reported in a despatch late in 1890, "The minister of foreign affairs. . . whilst dining at my home last evening took advantage of the opportunity to say that . . . he was satisfied that I had clearly demonstrated [the] claim to American citizenship." After Snowden called upon the prime minister, the authorities released the dual national to civilian life on Christmas Day, an undoubtedly welcome holiday present to him. Such was the substance and style of routine diplomacy in that period.[58]

Representative of major European consular posts' concerns during the early years of the decade are the activities of John M. Crawford, the linguistically capable consul general at St. Petersburg, and Consul General Adam E. King at Paris. A survey of messages sent at both St. Petersburg and Paris shows that commercial and trade matters dominated reporting other than on administrative matters, followed at a distance in numbers of messages by welfare and whereabouts questions. These consulates general did not report on political issues. A physician who later went on to a career in manufacturing and banking, Crawford sent only sixty-five despatches to Washington in 1890, covering subjects from routine administrative questions to substantive reports. An example of the latter is St. Petersburg's no. 115 (despatches were numbered serially throughout the incumbency of a principal officer) dated 20 November 1890 on lead and zinc mining in Russia. In 1891 one cable sent on 21 November reported a Russian prohibition on the import of wheat. The following year, Consul General Crawford loosened up a bit on telegrams; he sent four during the year, three of which were related to outbreaks of disease. The number of despatches dropped to sixty-four, perhaps in compensation for the "flurry" of cables.

Consul General King at Paris presided over a small staff of officers and clerks whose output of messages in 1890, sixty-two despatches, compared to that of the post at St. Petersburg. Wheat was a feature of Paris's commercial reporting as well. By his despatch no. 139 of 24 January 1890 the consul general informed the Department of State that the French army no longer would buy its wheat from foreign suppliers. Another report of that month deals in voluminous detail with the complexities of consular invoices, a major responsibility of posts in Europe. Under King, a Pennsylvania-born brigadier wounded during the Civil War who had held appointive positions at the Port of Baltimore, the reporting load declined from sixty-three despatches in 1891 to thirty-nine in 1892, plus three cables.[59]

The wealthy Philadelphian Charlemagne Tower served as minister to Austria-Hungary during the decade. As a final example of European post activities, his reporting from Vienna for the first six months of 1898 dealt with topics ranging from post administrative questions to the use of the Royal Library. Tower, a capable if sometimes prolix drafting officer, during that period sent forty despatches, a number of which are lengthy, and eight cables. The post was generally quiet, however, and most of his messages concerned routine matters. Few of the remainder covered substantive diplomatic issues, but he did send ten long messages on cases involving the protection of Americans and a half dozen directly addressing commercial questions. Eight of his despatches are related in one way or another to America's war with Spain, some simply recounting representations made on instructions to the Foreign Office. A striking exception, however, is a June despatch in which he reported a Vienna newspaper's editorial view on Germany's future role in the Philippines following Commodore Dewey's victory at Manila Bay. According to the daily, Germany "should and *will*" have a supply base there, and Berlin was sending warships to make sure. "The significant feature of this article," commented Tower, "is the thinly veiled menace contained in it toward the United States. . . . [A]lthough it bears upon it no stamp of authority, yet, it undoubtedly indicates what has been going on somewhere in the German mind."[60]

NEAR EAST

Even less well defined as to areawide policy than Europe was the Near East. Minister Solomon Hirsch in Turkey coped with problems generally similar to those of Ministers Denby in China and Snowden in Greece. He dealt with missionary difficulties, attempts to get officials to bring to justice bandits who attacked American citizens, and the protection of two naturalized Americans mistreated by soldiers in Jerusalem, still a part of the Ottoman Empire at that time. He concerned himself largely with protection and welfare cases. Hirsch was a Jewish immigrant from Germany who arrived in the United States in 1854. An Oregon wholesale dry goods merchant active in Republican circles, Hirsch was elected to the legislature in 1872 and served later in the state senate. He was fifty years old when appointed in 1889 to the legation at Constantinople, where he remained for three years. As the *New York Times* noted upon his appointment, Hirsch followed a fellow "Hebrew," the slight, elfinlike Oscar Straus, at the post.[61] Straus returned to Constantinople twice more, making it apparently one of the foreign service's few major "Jewish" posts of the day, somewhat in the manner that Port-au-Prince was a "black" post.

Another senior officer at Constantinople, Consul General Zachary Taylor Sweeny of Indiana, actually handled one of the protection problems; he coordinated reports on the Jerusalem protection case from the resident consul. Sweeny was a disappointed aspirant for the post of minister to Greece who settled for the consul generalship in Turkey. Educated at Eureka College in Illinois and at Asbury (DePauw) University, he had a prior career as a clergyman, educator, and writer. (One of his works was a Middle East travel guide.) In 1889 when President Harrison named him to the post at the age of forty, Sweeny was chancellor at Butler University.[62]

The erratic Texas lawyer and politician Alexander W. Terrell held the position of minister to Turkey throughout the second Cleveland term (it was he who presumed to advise the sultan to adopt an American-style government). Terrell studied at the University of Missouri, served as a brigadier in the Confederate army, practiced law, and was repeatedly elected to the Texas legislature. He was fifty-seven when assigned to Constantinople. The consul general under his jurisdiction was Luther Short, the owner and editor of a newspaper in Franklin, Indiana. Short graduated from Indiana University and the Michigan University Law School. A Civil War veteran also, he was briefly a member of the legislature. Probably his credentials as a member of the Executive Committee of the Democratic Editorial Association and as a national elector in 1892 served best in obtaining the post at Constantinople.[63]

The above abbreviated review of several major posts' activities suggests that senior officers around the world in the 1890s dealt with many of the kinds of problems facing the Foreign Service today. Consular questions centered on protection and welfare problems or trade promotion so often that there was an essential sameness about the work of many consuls general. The foremost exception to this overall assessment of consular problems is the importance at some posts of shipping and seamen problems. Most principal officers of major consular posts only occasionally reported on significant substantive matters; two of the few who routinely did were the consuls general at Apia and Havana. As indicated by the number of messages to Washington generated at most posts, the reporting workload was light.

Diplomatic missions, too, carried out routine duties, including, as noted from the Athens reports cited above, quasi-consular problems of protection and welfare. In Europe the flow of visitors from the United States who might need assistance was heavier than in other regions; in China and Turkey missionary problems were paramount. At virtually all posts, envoys became involved at least minimally with trade and investment, and many reported fairly frequently on other developments in their countries of accreditation. Not many chiefs of diplomatic mission were called upon to deal with fast-breaking crisis situations, although several instances of such circumstances have been recounted above, especially in Latin America.

One conclusion that can be drawn from this episodic treatment of the nineties—other than that Latin America was the area most important to the United States at the time—is that many of the senior officers concerned possessed energy and aptitude for service abroad. Often the demands on senior officers were light. And there were those who could not cope adequately with their duties: Mizner, Terrell, Baker, and Bayard come to mind. Yet a surprising number of others, including Crittenden, Egan, Stuart, Lee, Stevens, Denby, and Hirsch, showed ability and an understanding of their roles. Others will be discussed in the next chapter when the group as a whole is assessed. For purposes of the review to this point, however, we note that most officers performed at least adequately, an assessment not wholly to be expected from the critical studies of nineteenth-century American diplomacy.

That negative view is put by one scholar as follows: "With notable exceptions, U.S. diplomats during most of the era were clumsy amateurs at best."[64] Not so. The record at the end of the century suggests otherwise.

| 7 |

The Officer Corps Assessed

Political democracy, as it exists and practically works in America, with all its threatening evils, supplies a training school for making first-class men.

Walt Whitman, "Democratic Vistas" (1871)

In this consideration of the foreign service appointment patterns and record of the 1890s, a point begins to emerge with force and clarity: just prior to 1900 America had better diplomatic and consular representatives in senior positions than is generally recognized. Amateurs filled the ranks, but it is inaccurate to characterize the senior overseas positions of the era as refuges for elderly party workers or burying grounds for political liabilities. These ambassadors, ministers, and consuls general in the main did not come from among ward politicians, out-of-office congressmen, or out-of-work relatives of the politically influential, although there were a few in each of these categories in the diplomatic and consular services.

The human raw material was better than that. Not all gentleman amateurs became expert practitioners of the trade; some were unsuited to service abroad and reflected ill on the United States. But many performed creditably, and most adequately met the qualifications for their posts by the standards, expectations, and needs of the day. America possessed little real foreign policy or geographic area expertise then. Fortunately for the nation, however, the system managed to put forward for most of these senior assignments the best qualified people available, political appointees though they were. Those chosen were among the best educated and most experienced individuals the United States had to offer for public service.

To a large extent these men reflected an interest in foreign affairs and showed personal initiative by actively seeking assignment abroad, far from their hometowns of St. Louis or Chicago or Indianapolis. They sought political favor, but in nearly every instance they sought it overseas. North Carolina's J. G. Martin, mentioned earlier in this study, wished not for a Washington job or a position in the local post office, but rather he wanted a consular post abroad. For major public figures of more exalted standing than Martin, if the political favor could not be a cabinet post, then let it be a legation; for persons such as he with lesser claims, let it be a consulate general or consulate.

It is difficult to evaluate with precision and without dispute the worth to the nation of these 1890s senior officers as a group, or in some cases, individually. Assessing human beings is not an objective matter; judgments admit the possibility of differing interpretations, as everyone knows who has sat on a personnel review panel of any sort. Nevertheless, with information on their backgrounds as a basis, a listing of four general categories for these officers can be constructed from their records of service abroad. Appointees as senior diplomatic or consular officers could be: (1) demonstrably competent, whether wholly admirable in all respects or not; (2) demonstrably incompetent or ill suited to assignment abroad; (3) short-timers who left no appreciable record, including a few who probably should not have been sent in the first place; or (4) generally acceptable for the times, given the usually low level of Washington's need for expertise and activism abroad, in that they had unexceptional records and were without known major failings. This last grouping can be considered in the same light as Chester A. Arthur when he departed the White House in 1885; reformers agreed that he had done well, to their surprise, by not doing anything bad; the praise was somewhat faint, but it was praise nonetheless. (See appendix E for the lists by name of those officers in the first three categories; category number 4 comprising those who are not named and who were more or less acceptable is essentially a residual grouping and is the largest.)

The literature on diplomacy includes much comment on the qualifications of an envoy and many do's and don'ts for emissaries. Sir Earnest Satow, as one example, published in 1917 his volume *A Guide to Diplomatic Practice*. His commentary draws for advice upon, among others, François de Callières (1716) and the Earl of Malmsebury (1844). More recent publications on the subject include those of Charles O. Thayer and Abba Eban, both former diplomats, John R. Wood, an expert in consular affairs, and diplomatic historian Thomas A. Bailey.[1] They offer extensive lists of qualifications and much practical advice; Callières had ten printed pages, for instance, on what to do and what not to do as a newly arrived envoy.

Though opinions may vary, good performance abroad in this writer's view boils down to effectiveness in three general areas. The minister, ambassador, or consul general by his or her presence must "show the flag"—he or she is the very personification of all that is American, even if faced with very little else of importance during a tour. One must also report accurately and interpret for Washington what is going on politically, economically, and culturally in the country of assignment. And finally one must follow Washington's instructions carefully, tempered by judgment, especially in the conduct of negotiations. He or she should carry out or supervise the latter two responsibilities so that the desired results are achieved ably, knowledgeably, and ideally with aplomb. All else is elaboration on the content of these main activities or superfluous to the advancement of the nation's basic interests overseas.

This is the standard against which the members of the study group are now measured. Officers from the 1890s have been judged on the basis of one or more of the three criteria for effectiveness abroad—showing the flag, reporting, and implementing instructions. Their success in meeting these three criteria, measured subjectively, determined their placement in a category. Present-day views on the wisdom or unwisdom of the policies that they may have pursued on Washington's behalf do not enter into these determinations. The category of short-timers is self-explanatory. A residual list consists of those against whom neither a significant indictment or a mark of praise is entered; this latter group makes up the "acceptables" category.

These assessments may be in error, especially in the last category, and there is the danger of presenting numbers that appear overly precise. In the absence of detailed studies and judgments on each and every one of the 226 officers involved, some in the fourth, more-or-less acceptable, category may be overestimated as to ability; others in that group possibly are underestimated and were more successful at post than minimally adequate. Even with extensive service records on all, records which do not exist, different observers in any event likely would have different estimates of the same individuals.

The orders of magnitude are what are most important here. Of the 226 in the group biography, this study finds that some 18 were commissioned too short a period of time to permit a judgment on their performances. The information developed suggests that another 20 were demonstrably incompetent or an embarrassment or ill suited to service overseas. But the study indicates that nearly three times each of those figures, or a total of about 54 officers, were competent and effective representatives abroad during the decade. Another 134, evaluated on the basis of information compiled for this study (or in some cases, the absence of negative information), can be described as probably adequate to their often less-than-demanding responsibilities. Thus, less than one in ten of these 1890s officers clearly should not have been appointed to the senior foreign service, whereas a large majority, as many as four in five, on balance probably performed acceptably or better on the job.

On the basis of biographic information on the group, there seems further to be little doubt about the group's status as, at a minimum, a subelite in American life. The chief argument might be on semantics: Were they a true elite? If elite status is defined as deriving almost solely from exalted social status at birth, are they then as a group better described as a political-economic subelite? The difference hinges on the extent to which birthright, old money, and education enter into the definition. Not too many members of the prosopographical study qualified for the highest socioeconomic ranks from birth, but a large majority of the 226 officers were accomplished occupationally, or were college educated, or possessed of wealth, or had family political ties and social connections, or could claim some combination of those advantages. They were well above the average in these respects for Americans of the 1890s. The record shows that the foreign service drew some of even the least qualified for service abroad from a small, privileged segment of society—the educated professional middle class.

To illustrate the point, the emerging professions and a managerial class which would encompass the dozen planters in the study group were not then so heavily represented in the work force of the United States as now. Some 18.8 million males actively worked in 1890. Of this large number, the traditional professions of law, medicine, the clergy, and college and university teaching encompassed fewer than 300,000 men. About 205,000 more could be counted as belonging to emerging professions (journalists, government officials, bankers, wholesale merchants, and other company executives). The work force included an additional 96,500 male schoolteachers.[2] No other occupations readily fall into categories that can be termed "professional" at that time, the bulk of those remaining being in the fields of agriculture, fisheries, and mining.

The pool of males in the American professional class of the nineties therefore was comparatively small, not much more than 600,000 persons, or a little more than 3 percent of the gainfully employed male work force. This relatively limited cadre supplied the senior diplomatic and consular officer corps almost in its entirety.

In most instances, these officers' educational or occupational backgrounds alone would have set them apart. As to education, the United

States had some 120 colleges in 1850, a year during which many of the officers were receiving their educations, plus a number of law schools and theological seminaries. Twenty years later, in a period during which others of the group were still of school age, the total of enrolled college and university students in the United States stood at about 52,000. By the turn of the century, there were still fewer than a quarter of a million students, both male and female, at the college level—this in a population of seventy-six million. Henry Steele Commager has written that until well into the twentieth century, college life in America, unlike the European experience, placed "a stamp of distinction—we would now say elitism—on those fortunate enough to be associated with it." In 1900 less than one in five American boys and young men fifteen or older went to any school at all, much less to college. "A college degree," remarked Commager in 1976, "had a greater social and economic value then than it has now."[3]

Many appointees already had family money and status when appointed, men such as Bellamy Storer, who both inherited and married wealth, Charlemagne Tower, James B. Angell, Andrew D. White, Samuel R. Gummere, Wallace S. Jones, Horace Porter, William W. Phelps, and Herbert W. Bowen. The list could be continued of men in this group who personified at least second-generation money and inherited position. (See appendix A for a biographic register of these and all other officers included in the study.)

Numerous examples of acquired economic and social prominence can also be pointed out. These include men such as William S. Carroll, who made his own fortune and became a favorite with the court of Saxony. Whitelaw Reid, Frederic C. Penfield, John Hay, William Hayden Edwards, John G. A. Leishman, Albert G. Porter, and John E. Risley—all are men who married wealth or who, like Carroll, themselves amassed comfortable fortunes. All achieved a measure of social or financial prominence in their day that went beyond educational or prior professional attainments.

If one adds to this group those without exalted social backgrounds or riches but with attainments of education and profession in identifiable measure, the list encompasses more than 80 percent of the group. That is, this large majority pertains if the elitist definition is broadened to include individuals who either attended institutions of higher learning, whether or not they graduated, or practiced one of the recognized professions, including editing and publishing.

Of those left out, those with undistinguished backgrounds as to socioeconomic, educational, or professional status, half a dozen were like

Thomas Adamson, a quasi-career consular officer who started young and had a substantial number of years in the service, or like Ellis Mills, about whom a similar remark can be made. Background information is scanty on three or four officers. That leaves a maximum of only thirty-two (14.2 percent of the total) who from the record had no readily apparent claim to any kind of subelite status, under this broad definition, before appointment to the senior foreign service (see listing in appendix D). A number of these individuals, slightly more than one-half of whom were in the Consular Service, can be categorized as springing from the proverbial class of out-of-work politicians in need of a job. A few examples are Charles E. Turner, Thomas Moonlight, and Person C. Cheney, although they also followed occupations other than politics or held other responsibilities before appointment (appendix A).

The large majority of senior American foreign service officers of the 1890s therefore were cut from the "fine cloth" of a socioeconomic elite or an educational and professional subelite.[4] Out-of-office party hacks constituted only a small part of the group.

Personal characteristics also enter into an evaluation of this group. A number of officers had decidedly negative personality traits, and in some cases these traits affected performance. Not all were first-class human beings, any more than all were first-rate diplomats or consular officials in a strictly professional sense. Among others, Lewis Baker may well have been vain and Thomas Bayard, blundering (chapter 6). Minister and Consul General Herbert W. Bowen was notably contentious by nature; in 1905 he ran afoul of President Roosevelt, who summarily dismissed him from the Diplomatic Service. Consul General (later Ambassador) Frederic C. Penfield was one of the most "irrational, selfish, conceited, heartless" men career diplomat Joseph C. Grew ever met.[5] A colleague assessed the accomplished veteran diplomat W.W. Rockhill as the most difficult senior officer in the service to work for; he was "satiric and sneering . . . brusque and overbearing. He had no friends." The consul general at Hong Kong in the late 1890s, Rounseville Wildman, a former journalist, was notably ambitious and perhaps avaricious. He incurred the Department of State's disapproval for acting as a correspondent for the *New York Evening Journal* while a senior consular officer.[6] Henry M. Smythe at Port-au-Prince and Edmund W. P. Smith at Bogota had drinking problems. Van Leer Polk was implicated in the death of a Nashville, Tennessee, prostitute before taking up his post as consul general at Calcutta in 1893 (a jury had ruled that it was a suicide).[7]

Others had a mix of less-than-admirable traits along with good performance records. An example is Whitelaw Reid, minister to France under

Harrison and peace commissioner following the Spanish-American War, who died years later serving as ambassador to Great Britain. Tall and handsome, with a distinguished Vandyke beard, Reid incessantly sought high office and social status. He "had little genuine warmth. . . . [T]here was something artificial about his personality," wrote a diplomat who served with him as a junior officer. Nevertheless, Reid helped settle a trade controversy with France in the 1890s, he was cultured, "his manners were perfect, and he was always immaculately dressed." He was, "in his own way, a highly successful Ambassador," according to that same officer.[8]

The example of Reid illustrates a point. Some personal failings can detract from an officer's ability to show the flag abroad. But Secretary Hay regarded the "satiric and sneering" Rockhill as second in skill only to Henry White as an American diplomat. The much less well-known John Goodnow is another similar case. In 1904 an inspector of his post at Shanghai wrote that he was a "man of strong character and marked ability . . . [who] has performed the duties of the office exceedingly well." Yet the opinion of the "better element" of the American colony was unfavorable, and there were rumors of official improprieties during his eight years as consul general.[9] Goodnow was both admired and disliked, a common state of affairs for persons in high office.

The point here is that personal quirks, although they can stand out markedly in a small overseas foreign colony, do not invariably disqualify one for effective performance. On the basis of their overall records, Penfield, Reid, Rockhill, and Goodnow stand among those who performed effectively (see appendix E). Bowen, Baker, Bayard, Smythe, and Smith were ineffective or embarrassments, for different reasons, and Wildman's ambition and Polk's legal problems were irrelevant to their performances.

Certain individuals in the 1890s group under study enjoyed unalloyed good reputations, without significant reservation as to personal traits or professional controversies. A cadre of first-rate diplomats drawn from the ranks of well-known public figures was present during the decade. This group included the "learned and much travelled" Andrew D. White, renowned New York lawyer Joseph H. Choate, University of Michigan president James B. Angell, and New York businessman Oscar S. Straus, all of whom have been mentioned previously in the study. Each held more than one assignment over the years. (Choate had only one posting as an ambassador, but he was also chief delegate to the 1907 Hague Peace Conference.) The accomplished educator and historian White held diplomatic posts on increasingly responsible levels from 1854 to 1902. While on occasion Washington rebuked him for exceeding

John Goodnow, consul general at Shanghai, 1897–1905. Photographer un-known; taken in China ca. 1898 and inscribed to John Barrett, then U.S. min-ister to Siam. Note the portrait of President McKinley. (Courtesy Library of Congress.)

instructions, he was considered at worst a "safe" appointment to such positions; he was a "hardworking, highminded man who believed in all the right things."[10]

Choate, who turned seventy while at the London embassy, brought such "exceptional ability" to the post that he misses inclusion in Thomas A. Bailey's personal diplomatic hall of fame only because he was not faced with any significant problems during his six years in England. Other phrases used to describe Choate by one who knew him are "genial and shrewd" with a "penetrating wit and humor . . . [and a] supreme command of words . . . always at ease and self-possessed."[11]

Angell, like White, was a noted educator. He served capably not only twice as minister but also on several international commissions. Angell exhibited a sure touch in the world of diplomacy; within three months of his arrival at Constantinople in 1897 a staff member wrote that he had "made an excellent impression . . . everybody speaks very highly of him. . . . [H]e is surely gaining every inch of lost ground and prestige."

(Angell's predecessor was the unsuited and ineffective Alexander W. Terrell, one of those who should have stayed at home in a domestic political appointment.) Shortly thereafter he demonstrated his linguistic skills, according to the staff member, who wrote that he was "daily gaining a great deal of popularity among the colony and the general public. . . . He is getting on very well in his official relations with the government."[12]

Straus, a Democrat turned frequent Republican administration officeholder, succeeded Angell. Serious, ambitious, and articulate, Straus in Turkey was "a bright spot in an otherwise gloomy series" of envoys, in the opinion of one historian.[13] Along with his three tours at Constantinople, he served on The Hague Permanent Court of Arbitration and as secretary of commerce under Theodore Roosevelt.

Additional reasonably prominent figures can be cited who held senior posts in the Diplomatic Service. John Hay, Horace Porter, Frederick D. Grant, Charles Emory Smith, Robert Todd Lincoln, Wayne MacVeagh, William W. Phelps, and T. Jefferson Coolidge, among others, returned from tours abroad with their reputations intact.[14] All had made their names before taking up diplomacy.

Somewhat lesser figures, but examples of accomplished amateur officers, are Edwin H. Conger and Charlemagne Tower. Conger, who it so happens slightly resembled President Grant, entered the Diplomatic Service in 1890 as a forty-seven-year-old former Republican congressman from Iowa. After eleven years at three major posts over the next fifteen years, he suddenly resigned due to the expense of the embassy at Mexico. He died only two years later, at the age of sixty-four. Historians have treated Conger kindly; he receives high marks for his competence in political reporting in such disparate assignments as Brazil and China.[15] The other officer, Tower, was the Harvard-educated son of a Pennsylvania "iron millionaire."[16] After an active career in family-owned mining and steel firms, he first gained a senior post in 1897 at the age of forty-nine and held his third and last assignment, as ambassador to Germany, from 1902 to 1908. Shortly thereafter he was a founding member of the Carnegie Endowment for International Peace. In 1908 President Theodore Roosevelt subjected the Philadelphian to faint praise: "Tower is a good fellow, of great wealth & of rather cultivated tastes. [His replacement] is a . . . decidedly better man—but without the wealth."[17] Whether he measured up to Roosevelt's strenuous standards or not, he was generally regarded as an excellent overseas representative of the United States. No less an authority than Joseph C. Grew remarked that in 1907 Tower's "reputation in the Service stood very high."[18]

Added to these generally respected diplomats are a significant number of competent, experienced senior consular officers. Thomas R. Jernigan, a lawyer educated at the University of Virginia, was consul at Kobe for nine years before taking up the responsibilities of consul general at Shanghai in 1894; he held the favor of the local American community and came out well in consular inspections. Frank H. Mason was practically a Consular Service legend in his own day. A long-service consular official (from 1880 to 1914), in the 1890s he was said authoritatively to be an "excellent officer"; all consuls general "should be men of [such] experience and ability."[19] Felix A. Mathews of California in 1890 had strong political support for reappointment as consul general at Tangier, where he had served twice previously. He was widely acclaimed for his work on behalf of the Jews of Morocco.[20] His successor in 1893 was J. Judson Barclay, a linguistically capable, educated, and experienced third-generation consular official. Carl B. Hurst, the University of Tubingen Ph.D., served almost continuously from 1892 to 1927 at nine posts, mostly in Europe. Former Iowa banker Philip C. Hanna was consul at three Latin American posts in the nineties and then consul general at Monterrey for twenty years, beginning in 1899. James T. DuBois, a Cornell graduate and lawyer, held five consular assignments between 1877 and 1911, followed by service as minister to Colombia for two years. The well-regarded William H. Edwards of Ohio served almost without break from 1877 until his death in office in 1894 as consul general at Berlin.

Other consular officers rated almost as high. Wendell A. Anderson at Montreal, a physician, was "well posted" on regulations, and his office was in excellent condition, according to an inspector. Inspectors made similar comments on the distinguished-looking Consul General William S. Carroll at Dresden. One historian cites Warner P. Sutton favorably for his long, useful service as consul general at Matamoros. The former local government official, Arthur M. Beaupre of Illinois, who never attended college, rose from secretary of legation and consul general at Guatemala in 1897, when he was in his midforties, to minister to Colombia by 1903. Beaupre then held three other assignments as envoy in the years through 1913. Princeton-educated Samuel R. Gummere, who played a leading role in the 1904 Pedicaris incident, was consul general at Tangier for seven years (1898–1905) before Roosevelt named him minister to Morocco. Consul General Samuel H. M. Byers at St. Gall during the early 1890s previously had sixteen years of consular experience in Europe. A naturalized citizen, Richard Guenther of Wisconsin, while at Frankfort as consul general after Mason, was found by an inspector to be an "excellent official of a high order of intelligence, integrity and character."[21]

Comparative short-timers who the record indicates served ably include Daniel W. Maratta at Melbourne,[22] Thomas T. Crittenden at Mexico, and Charles de Kay at Berlin, all in office during the second Cleveland administration. Among others who evidently did well in office were Wakefield G. Frye at Halifax from 1882 to 1885 and again from 1889 to 1893, and Hezekiah A. Gudger at Panama from 1897 to 1905.[23] There were, in sum, senior Consular Service officers of the 1890s, unknown to the general public, who were capable and experienced.

None of the "typical" officers singled out in chapter 4 was noted for great acumen or for egregious errors in the performance of his duties. On the basis of a close reading of the reporting files, Thomas S. Harrison at Cairo rates among the competent and Samuel Merrill at Calcutta must be considered ill suited for his assignment. A case could be made for the abilities of William R. Finch at Montevideo, but his record is mixed. He is therefore included in the category of generally acceptable, as is John D. Washburn at Berne.

Some of those who turned out to have less-than-successful tours abroad still were not obviously mistakes as appointments from the outset. Lansing B. Mizner made a hash of his tour as minister to Guatemala, but the record shows that he had an appropriate background and that even he had some diplomatic success, particularly as a mediator. Patrick Egan was criticized for his actions while envoy to Chile, as was John L. Stevens in Hawaii. In both instances, however, they came under contemporary fire and incurred the later displeasure of historians mainly for excessive zeal, not for lack of ability or for failure to grasp the situation in their countries of accreditation.

Lewis Baker and Thomas F. Bayard can be indicted on the latter count with some justification; certainly they lacked the confidence of their superiors in Washington, a crippling drawback for any American diplomat. Both of these men merit inclusion in the list of unfortunate appointments. Nonetheless, they were far from the usual notion of out-of-office politicos feeding at the overseas public trough with little or no aptitude for diplomacy. Their records are poor for other reasons.

Following are further illustrative examples of the difficulties inherent in evaluating foreign service personnel; differences of opinion are possible in most, if not all, cases. John Stephens Durham, a black editor from Philadelphia, was perhaps not ideally suited for the foreign service. Early in the 1890s he showed too much zeal in protecting the interests of an American businessman and had to be reined in by Washington. Yet he was an engineering graduate of Pennsylvania and a lawyer, and he spoke several languages.[24] The brilliant orator and spokesman for blacks, Frederick Douglass, made many Haitian friends for the United States while serving at Port-au-Prince. At the same time, he was accused of excessive identification with Haitian interests—with what is called "clientitis," that is. While he was still in office, Washington replaced him in negotiations for base rights; ultimately, after two years at post, he resigned under a cloud.[25] Horace Newton Allen, a longtime (1890 to 1905) diplomatic and consular official at Seoul, was known for his aggressive temperament. In 1895 Secretary Olney reprimanded him for a policy stand he took on Japan. But Allen also had considerable political ability and was considered an important agent for American business groups in Korea.[26] The American envoy to Mexico from 1897 to 1905, Powell Clayton of Arkansas (originally from Pennsylvania), had a stormy career as a carpetbag railroad executive, governor, and United States senator. While in politics, his opponents accused him of fraud and corruption; a couple of indictments resulted. But his eight-year stint as ambassador was an uneventful sidelight to his domestic political career. There were no scandals during his long tour abroad.

Nevertheless, it must have been an unhappy official family at Mexico City at the turn of the century. The post's consul general during most of Clayton's period as ambassador was Andrew D. Barlow of Missouri, the scion of a wealthy railroad family. Barlow clashed with the local staff soon after arrival in 1897 and behaved so as to elicit sworn statements that he was a drunken boor. In 1898 the local English-language newspaper complained that "Uncle Sam [is] sending boys out to do men's work" (Barlow was thirty-five at the time). The uproar caused by his reported boorishness subsided, however; he stayed on at Mexico without further recorded incident until the spring of 1904, almost as long as Ambassador Clayton remained at post. Both lasted in office longer than average for the times. In a striking example of a mixed report on an officer, a former ranking Department of State official in 1895 described D. Lynch Pringle, consul general and secretary of legation at Guatemala, as "indolent and without marked ability." But in the same sentence he also characterized him as "a gentleman, a man of good sense [with] experience."[27] Pringle managed to hold responsible foreign service positions throughout the two Cleveland administrations.

Barlow, Pringle, and the others mentioned above are not the only senior officers abroad during the period who attracted at least sporadic adverse notice. Adam E. King and John K. Gowdy at Paris were so favored, King for supposedly drinking too much and Gowdy for allegedly charging exorbitant consular fees.[28] James R. Hosmer, Samuel Kimberly, and W. Godfrey Hunter, all at Guatemala at different times, incurred criticism. Hosmer, a lawyer, was tarred by the same brush of poor judgment in the Barrundia affair as Minister Mizner. His replacement, Kimberly, mishandled a relatively minor diplomatic approach to the government, to the department's displeasure. Some years later, Minister Hunter's son killed a man in a duel at post, and the minister himself was said to have been involved in shady financial dealings.[29] All of these officers had their redeeming features, but all came under criticism.

Most of those mentioned in the above paragraphs in unflattering personal terms nevertheless were reasonably acceptable as diplomatic or consular representatives in the 1890s, as were the majority of the remainder of the 226-man group under consideration. Vanity, brusqueness, cynicism, gushiness, contentiousness, even boorishness or lapsed judgment—none of these attributes necessarily disqualifies one for appointment as a senior officer. If these and other negative personal characteristics, including intemperate habits and indiscreet sexual mores, were disqualifying, the ranks of the diplomatic and consular services then, and the Foreign Service now, would be drawn from a much thinner pool of eligibles than was or is the case.[30] In filling the slots abroad which had to be staffed anew each time administrations changed, the nation benefited from the services of a better class of people than it had any reason to expect, given the nearly haphazard method of selection and the widespread lack of public interest in foreign affairs. Senior American diplomatic and consular officials' records of accomplishment before assuming office and their performances abroad belie—with the inevitable exceptions to any broad statement—the notion that the United States was ill served by its foreign service personnel.

Further, although the nation was entering a new age with professionalism on the increase, the method by which its representatives abroad were chosen was still generally appropriate for the times. One historian has similarly assessed another group of Americans in an earlier period: "By their amateur competence they made possible a continuing identification between political and social authority."[31] Changes were underway, but an amateur foreign service suited the American society and body politic in the closing years of the nineteenth century, the years during which America witnessed the twilight of amateurism in diplomacy.

| 8 |

The Officer Corps
Compared

Nine times out of ten, in the arts as in life, there is actually no
truth to be discovered; there is only error to be exposed.
H. L. Mencken, Prejudices, Third Series (1922)

The conclusions set forth in the foregoing chapter raise questions.
How is it that many observers, both contemporary and latter-day, mistak-
enly assessed America's senior officers abroad at the turn of the century?
Assuming the evaluation in this paper is substantially correct, that is,
why did reform-minded elements of the era and historians of our time so
frequently deride the quality of the patronage-system appointees at major
posts, particularly in comparison with their supposedly trained, skilled
European counterparts? Why have they routinely characterized the
American foreign service of the period as a refuge for elderly party workers, a haven for regularly inept hangers-on, and a burying ground for
political liabilities?[1] How is it that in the usual historiographical view the
subjects of this study fall into the category of "broken down men and
ignorant editors"[2] who were said to hold senior foreign service positions
in the 1890s?
Explanations of this seeming disparity between actual qualifications
and performance and the negative assessments of these officers lie in the
expectations and mind sets of the assessors. The explanations arise from
the evaluators' views on the promise of professionalization as a modern-
izing impulse in the conduct of foreign affairs and indeed in their understanding of the meaning of professionalism. Both reformers of the day
and historians of the twentieth century interested in reform saw heightened foreign policymaking needs emerging from an increasingly fast-
moving and complex international scene. This was especially clear after

1898 in the United States and certainly evident to even the highly ob-
tuse from 1914 onward in most of the industrialized world. Reacting to
the stirrings of Progressive intellectual currents and later utilizing hind-
sight on how the pace of organizational modernization in the United
States might have been advanced, detractors of the 1890s senior foreign
service applied heightened standards of efficiency in their assessments of
an amateur group. Reform elements and later commentators, approving
the added experience made possible by tenure in office, equated professionalism with a necessarily increased ability to further policy objectives
abroad.

Related to reformist beliefs was the widely held notion that the men
staffing the American diplomatic and consular services were less able
than those in the foreign affairs organizations of other major world powers. This is an arguable evaluation, however, despite the several assertions
along this line noted early in this study. In the 1890s some knowledge-
able Europeans, contrary to received wisdom, evidently believed that personnel of their own services did not perform as effectively as the
Americans. Also contrary to conventional wisdom, some few recent
scholars assess adversely the results of nineteenth-century European efforts at foreign service professionalization. A brief comparison of the
1890s foreign service with the diplomatic and consular corps of other
great powers, therefore, promises to shed additional light on the relative
status of American officers.

The American diplomatic and consular services themselves also contributed to the conviction that professionalization was both worthwhile
and necessary. By the 1920s professional "guilds," one of which was the
United States Foreign Service, "established [controls] over admission to
the occupation" at the lower levels, controls that were comprehensive and
unambiguous. There was both "an element of wanting to guarantee qualified personnel—and an element of limiting competition."[3] Many of
those holding commissions wanted to stay on, regardless of changes of
administrations in Washington, and other young men of a favored socioeconomic class sought to preserve their privileged entry into the under-
paid but prestigious lower diplomatic ranks.

Finally as an explanation of the negative views of 1890s officers, historical studies of the period sometimes show a lack of familiarity with
the individuals involved. Studies present relatively little information on
the backgrounds and qualifications of those who actually held the
seventy-odd senior officer positions abroad at any given time during the
decade, or even on who most of them were. The numerous references to

elderly party workers and inept hangers-on already cited suggest this lack of familiarity with the historical actors.

Historians of the period and contemporary critics unarguably were right about one thing: During the period under review, the 1890s, few if any true diplomatic or consular professionals had as yet appeared on the scene, no matter how professionalism might be defined. America made do year after year with a system of staffing foreign service posts with amateurs, a system that was geared to the fortunes and needs of political parties. Although there were aborted attempts at reform dating back to the 1860s and 1870s, the first meaningful consular examinations, those for midlevel officers, came in 1895, and in the Diplomatic Service, for entering junior officers in 1905.

Most European nations made the move earlier. By the 1890s administrative changes had been under way for some years in their small overseas establishments and foreign offices. Major countries generally took the route of examining and screening junior officers, both diplomatic and consular, well before the twentieth century began. The British first held examinations in 1856. (Shortly thereafter, the Liberal reformer John Bright characterized the diplomatic service as "a gigantic system of outdoor relief for the aristocracy of Great Britain.")[4] In 1872 the British system required written tests, unless the candidate was a university graduate, and a probationary period. The would-be diplomat had to be nominated for examination by the foreign secretary. The British added an oral examination in 1907. France also began examinations for the diplomatic and consular services in 1872. The Austro-Hungarian diplomatic service required all candidates to be university graduates, to have a year of government experience, and to take a stiff examination. Russian examiners by the early twentieth century required multiple oral and written tests. The upper class generally occupied the diplomatic positions, however, sometimes with careers almost handed down through families. The earliest selection procedures established in the Netherlands were in 1846; in 1860 diplomatic attachés came under an examination and probation system, and the beginning of professionalization in the Dutch consular service came in 1875. In 1868 Greece established by royal decree special tests for entry into the diplomatic service, although political affiliations continued to play a paramount role. In 1877 the Greek government reorganized the consular service.[5]

Exceptions to this schedule of reform in Europe can be found. As late as 1889 Belgium had only twenty-five career consuls—and five hundred honorary consuls—around the world; the organization was overhauled in

1896 and 1900 to put in more trained, university-educated careerists. Japan, the only non-Western nation considered here, began a merit system in 1894; before then diplomatic and consular appointments were made on the basis of personal contacts. An object of the 1894 reform was to establish one umbrella service covering the diplomatic and consular branches and the Japanese foreign office; it has remained the basic legislation since that time.

In all of these services, the emphasis was on small, homogeneous organizations and limited, if not always necessarily modest, facilities abroad. As late as 1914 the British foreign service had only 446 people abroad, including 150 diplomats. "The normal mission was a legation with a minister, one or two secretaries, an archivist, probably a locally engaged translator, one chancery servant . . . and sometimes a military or naval attaché," writes a British diplomatist. "The legation . . . was usually an unostentatious but dignified detached house in a quiet street, and the staff worked in two or three small rooms off the hall."[6] This description could well fit some of the larger American legations in the decade of the nineties.

In time, as junior diplomats came to professional maturity, London's examination of junior officers and system of probation resulted in a small group of excellent British ambassadors and ministers around the turn of the century, according to one observer. Yet not all scholarly assessments agree that the initiation of merit systems had favorable results. Britain drew her officers from "an exceedingly narrow social base," in the view of Zara Steiner, and there was a wide gulf between the diplomatic and consular services. "Even by the standards of pre-war Europe, the British diplomatic service was unduly restricted in its attitudes and interests. The Foreign Office would have been better informed had its agents been drawn from a wider circle of recruits." Raymond A. Jones writes, "The qualifying nominations excluded weak candidates, but did nothing to change the social background from which diplomats were drawn. . . . [T]he service continued to recruit from the political elite of Victorian England. As the composition of that elite changed and broadened in the late nineteenth century, so did that of the diplomatic service." British diplomats undoubtedly were drawn from a restricted group, but Jones concludes that by the turn of the century the service's "exclusivity was as much a function of professionalism and *esprit de corps* as of social class."[7]

Lamar Cecil's investigation of the German diplomatic and consular services also points up their narrow social origins. Even with a "rigorous examination schedule" for entering members of the foreign service, in the manner of the British system, other factors were more important in the German selection process. "It is doubtful . . . that the examinations, in spite of the terror they instilled in those who took them, were in fact very arduous. . . . The ease with which examinations could be diluted or avoided suggests that they were not taken entirely seriously by the Foreign Office. There is ample evidence to indicate that, as an index of a candidate's suitability, his performance on the tests was considered less important than the impression which he created." Germany in principle opened the services to talent, but in practice connections were indispensable. Not only were there exceptions to the requirements for entry, but similar requirements for advancement in rank could be bypassed. "Where talents or qualifications were pale, family and friends often proved effective surrogates."[8] This approach to filling the ranks of the German diplomatic and consular services added up to a preference for the nobility, especially Prussian Junkers. Not until 1906 did parliament members attack the system on the grounds that the selection bases were too narrow; only in 1908 did the German government abolish the formal requirement that candidates show evidence of private wealth.

The elite social backgrounds of the German foreign service members, as in the British system, gave a distinctive identity to the organization, but did not necessarily certify the officers' professional qualifications. The imperial foreign service was "an assemblage of men of real ability in some cases, of little other than luminous lineage in others." The two characteristics—meritorious achievement and elite status—are not the same and were by no means necessarily combined in the same person. For the officer who aspired to senior rank, however, "the correlation between noble birth and professional advancement persisted."[9]

In comparing the composition of the German and United States foreign services of the era, incidentally, the military was thinly represented in both. Over a period of forty-three years, 1871–1914, Berlin appointed only eight professional military officers, including seven generals, to senior positions in the pre–World War I German diplomatic service.[10] Washington named no career soldiers at all to senior positions in the American foreign service of the 1890s. A substantial number of American appointees had previous military service, especially during the Civil War, but all had shifted to civilian pursuits by the time they were appointed abroad. This was so even for such figures as Frederick D. Grant, who later resumed an interrupted army career and retired as a major general. In 1889, when named to Vienna, he had been out of the army and in the business world for eight years. Consul General Aulick Palmer at Dresden (1889–93) was a Marine Corps officer for thirteen years but a civilian when appointed to the Consular Service.

A point of organizational difference that emerges from this German-American comparison is the divergence in personnel between the consular and diplomatic services (a schism which in muted form persists to this day in the career American Foreign Service). The German services apparently did not have quite as wide a split between the services as the American and, from impressionistic data, the British, French, Russian, Greek and other overseas organizations of the times. Approximately one in four German officers served in both diplomatic and consular assignments in the more than forty years covered by Cecil's study.[11] Of the 226 American senior officers in service during the 1890s, less than one in five served in both types of assignments, including those who concurrently had dual diplomatic and consular appointments; 40 senior members of the United States foreign service held such positions. A few did not simply hold dual commissions but progressed, in a manner of speaking, from consul to diplomatic envoy. Among these were Pierce M. B. Young, the former Confederate general from Georgia, consul general at St. Petersburg in the 1880s and minister to Guatemala during the second Cleveland administration; Francis B. Loomis of Ohio, a consul in France in the early nineties and then minister successively to Venezuela and Portugal, 1897 to 1903; and Harold M. Sewall of Maine, who served as a vice consul in England and then consul general in Samoa from 1885 through 1892, followed by appointment as the United States' last minister to Hawaii. Dr. George H. Bridgman of New Hampshire, as noted earlier, made the reverse transition, from minister to Bolivia to consul at Kingston, Jamaica, but his case is unique for the nineties.

The senior imperial German foreign service accommodated precisely one recognized Jew, a member of the Rothschild family. Berlin admitted a few converted German ex-Jews in the more than forty years leading up to the First World War.[12] The record of the United States is not materially different in this respect; Washington appointed three known Jewish chiefs of mission or consuls general in the decade of the nineties—Oscar Straus and Solomon Hirsch at Constantinople, and Max Judd at Vienna. American blacks, while limited in numbers, were more heavily represented in the 1890s senior foreign service than Jews.

Available information on the foreign service establishments of other industrialized countries, with emphasis on those of Britain and imperial Germany, therefore suggests as the outstanding feature of recruitment efforts the narrow base from which junior candidates were drawn.[13] These junior officers—secretaries of legation, attachés, and vice consuls—were the pool from which came a large number of the senior officers by the turn of the century. In many cases they had developed skills and experience by the time they reached positions of senior responsibility, coming out of an organized system of selection and promotion as most did. Given the circumstances of their selection and maturation abroad, the judgment can be appreciated that Great Britain's system, for one, turned out a generation of first-rate envoys by about 1900.

The evidence compels one, however, to give credence as well to the judgment that virtually all European services of the time, including the British, were made up of small, wealthy elites whose status was largely based on exalted social standing. Scholars refer frequently to the importance that family and connections played in entry into the foreign services, including the consular corps, of European countries and of Japan as well. On occasion, influence served to overcome formal entry requirements. If in the selection process there was conflict between social status and test results, then the authorities found a way around the latter. In Germany, "For every rule there was an exception, for every seemingly insuperable barrier an avenue of appeal."[14] This clearly was not what American reformers had in mind when they strove for a professionalized foreign service like those of the European powers.

The Western nations thus began the systematic reorganization of their foreign services in nearly all cases before the United States.[15] They instituted professionalism, however, primarily in only one of its more limited senses—that is, as conscious moves toward elitist organizations—and their efforts did not always lead to heightened efficiency. Men of "real ability" gained entry into these services, as did men whose chief claim to appointment was "luminous lineage," in Cecil's phrase. "By the turn of the century the age of the great independent ambassador was over," remarks Zara Steiner in an assessment which denies that European nations produced a generation of unusually able senior officers. "The [British] diplomats were a very mixed group." Some were "men of mediocre ability" despite a generation of merit-based selection processes.[16] As a reflection of the interests of elite groups, the European appointing authorities recruited diplomats and consular officers from a narrower population base than even the relatively limited pool from which American officers came.

A chief failing of the European services was that they institutionalized self-imposed social class restrictions on the pool of eligibles, restrictions which in the contemporary United States services were not formal and were less sweeping in scope. As noted above in the British context, European foreign offices likely would have been better served if a wider group within the population had been the basic source of their envoys and senior consuls. Given the premium put on wealth, birth, and social station in the German diplomatic service's selection and promotion system, "in August 1914, when imperial Germany went to war," writes Cecil, "the Foreign Office, enveloped in its sacrosanct traditions, was undefiled by association with a world both at home and [through the foreign service] abroad which it could not comprehend."[17]

Consequently, not only is there doubt about the abilities of many European diplomats in the nineties, there is also reason to think that Americans in those years sometimes compared favorably, amateurs though they were. As the turn of the century approached, opinion actually was divided internationally on whether at least the United States' consular representatives were less adept than their European counterparts. Detractors and critics of the American foreign service there were in plenty, but one heard occasional praise at home for American officers. As Congressman Robert R. Hitt stated in a speech in 1894:

> It is easy to point out the faults in our [consular] service and its methods. They lie right on the surface. But . . . [many] men who have been employed in the service . . . were the equals of the consular officers of any other country in the world; in many respects superior to their colleagues. . . . Our officials . . . as a general rule, have been intelligent, vigorous, capable men. . . . The service has real merit; but the merit of the service lies, not in the method of appointment or in the method of removal, but in the inherent elements of the American character, in the intelligence and energy which so generally pervade our people.[18]

In middecade, the *New York Times* lauded an American consul in Jamaica, calling him hardworking, fair, and untiring in his representational duties, despite his low salary.[19] "Complaints of the consular service . . . of the incompetency of consuls . . . are not infrequently brought to the notice of the Department," wrote Secretary of State Olney in 1895. "That they are not always well founded is clear, and instances are by no means rare in which interested parties indulge in the severest condemnation of officials whose only fault has been a proper adherence to their line of duties."[20]

Observers occasionally drew favorable judgments on the patronage-era Diplomatic Service also. Hitt wrote: "There is an ignorant shamefacedness among us, often seen in the newspapers, about our politician diplomats, who are assumed to be inferior to foreigners. As I saw them, our representatives were among the very ablest in Europe, & so regarded by European statesmen, as I have heard them say. The training of action, prompt & responsible decision in public life in a popular govt. is the best for a really important public duty." In 1893 Europe-based American author Theodore Stanton similarly praised the "superior ability and wide experience" of United States diplomats abroad over the years. Many that he listed in a letter to the *New York Times* were "men of mark," he wrote, who often had "greater or less prominence in national politics." A few years later another man of letters resident in Europe wrote an assessment that supported this view: "The records which American diplomats have made in regard to actual international work accomplished," opined editor Chalmers Roberts in the early 1900s, "is almost wholly a creditable one, certainly a wonderful testimonial to their native ability." Roberts thought the Diplomatic Service needed training, but only in the social and protocol "half" of its duties, not in substantive matters.[21]

Some British, French, and German observers endorsed favorable estimates of the American Consular Service. In 1899 *The Consular Journal and Great Britain* and the French *La Revue Diplomatique* expressed envy of the Americans for their commercial reporting and initiative. "Other nations obtain much better and more reliable work from their officers than we do," complained the British publication. "Thus, a Consular officer of the United States' Government is . . . not so well paid as ours. But still . . . the work achieved by him is certainly superior to that done by our Consular officers abroad." As the French organ phrased it, "The American consul does not understand that he has a commercial situation to maintain, but always a commercial situation to conquer. . . . [A]bove all in Europe [they] are active and aggressive. . . . [T]he Americans have the art of putting life and initiative into a career where other people rest upon routine and immobility." A German trade publication of the day also praised the American Consular Service as being far in advance of other services in enterprise.[22]

An assessment of American consuls published years afterward also is positive in a comparative sense: "The [British] business world continued to complain," Harold Nicolson wrote about the period after 1887, "that the British diplomatic, consular and commercial officials did not display the same activity on behalf of their traders as was shown by the German and American services."[23] Nicolson was a careerist who advocated the professionalization of diplomacy. He noted these complaints in the context of changes in the Foreign Office's commercial department, a reorganization that was thought not thoroughgoing enough to get the job done in competition for world trade with the Germans and the Americans. In the summary comment of a British consular publication late in the 1890s, "It is plain that the perfect Consular Service is neither with us nor with the Americans. Certainly, if the present system of 'spoils' is departed from, there is more than a probability of 'social successes,' 'tea and tennis men,' finding their way to the ranks of Consuls, to the certain prejudice of the Service."[24]

Other Americans with experience in foreign affairs recognized, as did these overseas observers, the solid performances and qualifications for office of some senior diplomats and consuls. One-time Secretary of State John W. Foster, although an advocate of careerist principles, looked upon his own amateur qualifications for diplomacy and found them good: "I was not without some preparation for the new and important duties which I was about to assume," he wrote with regard to his appointment as minister to Mexico in 1872. "My training as a lawyer, my early participation [in the slavery question], my army service, my editorial work, my activity in politics and intercourse with public men, all tended to prepare me."[25] Many amateur chief of mission and consul general appointees of the 1890s could boast some variation on Foster's background.

Despite these favorable comparisons, the several factors cited at the outset of this chapter contributed to an overriding conviction that professionalism had been needed many years before the turn of the century. In the words of Bernard De Voto in another context, "Between the amateur and the professional, between the duffer and the expert, between the novice and the veteran there is a difference not only in degree but in kind."[26] Reformers and scholars both saw an improvement in kind as necessary for the American foreign service as the twentieth century dawned. Calls to professionalize the foreign service were linked explicitly or implicitly to ideas of occupational enhancement and bureaucratic development, tied to the belief basically that greater efficiency in the conduct of the United States' foreign affairs could thereby be promoted. Reformers equated proficiency with professionalism or careerism, with merit-based, standardized requirements for entry, promotion, assignment, and tenure. They likewise equated ineptness with amateurism and the associated lack of a personnel framework and bureaucratic organization.

As has been shown in chapter 2, however, professionalism is not so straightforward a concept. Professionalism incorporates a complex intermingling of ideas, not all of which concern efficient administrative operations. Recommendations for professionalization of the foreign service actually can lead in directions unanticipated by reformers; the idea of professionalism raises issues such as the significance of autonomy, credentialism, and controls over admission in any given reform proposal. Criticism of amateur diplomacy can leave unaddressed important questions of elitism versus merit-based systems, tenure versus administrative flexibility, and educational or social status versus the prestige of the exclusive traditional professions.

Historians of the period have been imprecise at best in their insistence on the need for diplomatic and consular professionals. In some instances, they, and contemporary reformers as well, mistook elitism for occupational qualifications; in others, they ignored factors making up the various less well-recognized meanings of professionalism. Often they seemed to confuse an absence of careerist status with ineptitude, and its presence with expertise. Critics and reformers rarely if ever saw the whole professionalization picture, but rather concentrated on improved bureaucratic performance as a goal. This was a fundamental misapprehension, but one which is understandable in light of the need perceived for greater administrative efficiency.

Practically all occupations during the past century have tended to move toward their versions of professionalization, but this frequently has meant striving toward higher status, greater autonomy, or some aspect of professionalization other than enhanced technical or bureaucratic expertise. Many observers have approved almost reflexively the century's thrust toward greater efficiency through increased organization. They would not be likely in principle to find merit, at that time or later, in the appointment of amateurs to important foreign service positions. Reformers sought to have standards established for merit-based selection and bureaucratized assignment and promotion, part—but only part—of the general idea of professionalization. Once these standards were finally imposed, historians tended to apply them retrospectively.

Thus both contemporary and later critics saw amateur senior diplomats and consuls of the late nineteenth century as what they were, the products of the patronage machinery; to critics, these appointees were inept party hacks, ignorant editors, or worse, almost by definition. Considering the increased complexity of American society and the need for administrative efficiency in the conduct of foreign relations, in the reformers' view, they should have been careerists. They were amateurs; detractors believed that in the interest of advancing American interests they should have been professionals.

| 9 |

Postscript: Amateur Diplomacy Today

The best diplomats . . . are born, not made. They can learn some lessons from books and from experience. . . . But if they do not have the proper qualities of mind, character, temperament, and personality, they are almost certain to fall short.

Thomas A. Bailey, The Art of Diplomacy (1968)

Even in those cases where success has attended the efforts of an amateur diplomatist, the example must be regarded as an exception, for it is a commonplace of human experience that skilled work requires a skilled workman.

François de Caillières, On the Manner of Negotiating with Princes (1716)

As reflected in the above remarks, opinions differ on the merits of career professionals versus amateurs in the most responsible overseas assignments—the ambassadorships (especially) and consul general assignments. The question arises whether careerism at that level is entirely necessary for today's Foreign Service. In other words, are the political appointments of nonprofessionals to those positions generally undesirable? Should careerists perforce receive the assignments?

This chapter's consideration of these questions should be read as a personal statement, an addendum to the preceding sections which deal primarily with research findings. Careerists, I conclude, have a claim to those top positions of chief of mission and consul general, but not necessarily at the expense of capable amateurs who are experienced in other professions. The demands of modern diplomacy are such that the nation must make use of its best people, from within and without the career Foreign Service. Note well, however, that this conclusion does not extend to the lower-ranking officers assigned to embassy and consulate general staffs; in the modern world those often-specialized positions call for training and experience that only careerists can provide.

More than six decades have passed since the Rogers Act of 1924 launched true professionalism among the junior and midlevel American diplomats and consuls. If one thinks that amateurism has been eradicated and appointment procedures to all positions have changed completely since the turn of the century, however, the words of a former ranking Department of State official provide a necessary corrective. In 1969, at the beginning of the Nixon presidency, U. Alexis Johnson, a senior career Foreign Service officer (FSO), assumed the duties of under secretary of state for political affairs. "Ambassadorial appointments occupied much of the new administration's attention," he writes. It could have been said just as well of the Harrison, Cleveland, or McKinley administrations. Johnson continues in words that sound familiar after our review of appointments in the 1890s:

> As the only career officer on the seventh floor [i.e., in top management], I had a fair amount of say on the decisions about career ambassadors. For political appointees, the White House, [Under Secretary Elliot L.] Richardson, and I set up an orderly screening system. We separately interviewed each of them . . . to get some sense of their background, character, and potential ability. Sometimes they had specific countries in mind, other times not. Many had family wealth, others had made fortunes in business. But all coveted that [ambassadorial] title.[1]

Johnson pays tribute to some of the distinguished political appointees of the past—Ellsworth Bunker, David K. E. Bruce, and W. Averell Harriman always are among those held up as models—but he comments as well on how "dense" many of the would-be Nixon ambassadors were. "Fortunately, we did not have to accept all of them, but neither could we reject them en masse."[2] His general disapproval of amateur ambassadorial applicants is the expected view of the careerist.

Such appointments to ambassadorships, and occasionally those to consul general positions at desirable locales, continue today to be made partially on the basis of political calculation or influence, service to the incumbent or incoming party, or size of campaign contributions—through the time-honored spoils system, in other words. The rule of thumb on senior staffing in recent decades has been that political-appointee ambassadors make up one-third of the envoys and career Foreign Service officers, two-thirds. This is a seemingly modest percentage of nonprofessionals, but one which is higher than that of other Western industrialized nations. Going back nearly a generation, the Kennedy administration surprisingly appointed even fewer careerists as envoys than this proportion. The Carter administration in recent years named relatively more. Under Secretary of State for Management Ronald I. Spiers, himself an FSO, noted in the fall of 1985 that the Reagan administration began a shift from the Carter pattern back toward what has come to be seen as the "normal" one-third to two-thirds breakdown. The secretary of state and the White House at the time agreed to a "target" of this ratio, according to Spiers, "but it will be possible to accomplish this [only] gradually."[3]

The ratio itself often is not so much called into question as the basic suitability of many of the nonprofessionals who are appointed. "The citizen-statesman tradition in the United States," further remarked Under Secretary Spiers, "has been a source of strength throughout our history. Yet I feel too many of our ambassadors have been appointed for reasons having little to do with their ability to meet the demands of the position. There are magnificent exceptions . . . [but] there are many who have no particular qualifications. The contention that these are better able to represent the President's policy is unpersuasive to me." The real issue, according to the American Foreign Service Association, the professional organization of American diplomacy, is not career versus noncareer envoys, "it is quality." "Where Do We Find These Envoy Clowns?" reads the title of a newspaper commentary of the early 1980s, one that reflects this professional skepticism. The writer, a retired career diplomat, as usual makes a bow in the direction of those political appointees who are highly regarded, the Bunkers and the Bruces, but the title of his piece unmistakably reveals his attitude on the need for a career service. Another career ambassador, after complimenting Bunker, Bruce, Sol Linowitz, Douglas Dillon, and others, writes that "one need only glance at the ambassadorial appointments over the last 20 years or so to recognize that the majority of political appointees have been clods with essentially no background in foreign affairs and nothing in their history or character that would lead one to expect that they would be effective representatives of U.S. interests."[4]

Complaints about amateurs thus clearly have not disappeared since the enactment of the Rogers Act. Proponents of professionalism in the conduct of foreign affairs such as these frequently decry the appointment especially of ambassadors on the basis of political favor and nothing much else. Criticism surfaces most noticeably when the nomination is gained as a result of substantial monetary favors granted to the party and the appointee has no discernible exposure to foreign affairs. "It is high time that the President stopped naming incompetents as ambassadors just because of their politics," thundered one retired FSO in a recent call for careerism.[5] This kind of comment, further examples of which abound, typifies those made repeatedly by today's foreign affairs professionals and clearly echoes the complaints aired by reformers in the late nineteenth century.

Arguments in this sense lead one to the proposition that the qualifications for the job of ambassador simply must include more than political favor or a record of donations to the party. The case against amateurish ambassadors and, to a lesser degree, consuls general, the case against inexperienced officers who are unfamiliar with foreign affairs and unable to cope effectively with their assignments, is almost self-evident and does not need to be stressed. In the modern world, nearly any country in which the United States maintains a Foreign Service post presents possibilities for trouble. An incompetent senior officer can be at least an embarrassment to his nation, if not a danger to harmonious relations. Diplomatic blunders that were simply mistakes of no great import a hundred years ago now have the potential for severe, if usually short-lived, consequences. Taken to its ultimate, the argument for professionalism in diplomacy supports the view expressed by Callières quoted at the beginning of this chapter—in diplomacy, "skilled work requires a skilled workman."

Callières's dogmatic assertion in favor of professionalism is not the last word, however; it can be refuted and the viewpoint at least partially reflected in Thomas A. Bailey's comment, also at the head of this chapter, can be substituted. Something can be said for amateurism in diplomacy—not amateurism in the limited meaning of ineptitude, but rather in the sense of an absence of career status. With the increased speed of world communications and air transport, one can argue that appointments of ambassadors and consuls general are less critical now than a hundred years ago, if for no other reason than that Washington is less likely to leave them on their own to make judgment calls. Washington now has virtually instantaneous cable and telephone contacts worldwide and the Department of State keeps envoys and principal consular officers on a short rein. In the 1890s, as previously noted, officers far from Washington often were left to their own devices. But as early as 1913, the acerbic former Secretary of State Richard Olney asserted a lack of independent authority as his reason for turning down a proffered assignment to London. "An ambassador is nobody these days. He sits at the end of a cable and does what he is told."[6] Olney's point is considerably more valid today.

Furthermore, too much can be made at the senior level of formal training and up-from-the-ranks experience in the foreign affairs field. Possession of diplomatic careerist credentials does not guarantee success in the Foreign Service, desirable as they often may be in conjunction with other qualities in today's age of experts and specialization. At the highest ranks, a broad background, independent attitude, sound judgment, and political affinity with the leadership in Washington can be equally important. Some experienced, trained FSOs turn out to be ineffective representatives abroad, even at midcareer levels of responsibility. Despite the service's elaborate screening procedures on entry and promotion, some persons rise to inappropriately high levels of authority or are assigned to positions for which they are not suited. Further, some senior officers, both career and noncareer, who might be generally capable fall eventually into the mind sets called in the modern Foreign Service "localitis" or "clientitis," an overidentification with the interests and problems of their country of assignment. They thereby lose effectiveness abroad and credibility at home.[7]

Critics of careerism have made these and other points, both in the setting of the 1890s and in more recent years. In 1896, for example, Illinois's Congressman Hitt, the sometime-chairman of the House Committee on Foreign Relations, characterized as "refreshing" a serving American ambassador's assessment that professionals were not needed at the highest diplomatic levels. Although in favor of a career consular corps, Hitt on this occasion expressed negative comments on the kind of American "who preferred other countries for residence." Hitt equated would-be expatriates who wanted to live outside the United States with careerists in diplomacy. "[They] press so hard at Wash[ington] for office abroad."[8]

At about the same time, Hitt's colleague, Democratic Congressman James B. McCreary of Kentucky, held similar anticareerist views on consuls as well as diplomats. "The most suitable persons for the consular service," he intoned on the floor of the House, "can not be selected under civil-service rules. . . . We should not inaugurate a consular aristocracy to hold office for life. . . . We want no permanent class of officers residing permanently abroad and giving up entirely their interest in our people, our business, and our Government." McCreary argued that both diplomatic and consular representatives abroad at any given time should belong to the political party then dominant in the United States (it was 1894, early in a Democratic presidential administration). One of our senior officers of that era, Francis B. Loomis, supported McCreary. He remarked that most consuls lived abroad for long stretches of time and "unconsciously drift[ed] away from the distinctive sentiment, thought and purposes of the United States." They often become "severe, habitual critics" of things American. "We have no reason to send abroad salaried apologists," he wrote in this period-piece indictment of "localitis."[9]

An academic colleague of Eben Alexander, minister to Greece during the mid-1890s, elaborated the argument for amateurism in diplomacy shortly after Alexander's death:

> Every now and then our wise men tell us that the American method of training diplomats is all wrong; that we need a school of diplomacy in which our consuls, ministers and ambassadors should be trained; and that the policy of selecting a man for this important service without long schooling in the art of diplomacy has sadly marred the standing of America in its relations with foreign countries. They are altogether wrong about this. . . . We can train clerks in diplomacy. No school of diplomacy can ever give us a Benjamin Franklin, a Thomas Jefferson, a John Quincy Adams.

The writer then cited the scholars in diplomacy, including Alexander, "who went from college halls or the world of letters to become better diplomats than all the technically trained consuls and ministers and ambassadors the schools could turn out in a century."[10] In 1898 a scholar took a similar position against the career principle for American diplomats at a gathering of the American Historical Association—this despite the professional bent of the organization which he addressed. He praised the amateur envoys' exceptionally high skills over the years and called attention to their diplomatic successes.[11]

Many Americans today still hold the notion that careerist principles are not always necessary, especially if those principles are equated with elitism. In 1982 a conservative daily newspaper in the Deep South scored the professionals of the "foreign service brotherhood" for questioning President Reagan's ambassadorial appointments and commented acidly that career officers may lack "the insight into America's free-enterprise system" that appointees from the business sector have. This Mississippi newspaper concluded that "new blood does a world of good" in the Foreign Service. Presidents should not choose "political hacks or those obviously unqualified," but careerists overstate their case when they claim that only they are capable of discharging the task of overseas representation.[12]

Evan G. Galbraith, an outspoken former banker who was ambassador to France from 1981 to 1985, would agree. He held that the president was entitled to have "his own men" (and women, presumably) in all major embassies and senior Department of State positions. According to him, only two basic requirements are essential for an ambassador: he must be intelligent and he must be closely identified with the president. Galbraith also asserted that the career Foreign Service "takes the guts out of people," a remark for which he was publicly rebuked by the secretary of state. He later said that his views had been distorted, but one can assume he meant that careerism encourages timid conformity, a charge which he was not the first to make.[13]

Thomas A. Bailey has endorsed professionalism in diplomacy, but he incorporates a point in favor of amateurs in one statement: "All embassies are now significant outposts, and diplomacy is much too important to be left solely to the [professional] diplomats." He sets forth the importance of broad-based participation in the conduct of foreign relations, as does a great-grandson of John Hay, himself a former high-level Department of State official; in a plea for popular involvement in foreign affairs, James W. Symington finds a place for careerists, albeit a limited one. Symington would leave technical questions to lower-ranking professionals, reserving policy matters to senior nonprofessionals.[14]

Bailey also touches on one of the most damning indictments of careerists in senior foreign policy positions, the supposed tendency of professionals to be stuck in preconceived modes of thought and operation, a charge similar to that of Galbraith's about a lack of guts among FSOs. In his paraphrase of the aphorism about war being too important to leave to the military, Bailey is particularly hard on "the overprofessionalized, overbureaucratized, overcautious, striped-pants variety" of diplomat, a point which underlies the opinions of many critics of the professional Foreign Service. Bailey concludes that a "judicious leavening by talented newcomers has its place."[15]

The above positions are representative of nonprofessional outsiders with an interest in diplomacy. Less to be expected is agreement on many of these points by an insider, retired career ambassador Charles W. Yost. Writing in the early 1970s, he made several suggestions for improved management of foreign affairs, including a requirement for "a staffing of the senior echelons . . . by a judicious mixture of experienced nonprofessionals enjoying the particular confidence of the President and the Secretary, outstanding professionals with a lifetime of training in foreign affairs, and 'in-and-outers' from the academic or business world with special expertise in certain relevant fields."[16] Yost's recommendations are hardly a plea for complete amateurism in the conduct of diplomacy, but he explicitly calls for a role for both professionals and nonprofessionals. This is a position, however, with which many confirmed careerists, including those quoted earlier in this chapter, probably would agree only in principle.

Positions taken either for or against professionalism in diplomacy frequently are self-serving or self-justifying. Some persons favor change in line with the rise of professionalism in American life; others see positive

merit in continuing the time-honored system of appointments from outside the career ranks. The discussants on either side sometimes are personally involved in the arguments. Careerists in diplomacy push for
professional standards, often to protect or validate their standing as in-
siders. They have the best interests of their country in mind when they
stress the need for professionalism, but they are also concerned about
their own careers and advancement. Under Secretary Spiers in 1985
hoped for a "steadier" ratio of career and noncareer appointments so as
to "ensure career opportunities at the top."[17] Likewise, the diplomatic
amateurs with roles as senior officers—past, present, or future—grind
their own axes of self-interest. Some noncareerists like former Ambassador Galbraith not only extol the virtues of amateurism per se, but also
often enough downgrade the usefulness of the careerists in their staff
capacities. Another Ambassador Galbraith, John Kenneth, a celebrated
Harvard economist but an amateur and greatly opinionated diplomat appointed during the Kennedy administration, also was notoriously critical
of FSOs. Criticism from such nonprofessional envoys, one suspects, de-
rives in some measure from a need to justify their own heady but relatively short visits as outsiders to the halls of diplomatic power.

Diplomacy, like engineering and other skilled occupations, may best
be served at most levels by practitioners with professional credentials, as
was suggested at the beginning of this section. Nearly all subordinate
diplomatic and consular positions today require backgrounds of skill, experience, and training that, while perhaps desirable in the foreign service of a hundred years ago, were not absolutely essential. The amateur
today would have a hard time coping with many of the complex, frequently specialized demands present since World War II—everything
from esoteric language requirements to visa fraud determinations to science and technology reporting to negotiations on the use of surplus cur-
rencies to international terrorism. It is a changed world from the 1890s.

The reader should note, however, that there is a fundamental difference between diplomacy as practiced at the highest ranks and other occupational fields. The conduct of foreign affairs abroad requires by long-
established custom the appointment to the capital of each country a
single person in an authoritative position—an ambassador—who is accredited to the host country chief of state and responsible technically to
his own head of state. Naming an ambassador therefore is more a personalized selection than many other senior bureaucratic appointments. In
America no legal or regulatory requirement specifies that FSOs make up
any proportion of total nominations to these unique ambassadorial slots.
A president could, in principle, name all political appointees as his

ambassadors. The ambassador's supporting staff abroad, on the other hand, now consists of selected, trained, and practiced diplomats and consular officers. In their subordinate roles, these careerists are comparable to graduate, credentialed engineers with experience. Here FSOs make their presence felt to the greatest advantage; it is difficult to imagine how posts abroad of any significance at all could function in the modern world without staffs of Foreign Service professionals. If well served by the staff and if a man or woman of good sense, an ambassador or a consul general need not necessarily be an experienced foreign affairs professional in every instance.

If amateur diplomats who have trained and practiced in other professional fields often can make valuable contributions in senior positions abroad, and if the foreign affairs professionals in truth often are narrowly focused and tend to be overly conservative, as charged by critics,[18] then one is tempted to find positive merit in diplomatic amateurism for the modern Foreign Service. The controversy would be resolved against the careerists; the ratio of career to noncareer ambassadors could be reversed, at least. The professionals' highest ambitions might be limited in all but clearly the most exceptional cases to perhaps a few minor ambassadorships at hardship posts, possibly most of the consul generalships, and virtually all of the deputy chiefs of mission, including those at major diplomatic missions. This finding in favor of noncareerists would be an especially viable principle if the Foreign Service and Department of State, backed by the White House, kept on for more than one assignment only those amateur ambassadors who demonstrated superior abilities, and encouraged those with indifferent talents or worse to return soon to their usual other pursuits.

Following this formulation, senior assignments abroad would be filled by the president's men (and women), as recommended by Evan Galbraith, and that would be that. "When an ambassador overseas negotiates, or speaks in private or in public," once argued a Senate subcommittee, "his audience needs to feel that he has the confidence and speaks with the authority of the President of the United States."[19] The president's ambassadors appointed by him directly from public life, including from the academic and business worlds and politics, presumably would have that confidence.

Clearly the issue is not resolved quite so simply or so cleanly; Washington unfortunately has made ill-considered nominations of diplomatic amateurs who actually had few of the desirable attributes of the nonprofessional. But the historical record, including particularly that of the period of the 1890s addressed in this study, nevertheless supports a contention that there is broad scope for effective diplomatic service by amateurs at senior levels. Without downgrading totally the benefits of experience, a career of preparation in foreign affairs is not indicated as an absolute prerequisite to a successful tour as the head of a diplomatic or large consular post. (I repeat that the same argument does not follow for subordinate support positions; as indicated above, detailed, often technical, knowledge is necessary for such assignments, and a backlog of practical experience is highly useful.) Other personal qualities can be more important than a background of career Foreign Service experience and training: character, ability, industry, dependability, and adaptability are among them. The noncareerist ambassador frequently also brings to the job the prestige and high-level contacts at home that are not available to the career diplomatist, who lives so long abroad.

The long list of amateurs in diplomacy who possessed those positive qualities in sufficient measure attests to the fact that successful assignments as the president's envoy abroad are by no means limited to Foreign Service professionals. Clare Booth Luce, a political-appointee ambassador herself, was correct when she asserted that "amateur diplomacy is the American method."[20] In 1985 an experienced retired careerist held that "the sources of the Service's current difficulties [a loss of prestige and effectiveness] are not to be found in the quality of the highest ranking officials." He found those officials, career and nonprofessional alike, to be "generally superior people, certainly vastly better than other countries' diplomats." In his view the fault lay rather in weaknesses in the management of the Foreign Service.[21]

To sum up, other factors being roughly equal, careerists in the American Foreign Service have valid claims to almost any senior assignment. They are the experienced product of a competitive selection, evaluation, and training system. They have been working away in the diplomatic or consular trenches for years, probably at considerable personal sacrifice, accumulating professional knowledge and experience. They deserve some reward from their nation. The envoy or consul general, amateur or professional, should be someone who is capable of getting things done if that is indicated, or alternatively, keeping the lid on if need be, adroitly doing nothing of consequence. Most responsibilities are variations on the three basic requirements already mentioned: projecting a suitable image of the United States, keeping Washington well informed on the local scene, and following policy guidance carefully and accurately. And very often career officers are the most competent, best prepared persons available to fill those responsibilities.

But I do not hold that increased professionalism answers all of the United States' diplomatic needs at the level of envoy or consul general. Ideally the issue of careerists versus noncareerists would not even enter into senior appointment calculations. Here I agree, probably for different reasons, with the American Foreign Service Association—the real issue is quality (see above in this chapter). Ideally there would be no overt considerations of a ratio between Foreign Service professionals and outsiders. As able as members of the American FSO corps are, there is too much evidence that the United States over the years has produced many gifted amateurs for the top diplomatic posts who were at least as accomplished as the professionals, the poor reputation of diplomatic outsiders in the historical literature notwithstanding. In the words of former Ambassador Luce, commenting on the multiplicity of American responsibilities in the post–World War II world, "Indeed, it is impossible to see how our democracy could conduct its foreign policy without the organized and unorganized assistance of amateurs."[22]

The same can be said of the nation's earlier years, including the 1890s. As phrased recently by Under Secretary Ronald Spiers, "The citizen-statesman tradition . . . has been a source of strength throughout our history."[23] Amateurs have had, and should continue to have, an important place in the highest ranks of the Foreign Service of the United States.

Appendix A

Biographic Register, Chiefs of Diplomatic Mission & Consuls General, 1890s

Entries are styled loosely after the Department of State *Biographic Register* which was published for decades until the early 1970s. Each entry includes, where known, the appointee's full name, state or country and year of birth, college-level education, filial relationship, military service if any, and profession or professions with the years they were followed. If the ending or beginning year of such professional experience is unknown or unclear, it is left blank. Included also is information on political experience, Diplomatic or Consular Service assignments by year from appointment to resignation, and locale from which named. If he was a published author or if there is documentary indication of language ability or travel abroad, those facts are noted. The year of death, where known, completes the biographic entry.

Many of the abbreviated terms and words in the *Register* are commonly used and do not require explanation. Examples are "atty." for attorney, "gov." for governor, the short forms of state names, "st." for state, "cand." for candidate, "lang." for language, and "phys." for physician. Following are some of the less obvious or less commonly used abbreviations:

AE&P	ambassador extraordinary & plenipotentiary
agt.	agent
BG	brigadier general
bvt.	brevet
C	consul
c.	circa
CG	consul general
clk.	clerk

co.	county
comm.	committee
commr.	commissioner
Cong.	Congress or Congressman
cons.	consular
couns.	counselor
conv.	convention
dep.	deputy
EE&MP	envoy extraordinary & plenipotentiary
LTC	lieutenant colonel
mfr.	manufacturer
MG	major general
MR	minister resident
off.	officer
sec. leg.	secretary of legation
supt.	superintendent
svc.	service
VC	vice consul

John True Abbott: b. N.H. 1850; educ. Bates Coll., Maine, grad. 1871; son of clergy & nephew of gov.; bar, law 1878–, business briefly in Columbia; EE&MP Colombia 1889–93; apptd. from Keene, N.H.; d. 1914.

Robert Adams, Jr.: b. Pa. 1849; educ. Univ. of Pa., grad. 1869, Wharton Sch., grad. 1884; U.S. Geol. Survey Yellowstone Park, journalist 1871–75, bar, law 1875–89; EE&MP Brazil 1889–90; U.S. Cong. 1892–1906; apptd. from Philadelphia, Pa.; d. 1906.

Thomas Adamson: b. Pa. 1827; business; C La Guaira 1861–62, Pernambuco 1862–69, Honolulu 1869–70; CG Melbourne 1871–77, Rio de Janeiro 1878–82, Panama 1882–93; apptd. from Philadelphia, Pa.; d. 1911.

Eben Alexander: b. Tenn. 1851; educ. Yale, grad. 1873; son of judge, grandson of U.S. Cong.; univ. prof. 1873–93, 1897–1900, dean 1900–1910; EE&MP Greece (also Romania & Serbia) 1893–97; apptd. from Chapel Hill, N.C.; lang., Greek, Fr.; d. 1911.

Horace Newton Allen: b. Ohio 1858; educ. Ohio Wesleyan, grad. 1881, Starling Med. Coll., Miami Med. Coll., Ohio, M.D. degree 1883; med. missionary to China, Korea; long residence abroad, court phys. Seoul 1885, adviser to Korean leg. Washington 1887; sec. leg. & dep. CG Seoul 1890–97, MR&CG Korea 1897–1901, EE&MP 1901–5; apptd. from Toledo, Ohio; author; d. 1932.

John Alexander Anderson: b. Pa. 1834; educ. Miami Univ., Ohio, grad. 1853; son and grandson of clergy; chaplain Civil War; clergy, pres. Kans. St.

Coll. 1873–78; U.S. Cong. 1878–91; CG Cairo 1891–92; apptd. from Junction City, Kans.; d. 1892.

Thomas Henry Anderson: b. Ohio 1848; educ. Mt. Union Coll., Ohio; sch. principal 1869, bar, law 1871–89, 1893–99; U.S. dist. atty. 1899–1901, assoc. justice D.C. sup. ct. 1901–; MR&CG Bolivia 1889–90, EE&MP 1890–92; apptd. from Mt. Vernon, Ohio; d. 1916.

Wendell A. Anderson: b. Maine 1840; educ. Bowdoin Coll., Maine, Coll. of Physicians & Surgeons, N.Y.; son of phys.; surgeon & bvt. LTC Civil War; phys.; chair Wis. Dem. Central Comm.; CG Montreal 1885–86, 1893–97; apptd. from La Crosse, Wis.; d. unknown.

James Burrill Angell: b. R.I. 1829; educ. Brown Univ., grad. 1849, study in Europe 1850–53; son of farmer & tavern keeper; coll. prof. 1853–60, editor 1860–66, pres. Univ. of Vt. 1866–71, Univ. of Mich. 1871–1909; EE&MP China 1880–81, Turkey 1897–98, int'l. commr.; apptd. from Ann Arbor, Mich.; author; d. 1916.

Lewis Baker: b. Ohio 1832; son of farmer; editor & publ. in Ohio, W.Va., Minn. 1852–93; W.Va. st. sen. 1870, nat. Dem. convs., chair Minn. Dem. Comm. 1892; EE&MP Nicaragua (also Costa Rica & El Salvador) 1893–97; apptd. from St. Paul, Minn.; d. 1899.

John Judson Barclay: b. Va. c. 1834; educ. in medicine, Philadelphia; son of med. missionary, grandson of CG; resided in Middle East; planter; dep. C Beirut 1858–59, C Cyprus 1859–65, CG Tangier 1893–96; apptd. from Lawrence Co., Ala.; lang., Arab, Gr.; d. unknown.

Andrew Dickson Barlow: b. Mo. c. 1863; son of RR pres.; post office exec.; CG Mexico 1897–1904; insurance business later; apptd. from St. Louis, Mo.; d. 1933.

John Barrett: b. Vt. 1866; educ. Dartmouth, grad. 1889; teacher, journalist 1889–94; MR&CG Siam 1894–98; EE&MP Argentina 1903–4, Panama 1904–5, Colombia 1905–7; dir. Int'l. Bureau of Amer. Republics 1907–20; apptd. from Portland, Oreg.; author; d. 1938.

George Sherman Batcheller: b. N.Y. 1837; educ. Harvard Law, grad. 1857; son of co. political leader; LTC Civil War; law 1857–75, 1885–89; judge Int'l. Tribunal Cairo 1875–85, 1898–1908, asst. Sec. of Treasury 1889–91, business 1895–96, pres. Universal Postal Cong. 1897; N.Y. st. legis. 1873–74, 1886, 1888–89; MR&CG Portugal 1891–93; apptd. from Albany, N.Y.; d. 1908.

Thomas Francis Bayard: b. Del. 1828; son and grandson of U.S. Sens.; bar, law 1851–69; U.S. Sen. 1869–85; Sec. of State 1885–89; AE&P Great Britain 1893–97; apptd. from Wilmington, Del.; d. 1898.

Truxtun Beale: b. Calif. 1856; educ. Columbia Law, grad. 1878; son of army officer, landowner and dipl.; bar, but managed large family landholdings Calif.; MR&CG Persia 1891–92, Greece 1892–93, EE&MP Greece 1893; apptd. from Bakersfield, Calif.; author & world traveller 1893–; d. 1936.

Arthur Matthias Beaupre: b. Ill. 1853; printer 1869–74, apptd. city, dep. co. clk. 1874–86, elected co. clk. 1886–97; bar; sec. leg. & CG Guatemala 1897–99, Bogota 1899–1903, EE&MP Colombia 1903–4, Argentina 1904–8, Netherlands 1908–11, Cuba 1911–13; apptd. from Aurora, Ill.; d. 1919.

John Lawrence Bittinger: b. Pa. 1833; maj. Civil War; journalist 1852–60, postmaster St. Joseph, Mo., 1860, 1862–65, editor 1865–97; Mo. st. legis. 7 terms, nat. Rep. convs. 1872, 1896; CG Montreal 1897–1903; apptd. from St. Joseph, Mo.; d. 1911.

James Henderson Blount: b. Ga. 1837, educ. Univ. of Ga., grad. 1857; LTC Civil War; bar, law, U.S. Cong. 1872–93; special rep. to Hawaii 1893, EE&MP 1893; apptd. from Macon, Ga.; law 1893–1903; d. 1903.

Benjamin F. Bonham: b. Tenn. c. 1856; bar 1856, Oreg. Terr. auditor & librarian 1858–59; circuit judge 1870–76, concurrently chief justice Oreg. sup. ct. 1874–76; st. legis. 1858; CG Calcutta 1886–90; apptd. from Salem, Oreg.

Augustus Osborn Bourn: b. R.I. 1834; educ. Brown, grad. 1855; son of mfr.; militia LTC Civil War; rubber mfr. 1867–83; R.I. st. sen. 1876–83, 1886–88, R.I. gov. 1883–85; CG Rome 1889–93; apptd. from Bristol, R.I.; d. 1925.

Herbert Wolcott Bowen: b. N.Y. 1856; educ. Yale, grad. 1878, Columbia, grad. 1881; son of publ.; law 1884–90; C Barcelona 1890–95, CG 1895–99, MR&CG Persia 1899–1901, EE&MP Venezuela 1901–5; apptd. from N.Y., N.Y.; author; d. 1927.

Sempronius Hamilton Boyd: b. Tenn. 1828; col. Civil War; bar, law 1855–90; mayor, Springfield, Mo., nat. Rep. conv. 1864, U.S. Cong. 1863–65, 1869–71; MR&CG Siam 1890–92; apptd. from Springfield, Mo.; d. 1894.

John P. Bray: b. Minn. 1859; educ. St. Cloud Coll., Minn.; co. & N.D. st. auditor 1883–92, postmaster Grand Forks, N.D., 1892; CG Melbourne 1897–1908, Sydney 1908–15, Johannesburg 1915–17; apptd. from Grand Forks, N.D.; d. 1917.

Clifton Rodes Breckenridge: b. Ky. 1846; educ. Wabash Coll., Va.; son of Vice Pres.; Civil War svc.; planter 1870–83; U.S. Cong. 1883–95: EE&MP Russia 1894–97; apptd. from Pine Bluff, Ark.; comm. to Indian tribes Okla. 1900–1905; d. 1932.

George Herbert Bridgman: b. N.H. 1853; educ. Dartmouth, grad. 1876, Harvard Med., grad. 1880; phys. 1880–97; EE&MP Bolivia 1897–1902, C Kingston 1901–6; apptd. from Elizabeth, N.J.; d. 1925.

James Overton Broadhead: b. Va. 1819; educ. Univ. of Va.; Civil War svc.; bar, law 1842–; U.S. dist. atty. 1862, spec. prosec. Whiskey Ring 1876; Mo. st. legis., U.S. Cong. 1883–85; spec. commr. French Spoilation Claims, EE&MP Switzerland 1893–95; apptd. from St. Louis, Mo.; d. 1898.

Charles Page Bryan: b. Ill. 1856; educ. Univ. of Va., Columbian (George Washington) Univ., D.C., grad. 1879; bar. 1878, editor & publ. 1879–84, law 1885–97; Colo. st. legis. 1880–84, Ill. st. legis. 1888–97; EE&MP Brazil 1898–1902, Portugal 1903–9, Belgium 1909–11, AE&P Japan 1911–12; apptd. from Elmhurst, Ill.; d. 1918.

William Insco Buchanan: b. Ohio 1852; business, exhibits mgr. 1880–94; dept. head Columbian Expo. 1890–93; EE&MP Argentina 1894–99, Panama 1903–5, dir. gen. Pan Amer. Expo. Buffalo 1901, deleg. int'l. confs. 1902, 1907; apptd. from Sioux City, Iowa; d. 1909.

Alfred Eliab Buck: b. Maine 1832; educ. Waterville Coll. (Colby), Maine, grad. 1859; bvt. col. Civil War; pres. elector 1868, U.S. Cong. 1869–71, nat. Rep. convs. 5 times; court clk. 1867–68, 1874–89, U.S. marshal 1889–93, business; EE&MP Japan 1897–1902; apptd. from Atlanta, Ga.; d. 1902.

David N. Burke: b. Vt. c. 1846; educ. Middlebury Coll., Vt., grad. 1867, St. Bonaventure Coll., N.Y., grad. c. 1903; teacher, principal 1867–85, clergy 1903–13; C Puerto Cabello 1886–88, Bahia 1888–91, Pernambuco 1893, Malaga 1893–96, CG Tangier 1896–97; apptd. from Mineville, N.Y.; d. 1913.

Samuel Hawkins Marshall Byers: b. Pa. 1838; bvt. maj. Civil War; bar; C Zurich 1869–84, CG Rome 1884–85, C St. Gall 1891–92, CG 1892–93; apptd. from Oskaloosa, Iowa; author; d. 1933.

Clark Ezra Carr: b. N.Y. 1836; educ. Knox Coll., Ill., grad. 1856, Albany Law Sch., grad. 1858; Civil War svc. on Ill. gov. staff; law 1858–94, nat. Rep. convs. 1864, 1884; MR&CG Denmark 1889–90, EE&MP 1890–93, apptd. from Galesburg, Ill.; d. 1919.

William Simpson Carroll: b. Pa. 1838; educ. Allegheny Coll., Pa.; teacher, law, oil business, banking; extensive travel abroad 1873–93; CG Dresden 1893–1905; apptd. from Baltimore, Md.; d. 1911.

George William Caruth: b. Ky. 1842; educ. Dickinson Coll., Pa., Univ. of Louisville, grad. 1863; son of banker; law 1873–93; EE&MP Portugal 1893–97; apptd. from Little Rock, Ark.; d. unknown.

Person Colby Cheney: b. N.H. 1828; lt. Civil War; son of mfr.; paper products mfr. 1854–, banker; RR commr. 1864–67, mayor Manchester, N.H. 1871, N.H. gov. 1875–76, U.S. Sen. 1886–87, nat. Rep. conv. 1888, nat. Rep. comm. 1892–1900; EE&MP Switzerland 1892–93; apptd. from Manchester, N.H.; d. 1901.

Joseph Hodges Choate: b. Mass. 1832; educ. Harvard, grad. 1852, Harvard Law, grad. 1854; son of phys.; bar, law 1855–97; cand. for U.S. Sen. 1897; AE&P Great Britain 1899–1905, head U.S. deleg. 2d Hague Peace Conf. 1907; apptd. from N.Y., N.Y.; author; d. 1917.

William Churchill: b. N.Y. 1859; educ. Yale, grad. 1882; teacher, editor 1891–96, 1897–1915; extensive travel abroad; CG Apia 1896–97; apptd. from Brooklyn, N.Y.; author; d. 1920.

Alexander G. Clark: b. Pa. 1826; educ. Iowa Univ. Law, grad. 1884; Civil War svc.; real estate business, also editor, lawyer, one-time barber; MR&CG Liberia 1890–91; apptd. from Muscatine, Iowa; d. 1891.

Powell Clayton: b. Pa. 1833; bvt. BG Civil War; civil engineer 1855–61, planter 1865–82, RR exec. 1882–97; Ark. gov. 1868–71, U.S. Sen. 1871–77, nat. Rep. comm. 1872–1913; EE&MP Mexico 1897–98, AE&P 1898–1905; apptd. from Eureka Springs, Ark.; d. 1914.

Patrick Andrew Collins: b. Ireland 1844; educ. Harvard Law, grad. 1871; son of laborer; bar, law 1871–; Mass. st. legis., st. sen. 1868–71, st. judge advocate 1875, U.S. Cong. 1883–89, mayor Boston 1902–3; CG London 1893–97; apptd. from Boston, Mass.; d. 1905.

Edwin Hurd Conger: b. Ill. 1843; educ. Lombard. Coll., Ill., grad. 1862, Albany Law Sch., grad. 1866; bvt. maj. Civil War; rancher, farmer, banking 1868–82; Iowa st. treasurer 1882–85, nat. elector 1896, U.S. Cong. 1885–90; EE&MP Brazil 1890–93, 1897–98, China 1898–1905, Mexico 1905; apptd. from Madison Co., Iowa; d. 1907.

Thomas Jefferson Coolidge: b. Mass. 1831; educ. in Europe, Harvard, grad. 1853; grandson of Pres.; import business, textiles, banking, briefly RR pres.; Mass. st. tax commr. 1892; EE&MP France 1892–93, int'l. comm. 1898–99; apptd. from Cape Ann, Mass.; lang., Fr.; author; d. 1920.

Frank Leslie Coombs: b. Calif. 1853; educ. Columbian (George Washington) Univ., D.C., grad. 1875; bar, law 1876–79, 1884–92; dist. atty. 1879–84, Calif. st. legis. 1887–93, 1897–99, U.S. Cong. 1901–3, U.S. atty.; EE&MP Japan 1892–93; apptd. from Napa, Calif.; d. 1934.

Jeremiah Coughlin: b. Ireland c. 1857; educ. Univ. of Mich., N.Y. Coll. of Phys. & Surgeons; phys. resident in Colombia; sec. leg. & CG Bogota 1892–93; apptd. from N.Y., N.Y.; remained Colombia; d. 1930.

Macgrane Coxe: b. Ala. 1859; educ. Yale, grad. 1879, Columbia Law, grad. 1881; bar, law 1881–85, asst. U.S. dist. atty. 1885–89, U.S. circuit court 1889–96, U.S. bankruptcy ref., univ. law lecturer 1906–; EE&MP Guatemala 1896–97; apptd. from N.Y., N.Y.; author; d. 1923.

John Martin Crawford: b. Pa. 1845; educ. Lafayette Coll., Pa., grad. 1871, Pulte Med. Coll., Ohio, grad. 1878, Miami Univ. Med., Ohio, grad. 1881; med. sch. registrar 1881–89, translator, banker, lecturer 1895–1916; CG St. Petersburg 1889–94; apptd. from Cincinnati, Ohio; lang., Russ., Finn., Estonian; author; d. 1916.

Thomas Theodore Crittenden: b. Ky. 1832; educ. Centre Coll., Ky., grad. 1855; nephew of gov. & U.S. Sen.; LTC Civil War; bar 1856, law 1857–62, 1865–73; Mo. st. atty. gen. 1865, U.S. Cong. 1873–75, 1877–81, Mo. gov. 1881–85, judge U.S. dist. ct. –1909; CG Mexico 1893–97; apptd. from Kansas City, Mo.; d. 1909.

Hector de Castro: b. Turkey 1849; educ. France, to U.S. 1885; vice pres. Commercial Cable Co. 1883–90, sec. Intercont. RR Commr., Washington, 1890–92; CG Rome 1897–1908, Zurich 1908–9; apptd. from Washington, D.C.; d. 1909.

Charles de Kay: b. D.C. 1848; educ. Yale, grad. 1868; son of Argentine naval off.; art & lit. editor 1876–94, 1898–; CG Berlin 1894–97; apptd. from N.Y., N.Y.; lang., Ger., Fr.; author; d. 1935.

Perry M. DeLeon: b. S.C. c. 1840; educ. USNA; Civil War svc.; CG Guayaquil 1897–1902; apptd. from Ga.; d. 1922.

Charles Denby: b. Va. 1830; educ. Georgetown Univ., Va. Military Inst., grad. 1850; son of shipping owner & naval agt.; LTC Civil War; bar 1855, editor briefly, law 1856–61, 1865–85; nat. Dem. conv. 1876, 1884; EE&MP China 1885–98, Philippine Commr. 1898; apptd. from Evansville, Ind.; lang., Fr.; author; d. 1904.

Charles Monroe Dickinson: b. N.Y. 1842; son of farmer & miller; bar, law 1865–77, editor & publ. 1878–1911, founder of Associated Press; pres. elector 1896; CG Constantinople 1897–1906, also dipl. agt. Bulgaria 1901–3, CG-at-large (insp.) 1906–8; apptd. from Binghamton, N.Y.; author; d. 1924.

George G. Dillard: b. Miss. c. 1838; Civil War svc.; law; Miss. st. sen., st. constit. conv. 1890; CG Guayaquil 1893–97; apptd. from Macon, Miss.; d. 1921.

Oliver Hart Dockery: b. N.C. 1830; educ. Wake Forest, Univ. of N.C., grad. 1848; son of local polit. leader; Civil War svc.; law-trained but planter; U.S. Cong. 1868–73, N.C. st. constit. conv. 1875, cand. for House of Rep., 1882, cand. for N.C. gov. 1888; CG Rio de Janeiro 1889–93; apptd. from Richmond Co., N.C.; d. 1906.

Joseph Gordon Donnelly: b. Wis. 1856; teacher, registrar of probate 1877–93, bar 1881; Irish nationalist, cand. for House of Rep., 1898, dist. judge 1901–; CG Nuevo Laredo 1893–98; apptd. from Milwaukee, Wis.; lang., Sp., Ger., Fr.; author; d. unknown.

Frederick Douglass: b. slave Md. c. 1817; editor & orator 1841–71; sec. Sto. Domingo Comm. 1871, U.S. marshal D.C. 1877–81, recorder of D.C. deeds 1881–89; extensive travel abroad; MR&CG Haiti, also chargé Domin. Rep. 1889–91; author; d. 1895.

William Franklin Draper: b. Mass. 1842; son of mfr.; bvt. BG Civil War; textile mach. mfr. 1865–92; U.S. Cong. 1892–97; AE&P Italy 1897–1900; apptd. from Hopedale, Mass.; d. 1910.

James Taylor DuBois: b. Pa. 1857; educ. Cornell, Columbian (George Washington) Univ. D.C.; printer, Rep. party editor 1872–77, 1886–97; cons. agt., C Aix-la-Chapelle 1877–83, Leipzig 1883–86, CG St. Gall 1897–1901, law clk. Dept. of State 1901–9, CG Singapore 1901–11, EE&MP Colombia 1911–13; apptd. from Spring Farm, Pa.; author; d. 1920.

Irving Bedell Dudley: b. Ohio 1861; educ. Kenyon Coll., Ohio, grad. 1882, Columbian (George Washington) Univ., D.C., grad. 1885; son of clergy; bar 1885, law 1888–91, city ct. judge 1891–95; Calif. st. Rep. exec. comm.; EE&MP Peru 1897–1907, AE&P 1907–11; apptd. from San Diego, Calif.; d. 1911.

Edwin Dun: b. Ohio 1848; grandson of U.S. Sen.; agric. bureau Japan 1873–84, oil business Japan 1897–; sec. leg. Tokyo 1884–93, EE&MP Japan 1893–97; apptd. from Ohio while in Japan; remained Japan; d. 1931.

John Stephens Durham: b. Pa. 1861; educ. Univ. of Pa., grad. 1886; editor 1887–90, planter Domin. Rep. 1893–; C Sto. Domingo 1890–91, MR&CG Haiti 1891–93; apptd. from Philadelphia, Pa.; d. 1919.

William Hayden Edwards: b. Ohio c. 1844; educ. Cincinnati Law Sch., grad. 1869; govt. clk. 1870–76; sec. leg. Rio de Janeiro 1877–78, CG St. Petersburg 1878–81, int'l. commr. 1882, dipl. bureau chief Dept. of State 1884–85, cons. agt. Schiedam 1885–89, CG Berlin 1889–94; apptd. from Ripley, Ohio; d. 1894.

Patrick Egan: b. Ireland 1841; son of engineer; polit. activist, elected to Parliament, business, to U.S. 1883, grain & milling business 1883–89; nat. Rep. conv. 1888; EE&MP Chile 1889–93; apptd. from Lincoln, Neb.; d. 1919.

James Biddle Eustis: b. La. 1834; educ. Harvard Law, grad. 1854; son of judge; Civil War svc.; law, prof. of law 1879–84; La. st. legis. & sen. 1872, 1874–78, U.S. Sen. 1877–79, 1885–91; AE&P France 1893–97; apptd. from New Orleans, La.; d. 1899.

James Stevenson Ewing: b. Ill. 1835; educ. Centre Coll., Ky., grad. 1858; bar, law 1859–93; nat. elector 1860, nat. Dem. conv. 6 times; EE&MP Belgium 1893–97; apptd. from Bloomington, Ill.; d. 1918.

Thomas Barker Ferguson: b. S.C. 1841; educ. S.C. Mil. Acad., grad. 1861; son of army col.; maj. Civil War; govt. fisheries 1870–87, asst. commr. to Paris Expo. 1878, inventor; EE&MP Sweden & Norway 1894–98; apptd. from Baltimore, Md.; d. 1922.

William Rufus Finch: b. Wis. 1847; son of farmer; journalism, editor & publ. 1865–97; EE&MP Uruguay & Paraguay 1897–1905; apptd. from LaCrosse, Wis.; d. 1913.

John Gilman Foster: b. Vt. 1859; educ. Tufts, grad. 1880; bar, 1881, banker 1881–97; Vt. st. legis. 1892–94; CG Halifax 1897–1903, Ottawa 1903–27; apptd. from Derby Line, Vt.; d. 1931.

Wakefield G. Frye: b. Maine; coll. (unknown) grad.; law, court clk., customs collector; CG Halifax 1882–85, 1889–93; apptd. from Belfast, Maine; d. 1893.

Julius Goldschmidt: b. Germany c. 1846; to U.S. c. 1858, foundry business 1867–89, garment business 1893–97; pres. elector 1888; CG Vienna 1889–93, Berlin 1897–98; apptd. from Milwaukee, Wis.; lang., Ger., Fr.; d. 1898.

John Goodnow: b. Ind. 1858; educ. Univ. of Minn., grad. 1874; son of army col.; coal & wood business 1880–97; CG Shanghai 1897–1905; apptd. from Minneapolis, Minn.; d. 1907.

John Kennedy Gowdy: b. Ind. 1843; son of st. legis.; Civil War svc.; sheriff 1871–75, co. auditor 1883–91, farmer; chair Ind. st. Rep. comm. 1891–97; CG Paris 1897–1905; apptd. from Rushville, Ind.; d. 1918.

John F. Gowey: b. Ohio; law, dist. atty., land office registrar, banker; Ohio st. legis., nat. Rep. conv.; CG Yokohama 1897–1900; apptd. from Olympia, Wash.; d. 1900.

Frederick Dent Grant: b. Ill. 1850; educ. USMA, grad. 1871; son of Pres.; army off. 1871–81; 1898–1912, MG; business 1886–89, police commr. 1894–98; EE&MP Austria-Hungary 1889–93; apptd. from N.Y., N.Y.; d. 1912.

Frederick James Grant: b. Ohio c. 1862; editor 1882–92; Wash. st. legis.; EE&MP Bolivia 1892–93; apptd. from Seattle, Wash.; lang., Fr., Ger.; d. 1894.

Isaac Pusey Gray: b. Va. 1828; col. Civil War; business 1848–60; bar, law 1860–; Ind. st. legis. 1868–72, Ind. lt. gov. 1876–80, gov. 1880–81, 1885–89; EE&MP Mexico 1893–95; apptd. from Union City, Ind.; d. 1895.

Edward Burd Grubb: b. N.J. 1841; educ. Burlington Coll., N.J., grad. 1860; son of mfr.; bvt. BG Civil War; iron mfr., mining 1865–90; cand. for gov. 1888; EE&MP Spain 1890–92; apptd. from Burlington, N.J.; d. 1917.

Hezekiah A. Gudger: b. N.C. 1850; educ. Weaverville Coll., N.C., grad. 1870, Bailey's Law Sch., grad. 1871; law 1871–77, 1885–97, sch. principal

1877–83; N.C. st. legis. 1871–77, st. sen. 1885; CG Panama 1897–1905, chief justice Panama Canal Zone Sup. Ct. 1905–14; apptd. from Asheville, N.C.; d. 1917.

Richard Guenther: b. Germany 1845; to U.S. 1866, pharmacy business 1867–81; U.S. Cong. 1881–89; CG Mexico 1890–93, Frankfort 1898–1910, Capetown 1910–13; apptd. from Oshkosh, Wis.; lang., Ger.; d. 1913.

Samuel René Gummere: b. N.J. 1853; educ. Princeton, grad. 1870; son of lawyer; bar, law 1874–81, 1885–98; sec. to U.S. min. to Netherlands 1881–84, CG Tangier 1898–1905, EE&MP Morocco, 1905–9, delegate to Algeciras Conf. 1905; apptd. from Trenton, N.J.; d. 1920.

Philip C. Hanna: b. Iowa 1857; banking 1880–91; C La Guaira 1891–94, Trinidad 1897, San Juan 1897–98, CG Mexico 1899–1919; apptd. from Waterloo, Iowa; d. 1929.

Arthur Sherburne Hardy: b. Mass. 1847; educ. Amherst, USMA, grad. 1869, study in France; son of shipping owner; army 1869–70, coll. prof. 1871–93, editor 1893–95; MR&CG Persia 1897–99, EE&MP Greece (also Romania & Serbia) 1899–1901, Switzerland 1901–3, Spain 1903–5; apptd. from Hanover, N.H.; author; lang., Fr.; d. 1930.

Addison Clay Harris: b. Ind. 1840; educ. Northwestern Christian Univ., Ind., grad. 1862; son of farmer & st. legis.; bar, law 1865–99; Ind. st. sen. 1877–79, cand. for House of Rep. 1888; EE&MP Austria-Hungary 1899–1901; apptd. from Indianapolis, Ind.; d. 1916.

Thomas Skelton Harrison: b. Pa. 1837; son of mfr.; Civil War svc.; chemicals mfr. 1864–1902; extensive travel abroad; CG Cairo 1897–99; apptd. from Philadelphia, Pa.; author; d. 1919.

Charles Burdett Hart: b. Md. 1851; teacher 1868–69, law-trained but editor & publ., 1871–97; EE&MP Colombia 1897–1903; apptd. from Wheeling, W.Va.; d. 1930.

Seneca Haselton: b. Vt. 1848; educ. Univ. of Vt., grad. 1871, Univ. of Mich. Law, grad. 1875; son of clergy; univ. instr. 1873–75, bar, law 1875–78, city judge 1878–86, law 1895–1900; Vt. st. legis. 1886, mayor Burlington, Vt., 1891–94; EE&MP Venezuela 1894–95; st. sup. ct. 1900–19; apptd. from Burlington, Vt.; d. 1921.

John Milton Hay: b. Ind. 1838; educ. Brown, grad. 1858; son of phys.; bvt. col. Civil War; law 1858–61, editor 1870–79, 1881–97; sec. leg. Paris 1865–67, Vienna 1867–68, Madrid 1869–70, asst. Sec. of State 1879–81; AE&P Great Britain 1897–98; Sec. of State 1898–1905; author; d. 1905.

William Haywood: b. D.C. 1863; law clk. 1882–85, govt. clk. 1890–97; sec. leg. & CG Honolulu 1897–98, revenue collector Honolulu; apptd. from Washington, D.C.; d. 1906.

Augustine Heard: b. Mass. 1827; educ. Harvard, grad. 1847; nephew of shipper-merchant; China trade 1847–; extended residence abroad; EE&MP Korea 1890–93; apptd. from Mass.; d. 1905.

William Henry Heard: b. slave Ga. 1850; educ. Atlanta Univ., Univ. of S.C., Allen Univ., grad. 1891; teacher 1870–82, clergy 1882–; S.C. st. legis. 1876; MR&CG Liberia 1895–98; apptd. from Harrisburg, Pa.; author; d. 1937.

William B. Hess: b. Ohio c. 1842; lt. Civil War; law 1865–85, prosec. atty., circuit judge 1885–92; CG Constantinople 1892–93; apptd. from Plymouth, Ind.; d. unknown.

John Hicks: b. N.Y. 1847; son of stone mason & farmer; editor & publ. 1867–89, 1893–1905; EE&MP Peru 1889–93, Chile 1905–9; apptd. from Oshkosh, Wis.; author; d. 1917.

Solomon Hirsch: b. Germany 1839; to U.S. 1854, dry goods business 1859–89; Oreg. st. legis. 1872, st. sen. 1874–76; EE&MP Turkey 1889–92; apptd. from Portland, Oreg.; d. 1902.

Ethan Allen Hitchcock: b. Ala. 1835; son of judge; China trade 1860–72, glass, steel mfr., mining, RRs 1874–97; extended residence in Far East, travel; EE&MP Russia 1897–99; apptd. from St. Louis, Mo.; U.S. Sec. of Interior 1899–1907; d. 1909.

William Robeson Holloway: b. Ind. 1836; son of U.S. Cong.; sec. to Ind. gov. 1860–64, editor 1864–69, 1880–86, postmaster Indianapolis 1869–81; CG St. Petersburg 1897–1903, Halifax 1903–7; apptd. from Indianapolis, Ind.; d. 1911.

James Ray Hosmer: b. N.Y. 1834; educ. Columbia Univ.; Civil War & Spanish-Amer. War svc.; bar, editor, business; VC Southampton 1886–87, sec. leg. & CG Guatemala 1887–88; apptd. from N.Y., N.Y.; d. 1923.

Whiteside Godfrey Hunter: b. Ireland 1841; educ. in medicine, Philadelphia; Civil War svc.; phys. & druggist 1865–95, business 1902–17; Ky. st. legis. 1873–75, 1881–82, nat. Rep. convs. 1880, 1892, U.S. Cong. 1887–89, 1895–97, 1903–5; EE&MP Guatemala, also Honduras 1897–1902; apptd. from Burkesville, Ky.; d. 1917.

Carl Bailey Hurst: b. Germany of Amer. parents 1867; educ. Harvard, Univ. of Tubingen; son of univ. pres. & Method. bishop; C Catania 1892, Crefield 1893–95, Prague 1895–97, CG Vienna 1897–1903, C La Guaira 1904–5, Plauen 1905–10, Lyon 1910–13, CG Barcelona 1913–20, Havana 1920–27; apptd. from Washington, D.C.; d. 1943.

Darius Holbrook Ingraham: b. Maine 1837; educ. USNA; son of merchant; bar 1859, law & banking; Maine st. legis. 1879, mayor Portland, Maine 1892–

93, cand. for House of Rep. 1892; extensive travel abroad; C Cadiz 1885–89, CG Halifax 1893–97; apptd. from Portland, Maine; d. 1923.

John Nichol Irwin: b. Ohio 1847; educ. Miami Univ., Ohio, Dartmouth, grad. 1867; Civil War svc.; law-trained but wholesale grocery business; Idaho terr. gov. 1883, Ariz. terr. gov. 1890; EE&MP Portugal 1899–1900; apptd. from Keokuk, Iowa; d. 1905.

Thomas R. Jernigan: b. N.C.; educ. Univ. of Va.; law-trained but business; N.C. st. sen. 1874–75; C Osaka 1885–94, CG Shanghai 1894–97; apptd. from Hertford Co., N.C.; author; remained in China; d. 1920.

Wallace S. Jones: b. Ga. 1845; educ. Sorbonne, grad. 1863, St. Cyr, grad. 1866; bar 1869, planter, business; vice pres. Fla. Dem. conv. 1884, nat. Dem. convs. 1884, 1892, Fla. constit. conv. 1885; C Messina 1885–91, CG Rome 1893–97; delegate to int'l. conf. 1897; apptd. from Lloyd, Fla.; lang., Fr., Ital.; d. unknown.

Max Judd: b. Austria-Hungary 1852, to U.S. as child; lumber, clothing business 1880–93; CG Vienna 1893–97; apptd. from St. Louis, Mo.; d. 1906.

John Karel: b. Bohemia c. 1851; real estate & insurance business 1876–93; Wis. st. legis. 1879; C Prague 1893–94, CG St. Petersburg 1894–97; lang., Ger.; apptd. from Chicago, Ill.; d. unknown.

Samuel Kimberly: b. Md.; educ. Univ. of Md.; wholesale grocery business, court clk. 1883–89, Norfolk, Va. city council, cand. for mayor; sec. leg. & CG Guatemala 1890–93; apptd. from Norfolk, Va.; d. unknown.

Adam E. King: b. Pa.; bvt. BG Civil War; port official Baltimore; CG Paris 1890–93; apptd. from Baltimore, Md.; d. 1910.

Hamilton King: b. Canada 1852; educ. Olivet Coll., Mich., grad. 1878, Chicago Theol. Sem. 1878–79, Chicago Univ. 1881, study in Europe 1883–84; coll. prof. 1879–98; nat. Rep. conv. 1896; MR&CG Siam 1898–1903, EE&MP 1903–12; apptd. from Olivet, Mich.; author; d. 1912.

Charles Luman Knapp: b. N.Y. 1847; educ. Rutgers, grad. 1869; son of farmer; bar, law 1873–89, law & banking 1893–1901, 1911–29; N.Y. st. legis. 1886–87, U.S. Cong. 1901–11; CG Montreal 1889–93; apptd. from Lowville, N.Y.; d. 1929.

Julius Gareche Lay: b. D.C. 1872; son of army off.; cons. clk. Ottawa 1889–93, vice CG 1893–96, C Windsor 1896–99, CG Barcelona 1899–1904, Canton 1904–6, Capetown 1906–10, Rio de Janeiro 1910–14, Berlin 1914–17, Dept. of State 1917–20, CG Calcutta 1924–27, couns. of embassy Santiago 1927–29, EE&MP Honduras 1930–34, Uruguay 1934–37; apptd. from Washington, D.C.; banking 1920–24; d. 1939.

Richard Gregory Lay: b. D.C.; col. Civil War; CG Ottawa 1889–93; apptd. from Washington, D.C.; d. unknown.

Fitzhugh Lee: b. Va. 1835; educ. USMA, grad. 1856; son of naval off., nephew of R.E. Lee; MG Civil War; army 1856–65, 1898–1901, planter 1865–, revenue collector 1894–96; Va. gov. 1886–90; CG Havana 1896–98; apptd. from Richmond, Va.; military gov. Cuba, 1899–1900; author; d. 1905.

John G. A. Leishman: b. Pa. 1857; orphan; steel business executive 1870–97; EE&MP Switzerland 1897–1901, Turkey 1901–9, AE&P Italy 1909–11, Germany 1911–13; apptd. from Pittsburgh, Pa.; d. 1924.

Joseph Alexander Leonard: b. Md. 1830; educ. Phila. Med. Coll., grad. 1851; Civil War svc.; phys. 1852–54, editor 1854–57, bar, law 1858–64, 1865–, land registrar 1874–75, probate judge 1897–1903; C Edinburgh 1881–83, CG Calcutta 1884, Shanghai 1889–93; apptd. from Rochester, Minn.; d. unknown.

George F. Lincoln: b. Conn. c. 1850; educ. Yale, grad. 1870, Columbia Law, grad. 1880; law 1880, 1885–92; C Stettin 1880–83, Aix-la-Chapelle 1883–85, Antwerp 1892–93, 1897–98, CG 1898–1903; lang., Ger., Fr.; d. 1903.

Robert Todd Lincoln: b. Ill. 1843; educ. Harvard, grad. 1864; son of Pres.; capt. Civil War; bar, law 1867–81, business, banking 1885–89, 1893–1911; Sec. of War 1881–85; EE&MP Great Britain 1889–93; apptd. from Chicago, Ill.; d. 1926.

Edward Campbell Little: b. Ohio 1858; educ. Univ. of Kans., grad. 1883; LTC Spanish-Amer. War; bar, law 1886–; nat. Rep. conv. 1892, co. atty. 1892, cand. for U.S. Sen. 1897, U.S. Cong. 1917–24; dipl. agt. & CG Cairo 1892–93; apptd. from Abilene, Kans.; d. 1924.

Francis Butler Loomis: b. Ohio 1861; educ. Marietta Coll., Ohio, grad. 1883; son of judge; journalist, Ohio st. librarian 1884–88, editor 1888–90, 1893–97; C St. Etienne 1890–93, EE&MP Venezuela 1897–1901, Portugal 1901–3, asst. Sec. of State 1903–5, deleg. int'l. expos. 1908, 1912; apptd. from Marietta, Ohio; d. 1948.

William Paine Lord: b. Del. 1838; educ. Fairfield Coll., N.Y., grad. 1860, Albany Law Sch., grad. 1866; maj. Civil War, army 1867–68, law 1868–80; Oreg. st. sup. ct. 1880–94, st. sen. 1878, Oreg. gov. 1895–99; EE&MP Argentina 1899–1903; apptd. from Salem, Oreg.; author; d. 1911.

William D. McCoy: b. Ind. 1853; teacher & principal 1875–90; cand. for Ind. st. legis.; MR&CG Liberia 1892–93; apptd. from Indianapolis, Ind.; d. 1893.

Alexander McDonald: b. Va. c. 1827; editor 1850–93; dep. postmaster, Va. st. sen. 1891, commr. to Vienna & Paris Expos.; MR&CG Persia 1893–97; apptd. from Lynchburg, Va.; d. 1897.

Nicholas Williams McIvor: b. S.C. 1860; educ. Trinity Coll., Conn., grad. 1882, Harvard Law, grad. 1885; law, Iowa st. adj. gen. 1885–92; CG Yokohama 1893–97; apptd. from Cedar Rapids, Iowa; d. 1915.

James Andrew McKenzie: b. Ky. 1840; educ. Centre Coll., Ky.; Civil War svc.; har 1861, farmer; Ky. st. legis. 1867–71, U.S. Cong. 1877–83; EE&MP Peru 1893–97; apptd. from Long View, Ky.; d. 1904.

Luther Franklin McKinney: b. Ohio 1841; educ. St. Lawrence Coll., N.Y., grad. 1870; Civil War svc.; teacher 1865–67, clergy 1871–85, 1908–22, business 1885–87, 1897–1908; U.S. Cong. 1887–89, 1891–93, cand. for N.H. gov. 1892; Maine st. legis. 1907–8; EE&MP Colombia 1893–96; apptd. from Manchester, N.H.; d. 1922.

James Clifford McNally: b. England 1865; educ. St. Vincent's Coll., Pa., Univ. of Mich. Law Sch., grad. 1891; law, Utah 1891–93, U.S. commr. 1893–94, probate judge 1894–96; sec. leg. & CG Bogota 1898–99, CG Guatemala 1899–1902, C Liège 1902–7, Nanking 1907–10, Tsingtau 1910–14, VC Kehl 1915–16, Hamburg 1916–17, CG Zurich 1917–20; apptd. initially from Pa.; d. 1920.

Isaac Wayne MacVeagh: b. Pa. 1833; educ. Yale, grad. 1853; son of army maj.; maj. Civil War; law 1856–93, dist. atty., U.S. Atty. Gen. 1881; EE&MP Turkey 1870–71; AE&P Italy 1893–97, couns. The Hague Tribunal 1903; apptd. from Philadelphia, Pa.; author; d. 1917.

Rowland Blennerhassett Mahany: b. N.Y. 1864; educ. Hobart Coll., Harvard, grad. 1888; editor, teacher 1888–90, law, solicitor U.S. Dept. of Labor 1918, int'l. law; U.S. Cong. 1895–99, nat. Dem. convs. 1924, 1928; EE&MP Ecuador 1892–93; apptd. from Buffalo, N.Y.; d. 1937.

George Earl Maney: b. Tenn. 1826; educ. Univ. of Nashville, grad. 1845; Mex. War svc., BG Civil War; law 1850–61, RR pres. 1866–81; Tenn. st. legis.; MR Colombia 1881–82, Bolivia 1882–89, Uruguay & Paraguay 1889–90, EE&MP 1890–94; apptd. from Nashville, Tenn.; d. 1901.

Daniel W. Maratta: b. unknown; steamboat capt. Ohio River, U.S. marshal Dakota terr. 1886–; CG Melbourne 1893–97; apptd. from Bismarck, N.D.; d. unknown.

Frank Holcomb Mason: b. Ohio 1840; educ. Hiram Coll., Ohio; capt. Civil War; editor & publ. 1865–80; C Basle 1880–84, Marseilles 1884–89, CG Frankfort 1889–98, Berlin 1898–1905, Paris 1905–14; apptd. from Cleveland, Ohio; lang., Fr., Ger.; d. 1916.

Felix A. Mathews: b. Morocco c. 1834; Civil War svc.; navy 1852–58, county assessor 1867–69; C Tangiers 1869–70, 1876–87, CG 1890–93; apptd. from Cal.; lang., Fr., Sp., It., Port., Arabic; d. 1899.

Campbell L. Maxwell: b. Ohio c. 1841; educ. Wilberforce Univ., Ohio; law, univ. atty.; C Sto. Domingo 1892–93, CG 1898–1904; apptd. from Xenia, Ohio; d. unknown.

Samuel Merrill: b. Ind. 1831; educ. Wabash Coll., Ind., grad. 1851; son of publ. & banker; bvt. col. Civil War; publ. & book business 1852–90, 1893–; CG Calcutta 1889–93; apptd. from Indianapolis, Ind.; author; d. 1924.

William Lawrence Merry: b. N.Y. 1842; son of sea capt. & merchant; sea capt., shipping business 1874–97; extensive travel abroad; EE&MP Costa Rica (also Nicaragua & El Salvador) 1897–1907, Costa Rica (also Nicaragua) 1907–8, Costa Rica 1908–11; apptd. from San Francisco, Calif.; author; d. 1911.

Ellis Mills: b. England, c. 1856; govt. clk., Cong. staff 1879–86, Dept. of State clk. 1886–93; sec. leg. & CG Honolulu 1893–97; apptd. from Rapidan, Va.; d. 1914.

Lansing Bond Mizner: b. Ill. 1825; educ. Shurtleff Coll., Ill.; Mex. War svc.; bar 1850, co. judge, customs collector 1853–, law & real estate holdings; Calif. st. sen. 1865; legation clk. Bogota 1840–44, EE&MP Central American States 1889–90; apptd. from Calif.; d. 1893.

Thomas Moonlight: b. Scotland 1833, to U.S. 1856; son of farmer; bvt. BG Civil War; farmer & factory worker Scotland; surveyor, Kans. sec. of state, st. sen. 1873–74, town marshal Leavenworth, Kans., 1877–80, st. adj. gen. 1883–84, cand. for Kans. gov. 1886; Wyo. terr. gov. 1888–90; EE&MP Bolivia 1894–98; apptd. from Leavenworth, Kans.; d. 1899.

Samuel E. Morss: b. Ind. 1852; son of mayor; editor 1871–82, 1883–88; nat. Dem. convs. 1892, 1900; travel abroad 1882–83; CG Paris 1893–97; apptd. from Indianapolis, Ind.; d. 1903.

Robert Alexander Moseley, Jr.: b. Ala. c. 1842; educ. Howard Coll., Ala., Jefferson Med. Coll., Pa.; capt. Civil War; editor; U.S. dist. comm., alderman, mayor & postmaster Talladega, Ala., chair st. Rep. comm.; CG Singapore 1899–1900; apptd. from Birmingham, Ala.; d. 1900.

James Hilary Mulligan: b. Ky. 1844; educ. St. Mary's Coll., Canada, grad. 1864, Univ. of Ky. Law, grad. 1869; law 1869–94, 1896–1904, also editor 1893–94; Ky. st. legis. 1881–88, st. sen. 1890–94; CG Apia 1894–96; apptd. from Lexington, Ky.; author; d. 1916.

John Chalfant New: b. Ind. 1831; educ. Bethany Coll., Va., grad. 1851; law 1852–62, banking 1865–75, editor 1878–82; Ind. st. sen. 1862, Treasurer of the U.S. 1875–76, asst. Sec. of Treasury 1882–84, chair st. Rep. comm. 1880, 1884, Nat. Rep. Comm. 1878–92; CG London 1889–93; apptd. from Indianapolis, Ind.; d. 1906.

Stanford Newel: b. R.I. 1839; educ. Yale, grad. 1861, Harvard Law, grad. 1864; law 1864–97; chair st. Rep. comm. 6 yrs.; nat. Rep. conv. 1884, 1892; EE&MP Netherlands 1897–1903, Netherlands & Luxembourg 1903–5; apptd. from St. Paul, Minn.; d. 1907.

Luther W. Osborn: b. N.Y. c. 1844; Civil War svc.; bar, law 1869–95, co. atty. 3 yrs.; Neb. st. sen. 1873, nat. Rep. conv. 1876; CG Apia 1897–1901; apptd. from Blair, Neb.; d. 1901.

William McKinley Osborne: b. Ohio 1842; educ. Allegheny Coll., Pa., Univ. of Mich. Law; Civil War svc.; cousin of Pres.; bar, law 1864–85; mayor Youngstown, Ohio, 1874–75, Boston police board 1885–93, sec. Nat. Rep. Comm. 1896; CG London 1897–1902; apptd. from Boston, Mass.; d. 1902.

Romualdo Pacheco: b. Calif. (Mexico) 1831, oath of allegiance to U.S. 1846; stepson of sea capt.; sailing master 1847–51, co. judge 1854–58, travel Europe 1859–61, rancher 1883–89; Calif. st. legis. 1853, st. sen. 1858–70, Calif. gov. staff 1861, st. treas. 1865–69, Calif. lt. gov. 1870, gov. 1874, U.S. Cong. 1877–83; EE&MP Central American States 1890–91, Guatemala and Honduras 1891; apptd. from Sacramento, Calif.; d. 1899.

Aulick Palmer: b. D.C. 1843; son of U.S. Surgeon Gen.; Marine off. 13 yrs.; C Dresden 1889–92, CG 1892–93; apptd. from Washington, D.C.; d. 1925.

Thomas Witherall Palmer: b. Mich. 1830; educ. Univ. of Mich.; son of businessman; mercantile & real estate business 1850–73, banker 1891–; extensive travel abroad; Detroit board of estimates 1873; Mich. st. sen. 1876, U.S. Sen. 1883–89; EE&MP Spain 1889–90, Columbian Expo. Commr. 1892; apptd. from Detroit, Mich.; author; d. 1913.

Frank Charles Partridge: b. Vt. 1861; educ. Amherst Coll., grad. 1877, Columbia Law, grad. 1884; law 1885–89, 1900–, business 1885–90; sec. to Sec. of War 1889–90, Solicitor Dept. of State 1890–93, EE&MP Venezuela 1893–94, CG Tangier 1897–98; Vt. st. sen. 1898–1900; deleg. Pan-Amer. Conf. Chile 1923, U.S. Sen. 1830–31; apptd. from Middleburg, Vt.; d. 1943.

Robert Franklin Patterson: b. Maine 1836; bvt. BG Civil War; tax collector 13 yrs., postmaster Memphis, Tenn., 1889–93; CG Calcutta 1897–1905; apptd. from Memphis, Tenn.; d. c. 1908.

John Lee Peak: b. Ky. 1839; educ. Georgetown Coll., Ky., grad. 1858, Louisville Law Sch., grad. 1860; bar, law 1861–87, co. prosecuting atty. 1887–91; EE&MP Switzerland 1895–97; apptd. from Kansas City, Mo.; d. 1911.

Frederic Courtland Penfield: b. Conn. 1855; educ. in Europe; journalist 1880–85; vice & dep. CG London 1885–87, CG Cairo 1893–97, AE&P Austria-Hungary 1913–17; apptd. from Hartford, Conn.; author; d. 1922.

William Walter Phelps: b. Pa. 1839, educ. Yale, grad. 1860, Columbia Law, grad. 1863; son of RR owner & businessman; law 1863–69, family import business 1869–, ct. of appeals judge 1894; U.S. Cong. 1873–75, 1883–89, nat. Rep. convs. 1880–1884; EE&MP Austria-Hungary 1881–81, Germany 1889–93; apptd. from Englewood, N.J.; lang., Ger.; d. 1894.

Gilbert Ashville Pierce: b. N.Y. 1841; educ. Univ. of Chicago; son of merchant; col. Civil War; editor 1871–84, 1891–94; Ind. st. legis. 1869–69, Dakota terr. gov. 1884–86, U.S. Sen. 1889–91; MR&CG Portugal 1893; apptd. from Minneapolis, Minn.; author; d. 1901.

John Robert Graham Pitkin: b. La. 1841; educ. Univ. of La., grad. 1860; travel abroad; bar 1861, school principal, law 1863–, ct. registrar 1867–71, U.S. marshal La. 1876–77, 1882–85, postmaster New Orleans 1898–1901; EE&MP Argentina 1889–93; apptd. from New Orleans, La.; d. 1901.

Van Leer Polk: b. Tenn. c. 1857; educ. Europe, travel abroad; editor; Tenn. st. sen. 1890–92, nat. Dem. conv. 1892; CG Calcutta 1893–97, 3d Int'l. Cong. of Amer. States Rio de Janeiro 1906; apptd. from Nashville, Tenn.; lang., Fr., Sp., Ital.; d. unknown.

John Kilby Pollard: b. Ohio c. 1844; st. official; sheriff, Ohio st. sen.; CG Monterrey 1898–99; apptd. from Delaware, Ohio; d. 1899.

Albert Gallatin Porter: b. Ind. 1824; educ. Asbury Coll. (DePauw), grad. 1843; son of farmer; law 1845–53, city official 1851–53, 1857–59, clk. Ind. st. sup. ct. 1853–56; U.S. Cong. 1859–63, U.S. Compt. of Currency 1878–80, Ind. gov. 1881–85, nat. Rep. conv. 1888; EE&MP Italy 1889–92; apptd. from Indianapolis, Ind.; d. 1897.

Horace Porter: b. Pa. 1837; educ. USMA, grad. 1860; son of gov. & mfr.; BG Civil War; asst. Sec. of War 1866, military sec. to Pres. 1869–73; RR pres. 1873–97; AE&P France 1897–1905; apptd. from N.Y., N.Y.; author; lang., Fr.; d. 1921.

James Davis Porter: b. Tenn. 1828; educ. Univ. of Nashville, grad. 1846, Cumberland Univ., Tenn.; son of phys.; Civil War svc.; law 1850–70, judge 1870–74, RR pres. & business 1879–83, univ. chancellor 1901–9; Tenn. st. legis. 1859–61, Tenn. gov. 1875–79; asst. Sec. of State 1885–87, EE&MP Chile 1893–94; apptd. from Paris, Tenn.; lang., Fr.; d. 1912.

William Potter: b. Pa. 1852; educ. Univ. of Pa.; son of mfr.; dir. of cloth mfg. co., pres. med. coll., Philadelphia; cand. for mayor; special commr. Dept. of State 1890, delegate to Universal Postal Union Vienna 1891, EE&MP Italy 1892–94; apptd. from Philadelphia, Pa.; d. 1926.

William Frank Powell: b. N.Y. 1848; govt. clk. 1881–83, teacher, sch. supt.; EE&MP Haiti 1897–1905, also Dom. Rep. 1898–1904; apptd. from Camden, N.J.; d. 1920.

Edward Spencer Pratt: b. Ala. c. 1850; educ. in Europe in medicine; son of banker; extended residence abroad; phys.; MR&CG Persia 1886–91, CG Singapore 1893–99; apptd. from Mobile, Ala.; lang., Fr.; d. 1925.

D. Lynch Pringle: b. S.C. c. 1846; educ. in Europe; C Tegucigalpa 1885, sec. leg. & CG Guatemala 1885–87, CG Constantinople 1887–89, sec. leg. & CG Guatemala 1893–97; apptd. from N.Y.; lang., Ger., Fr.; d. unknown.

William Emory Quinby: b. Maine 1835; educ. Univ. of Mich., grad. 1858; son of editor; bar 1859, but editor & publ. 1861–93; EE&MP Netherlands 1893–97; apptd. from Detroit, Mich.; d. 1908.

Matt Whitaker Ransom: b. N.C. 1826; educ. Univ. of N.C., grad. 1847; MG Civil War; bar, law, planter; N.C. st. atty. gen., st. legis., U.S. Sen. 1872–95, Nat. Dem. Comm. 1876–95; EE&MP Mexico 1895–97; apptd. from Weldon, N.C.; d. 1904.

Jared Lawrence Rathbone: b. N.Y.; educ. USMA, grad.; maj. Civil War; stepson of U.S. Sen., son of Albany, N.Y. mayor; travelled abroad; regular army, planter & stockman, mining interests; CG Paris 1887–90; apptd. from San Francisco, Calif.; lang., Fr.; d. 1907.

Whitelaw Reid: b. Ohio 1837; educ. Miami Univ., Ohio, grad. 1856; son of farmer; govt. clk., editor & publ. 1858–1905; cand. for U.S. Vice Pres. 1892; EE&MP France 1889–92, Sp.-Amer. War Peace Commr. 1898; AE&P Great Britain 1905–12; apptd. from N.Y., N.Y.; author; d. 1912.

Irving Berdine Richman: b. Iowa 1861; educ. Iowa St. Coll., grad. 1883; law 1885–93, 1898–; Iowa st. legis. 1889–93; CG St. Gall 1893–98; apptd. from Muscatine, Iowa; author; d. 1938.

John B. Riley: b. N.Y. 1852; bar, law 1879–85, mayor Plattsburg, N.Y., 1883–84, supt. U.S. Indian Schs. 1885–88, N.Y. st. civil svc. comm. 1888–93, law, county judge 1910–12, supt. N.Y. st. prisons 1912–16; CG Ottawa 1893–97; apptd. from Plattsburg, N.Y.; d. 1919.

John Ewing Risley: b. Ind. 1840; educ. Wabash Coll., Ind.; son of farmer; bar, law 1861–93, 1897–; EE&MP Denmark 1893–97; apptd. from N.Y., N.Y.; d. unknown.

William Woodville Rockhill: b. Pa. 1854; educ. St. Cyr, France, grad. 1873; son of lawyer; French army 3 yrs., Smithsonian expedit. China & Tibet 1888–92; sec. leg. Peking 1885–88, chargé Seoul 1886–87, chief clk. Dept. of State 1893–94, asst. Sec. of State 1894–97, EE&MP Greece, also Serbia & Romania 1897–99, dir. Int'l. Bureau of Amer. Rep. 1899–1905, EE&MP China 1905–9, AE&P Russia 1909–11, Turkey 1911–13; apptd. from Washington, D.C.; lang., Fr., Chin.; author; d. 1914.

Theodore Runyon: b. N.J. 1822; educ. Yale, grad. 1842; bvt. MG Civil War; bar 1846, city atty. Newark, N.J., 1853–61, mayor 1864–66, law 1866–73, 1887–93, N.J. st. chancellor 1873–87; AE&P Germany 1893–96; apptd. from Newark, N.J.; d. 1896.

Thomas Ryan: b. N.Y. 1837; educ. Dickinson Sem., Pa.; capt. Civil War; bar, co. atty. Kans. 1865–73, asst. U.S. dist. atty. 1873–77, U.S. Cong. 1877–89, asst. U.S. Sec. of Interior 1897–1908; EE&MP Mexico 1889–93; apptd. from Topeka, Kans.; d. 1914.

Archibald Johnson Sampson: b. Ohio 1839; educ. Mt. Union Coll., Ohio, grad. 1861, Cleveland Law Sch., grad. 1866; son of farmer; capt. Civil War; sch. supt. 1862–63, bar, law 1865–89, 1893–97; pres. elector 1872, co. atty., Colo. st. atty. gen. 1876–; C El Paso del Norte 1889–93, EE&MP Ecuador 1897–1907; apptd. from Phoenix, Ariz.; lang., Sp.; d. 1921.

William Lindsay Scruggs: b. Tenn. 1836; educ. Strawberry Plains Coll., Tenn.; son of planter; bar 1858, editor 1862–66, 1870–72, int'l. law 1894–98; MR Colombia 1873–76, 1882–84, EE&MP 1884–85, C Chinkiang 1879–80, CG Canton 1880–82, EE&MP Venezuela 1889–92; apptd. from Atlanta, Ga.; lang., Sp.; author; d. 1912.

Eugene Seeger: b. Germany 1853, to U.S. 1870; journalist, editor 1870–86, city official Chicago 1886–, export business Brazil 1906–; CG Rio de Janeiro 1897–1906, U.S. Commr. Brazilian Expo. 1908; apptd. from Chicago, Ill.; d. 1941.

Henry W. Severance: b. Maine c. 1839; son of U.S. Cong. & dipl.; Hawaiian C San Francisco 1868–85; CG Honolulu 1889–93; apptd. from San Francisco, Calif.; d. unknown.

Harold Marsh Sewall: b. Maine 1860; educ. Harvard, grad. 1882, Harvard Law, grad. 1885; son of shipping co. owner & RR pres.; bar 1892; nat. Rep. conv. 1896, Maine st. legis. 1896, 1903–7, st. sen. 1907–9, cand. for House of Rep., 1914; VC Liverpool 1885–87, CG Apia 1887–89, 1890–92; apptd. from Bath, Maine; d. 1924.

Henry Cutts Shannon: b. Conn. 1839; educ. Colby Coll., Maine, grad. 1862, Columbia Law, grad. 1885; LTC Civil War; business in Brazil 1876–83, bar 1886; U.S. Cong. 1895–99; sec. leg. Rio de Janeiro 1871–75, EE&MP Nicaragua, also Costa Rica & El Salvador 1891–93; apptd. from Brockport, N.Y.; d. 1920.

Luther Short: b. Ind. 1845; educ. Ind. Univ., Mich. Law Sch.; Civil War svc.; travel abroad; law 10 yrs., editor & publ. c. 1880–; Ind. st. legis. 1891, nat. elector 1892, nat. Dem. Editorial Assn.; CG Constantinople 1893–97; apptd. from Franklin, Ind.; d. 1925.

John Mahelm Berry Sill: b. N.Y. 1831; educ. Mich. St., grad. 1854; son of farmer; coll. prof. 1854–63, sch. principal 1863–65, 1886–93, teacher 1865–75, sch. supt. 1875–86, part-time clergy 1890–93; MR&CG Korea 1894–97; apptd. from Lansing, Mich.; author; d. 1901.

Jacob Sleeper: b. Mass. 1869; educ. in Europe; son of merchant & philanthropist; sec. to gov. of Puerto Rico; sec. leg. & CG Bogota 1893–98, sec. leg. Havana 1902–6, Caracas 1906–8, Berne 1908–10; apptd. from Boston, Mass.; d. 1930.

Charles Emory Smith: b. Conn. 1842; educ. Union Coll., N.Y., grad. 1861; son of mfr.; Civil War svc.; editor & publ. 1865–90; nat. Rep. convs. 1876, 1888; EE&MP Russia 1890–92; apptd. from Philadelphia, Pa.; U.S. Postmaster Gen. 1898–1902; d. 1908.

Edmund W. P. Smith: b. Ind.; sec. to Ind. gov., journalist, govt. clk. c. 1872–77, business in Colombia 1877–89; commercial agt. Carthagena 1879–81, C 1881–82, C Sabanilla 1882–83, sec. leg. & CG Bogota 1890–91; apptd. from Washington, D.C.; lang., Sp.; d. 1891.

Owen Lun West Smith: b. slave N.C. 1851; educ. Univ. of S.C.; teacher 1871–73, magistrate 1873–74, clergy 1881–98; MR&CG Liberia 1898–1902; apptd. from Wilson, N.C.; d. unknown.

Henry Maxwell Smythe: b. Va. 1844; educ. Washington Coll., Tenn., Emory & Henry Coll., Va.; Civil War svc.; law 1872–89, sch. supt. 1889–90, editor 1890–93, farming & stockraising 1897–; MR&CG Haiti 1893–97; apptd. from Graham, Va.; d. 1932.

Archibald Loudon Snowden: b. Pa. 1837; educ. Jefferson Coll., Pa., grad. 1856, Univ. of Pa. Law; son of phys.; LTC Civil War; U.S. Mint official, postmaster Philadelphia 1877–79, supt. U.S. Mint 1879–85; EE&MP Greece, also Serbia & Romania 1889–92, Spain 1892–93; apptd. from Philadelphia, Pa.; author; d. 1912.

William Brooks Sorsby: b. Miss. 1858; educ. Miss. Coll.; editor & publ. c. 1880–, mining in Ecuador 1893–98; CG Guayaquil 1889–93, C San Juan del Norte 1897–1901, Kingston 1901–2, EE&MP Bolivia 1902–8; apptd. from Clinton, Miss.; d. 1912.

Watson Robertson Sperry: b. N.Y. 1842; educ. Yale, grad. 1871; son of clergy; journalist, editor 1871–92, 1893–1918; MR&CG Persia 1892–93; apptd. from Hartford, Conn.; d. 1926.

John Leavitt Stevens: b. Maine 1820; educ. Maine Wesleyan Sem.; son of farmer; clergy 1845–55, editor & publ. 1855–69; Maine st. legis. 1865–70, nat. Rep. convs. 1865, 1876; EE&MP Uruguay & Paraguay 1870–73, Sweden & Norway 1877–83, MR&CG Hawaii 1889, EE&MP 1889–93; apptd. from Kennebec, Maine; lang., Fr.; author; d. 1895.

Bellamy Storer: b. Ohio 1847; educ. Harvard, grad. 1867, Cincinatti Law Sch., grad. 1869; son of judge; bar, law 1869–90; U.S. Cong. 1891–95; EE&MP Belgium 1897–99, Spain 1899–1902, AE&P Austria-Hungary 1902–6; apptd. from Cincinnati, Ohio; d. 1922.

James Gardner Stowe: b. R.I. 1843; machinist, inventor 1861–65, iron, loco-motive, agric. implement business 1865–98; city council Cincinatti, Ohio, 1879–85; CG Capetown 1898–1901; apptd. from Kansas City, Mo.; author; d. unknown.

Oscar Solomon Straus: b. Germany 1850, to U.S. 1854; educ. Columbia, grad. 1871, Columbia Law, grad. 1873; son of merchant; law 1873–81, import business 1881–1901; EE&MP Turkey 1887–89, 1898–99, 1909–10, Hague Tri-bunal 1901–6, U.S. Sec. of Commerce 1906–9; apptd. from New York, N.Y.; author; d. 1926.

Edward Henry Strobel: b. S.C. 1855; educ. Harvard, grad. 1877, Harvard Law, grad. 1882; son of banker; law 1883–85, law prof. 1898–1906, Hague Tri-bunal 1903; resided in Europe; sec. leg. Madrid 1885–90, asst. Sec. of State 1893–94, EE&MP Ecuador 1894, Chile 1894–97; apptd. from N.Y., N.Y.; au-thor; d. 1908.

Granville Stuart: b. Va. 1843; son of prospector; vol. military svc. 1855; miner, trader, rancher 1852–87; Mont. st. land agt. 1891–94, st. librarian 1904–16; EE&MP Uruguay & Paraguay 1894–98; apptd. from Butte, Mont.; lang., Fr., Sp., Indian dialects; author; d. 1918.

Warner Perrin Sutton: b. Mich. c. 1847; sch. supt. 1868–78; commercial agt. Matamoros 1878–79, C 1879–83, CG 1883–89, CG Nuevo Laredo 1889–93; apptd. from Saugatuck, Mich.; d. 1913.

Zachary Taylor Sweeney: b. Ky. 1849; educ. Eureka Coll., Ill., Asbury Coll. (DePauw), Ill.; son of clergy; teacher 1866–69, clergy 1869–96, chancellor But-ler Univ. 1889; extensive travel abroad; CG Constantinople 1889–93; Ind. st. game & fish commr. 1899–1911; apptd. from Columbus, Ind.; author; d. 1926.

Laurits Selmer Swenson: b. Minn. 1865; educ. Luther Coll., Iowa, grad. 1886, Johns Hopkins Univ.; son of st. legis.; sch. principal 1888–97, banker; nat. Rep. conv. 1896; EE&MP Denmark 1897–1905, Switzerland 1909–11, Norway 1911–13, 1921–30, Netherlands 1931–34; apptd. from Minneapolis, Minn.; author; d. 1947.

John Franklin Swift: b. Mo. 1829; tinsmith, business, law 1857–89; U.S. Cong. 1877–79; commr. to negotiate China treaty 1880; cand. for Calif. gov. 1886; extensive travel abroad; EE&MP Japan 1889–91; apptd. from San Fran-cisco, Calif.; d. 1891.

Hannis Taylor: b. N.C. 1851; educ. Univ. of N.C.; son of merchant; bar, law 1870–92; EE&MP Spain 1893–97, int'l. commr. 1902, 1903; apptd. from Mo-bile, Ala.; author; d. 1922.

Alexander Watkins Terrell: b. Va. 1827; educ. Univ. of Mo.; BG Civil War; law 1849–57, dist. judge 1857–62, law 1865–93; Tex st. legis. 4 yrs., st. sen. 10 yrs.; EE&MP Turkey 1893–97; apptd. from Austin, Tex.; d. 1912.

Edwin Holland Terrell: b. Ind. 1848; educ. Asbury Coll. (DePauw), Ill., grad. 1871, Harvard Law, grad. 1873, in Europe 1873–74; son of clergy; law 1874–89, 1893–; nat. Rep. convs. 1880, 1888, 1904, Tex. st. Rep. Comm. 1894–1900; EE&MP Belgium 1889–93; apptd. from San Antonio, Tex.; d. 1910.

Samuel Richard Thayer: b. N.Y. c. 1837; educ. Union Coll., N.Y., grad. 1860; bar, law 1864–89, 1893–; EE&MP Netherlands 1889–93; apptd. from Minneapolis, Minn.; d. 1909.

Allen Thomas: b. Md. 1830; educ. Princeton, grad. 1850; son of phys. & farmer; BG Civil War; planter 1865–82, univ. prof. of agric. 1882–84, U.S. Mint New Orleans 1885–89; pres. elector 1872, 1880; C La Guaira 1894–95, EE&MP Venezuela 1895–97; apptd. from Osceola Co., Fla.; d. 1909.

William Widgery Thomas, Jr.: b. Maine 1839; educ. Bowdoin Coll., Maine, grad. 1860, Harvard Law, grad. 1866; law, Maine st. commr. of public lands, st. commr. on immigration 1866–73; Maine st. legis. 1873–75, st. sen. 1879, nat. Rep. conv. 1880; courier, vice CG Constantinople, acting C Gothenburg, Galatz 1862–65, MR Sweden & Norway 1883–85, EE&MP 1889–94, 1897–1905; apptd. from Portland, Maine; lang., Swed.; author; d. 1927.

David Preston Thompson: b. Ohio 1834; son of miller; surveyor, contractor, banker 1853–90; Oreg. st. sen. 1868–72, st. legis. 1878–79, 1889–90, mayor Portland, Oreg. 1879, 1881, Idaho terr. gov. 1875–76, cand. for Oreg. gov. 1890; EE&MP Turkey 1892–93; apptd. from Portland, Oreg.; d. 1901.

Thomas Larkin Thompson: b. Va. 1838; son & grandson of U.S. Cong.; editor & publ. 1855–58, 1860–86, post office 1858–60; nat. Dem. convs. 1880, 1892, Calif. sec. of state; U.S. Cong. 1887–89; EE&MP Brazil 1893–97; d. 1898.

James Davidson Tillman: b. Tenn. 1841; educ. Univ. of Nashville, grad. 1860; col. Civil War; law 1865–95; Tenn. st. legis. 1870, st. sen. 1873, 1893, 1903; EE&MP Ecuador 1895–98; apptd. from Fayetteville, Tenn.; d. unknown.

Willard D. Tillotson: b. Ohio c. 1860; law 1883–91; Wash. st. legis.; CG Yokohama 1891–93; apptd. from Tacoma, Wash.; d. unknown.

Charlemagne Tower: b. Pa. 1848; educ. Harvard, grad. 1872, in Europe 1872–76; son of mfr.; bar, law 1878–82, RR, mining, iron mfg. 1882–97; EE&MP Austria-Hungary 1897–99, AE&P Russia 1899–1902, Germany 1902–8; apptd. from Philadelphia, Pa.; author, d. 1923.

William T. Townes: b. Va. b. unknown; tobacco business, planter 1886–93, tobacco sales West Indies 1899–; CG Rio de Janeiro 1893–97; apptd. from Danville, Va.; d. unknown.

Lawrence Townsend: b. Pa. 1860; educ. Univ. of Pa., in Europe; rancher 1886–92; sec. leg. Vienna 1893–97, EE&MP Portugal 1897–99, Belgium 1899–1905; apptd. from Philadelphia, Pa.; lang., Fr., Ger.; d. 1954.

Bartlett Tripp: b. Maine 1842; educ. Waterville Coll. (Colby), Maine, Albany Law Sch., grad. 1867; teacher, RR engineer, univ. law lecturer, chief justice S.D. terr. sup. ct. 1885–89; EE&MP Austria-Hungary 1893–97, Samoan commr. 1899; apptd. from Yankton, S.D.; d. 1911.

Charles E. Turner: b. Conn.; business; Conn. gov. staff, st. Rep. Comm.; CG Ottawa 1897–1903; apptd. from Waterbury, Conn.; d. unknown.

Edwin Fuller Uhl: b. N.Y. 1841; educ. Univ. of Mich., grad. 1862; son of farmer; bar 1864, law 1866–90, 1897–1901; mayor Grand Rapids, Mich. 1890–92, cand. for U.S. Sen. 1894; asst. U.S. Sec. of State 1893–96; AE&P Germany 1896–97; apptd. from Grand Rapids, Mich.; d. 1901.

Victor Vifquain: b. Belgium c. 1836; BG Civil War, LTC Sp.-Amer. War; editor 1870–85; cand. for Nebr. st. office; C Barranquilla 1886–87, Colon 1887–90, CG Panama 1893–97; apptd. from Lincoln, Neb.; lang., Fr.; d. 1904.

George H. Wallace: b. Ohio 1842; Yellowstone Expedit. 1859–60, army teleg. 1861–64, business 1865–75, rancher, pres. Mo. Wool Growers' Assoc. 1875–89; cand. for Mo. lt. gov.; CG Melbourne 1890–93; apptd. from Fayette, Mo.; d. unknown.

John Davis Washburn: b. Mass. 1833; educ. Harvard, grad. 1853, Harvard Law, grad. 1856; insurance atty. 1866–89, banking; Mass. st. legis. 1876–79, st. sen. 1884; EE&MP Switzerland 1889–92; apptd. from Worcester, Mass.; d. 1903.

Andrew Dickson White: b. N.Y. 1832; educ. Yale, grad. 1853, in Europe; son of banker; univ. prof. 1857–67, univ. pres. 1867–85; N.Y. st. sen. 1863–67; attaché St. Petersburg 1854–55, int'l. commr. 1871, 1878, 1896–97, EE&MP Germany 1879–81, Russia 1892–97, AE&P Germany 1897–1902, The Hague Peace Conf. 1899; apptd. from Ithaca, N.Y.; author; d. 1918.

Rounseville Wildman: b. N.Y. 1863; educ. Syracuse Univ.; son of clergy; editor 1885–90; C Singapore 1890–93, Barmen 1893–97, Hong Kong 1897–98, CG 1898–1901; apptd. from Calif. but resided Boise, Idaho, upon initial appointment; d. 1901.

Ramon O. Williams: b. D.C. c. 1827; sugar trade in Cuba, long residence there; vice CG Havana 1874–84, CG 1884–96; apptd. from Brooklyn, N.Y.; lang., Sp.; d. 1913.

Albert Shelby Willis: b. Ky. 1843; educ. Louisville Law Sch.; son of phys.; teacher, law 1864–77, 1887–93; pres. elector 1872, co. atty. 1874–77; U.S. Cong. 1877–87; EE&MP Hawaii 1893–97; apptd. from Louisville, Ky.; d. 1897.

Henry Lane Wilson: b. Ind. 1856; educ. Wabash Coll., Ind., grad. 1879; son of Cong., army off. & dipl.; editor 1882–85, law, banking 1885–96; EE&MP Chile 1897–1904, Belgium 1905–9, AE&P Mexico 1909–13; apptd. from Spokane, Wash.; author; d. 1932.

Edward Delbert Winslow: b. Ill. 1858; educ. St. Ignatius Coll., Ill., grad. 1877, Northwestern Univ. Law, grad. 1879; grain business 1880–97, stockbroker 1901–8, insurance broker 1922–30; CG Stockholm 1897–1900, sec. leg. 1900–1901, CG 1909–10, C Plauen 1910–11, CG Copenhagen 1911–17; apptd. from Chicago, Ill.; d. 1941.

Stewart Lyndon Woodford: b. N.Y. 1835; educ. Yale, Columbia, grad. 1854; bvt BG Civil War; bar, law 1857–, 1898–1913; nat. Rep. conv. 1860, 1876; asst. dist. atty. 1861–62, N.Y. lt. gov. 1866–68, cand. for gov. 1870, U.S. Cong. 1873–74, U.S. dist. atty. 1877–83; EE&MP Spain 1897–98; apptd. from N.Y., N.Y.; d. 1913.

Pierce Manning Butler Young: b. S.C. 1836; educ. USMA; son of phys.; MG Civil War; planter 1865–85, 1887–93; U.S. Cong. 1868–75, int'l. commr. 1878; CG St. Petersburg 1885–87, EE&MP Guatemala (also Honduras)1893–96; apptd. from Cartersville, Ga.; d. 1896.

Appendix B

U.S. Diplomatic Missions & Consulates General 1890, 1899

I. Legations as of 5 April 1890

Athens, Greece[1]
Bangkok, Siam[2]
Berne, Switzerland[2]
Berlin, Germany
Bogota, Colombia
Brussels, Belgium
Buenos Aires, Argentina
Caracas, Venezuela
Constantinople, Turkey
Copenhagen, Denmark[2]
Guatemala, Guatemala[3]
Honolulu, Hawaiian Islands
La Paz, Bolivia[2]
Lima, Peru
Lisbon, Portugal[2]
London, Great Britain
Madrid, Spain

Mexico, Mexico
Monrovia, Liberia[2]
Montevideo, Uruguay[4]
Paris, France
Peking, China
Port-au-Prince, Haiti[5]
Rio de Janeiro, Brazil
Rome, Italy
St. Petersburg, Russia
Santiago, Chile
Seoul, Korea[2]
Stockholm, Sweden & Norway
Tehran, Persia[2]
The Hague, Netherlands
Tokyo, Japan
Vienna, Austria-Hungary

Total legations = 33

NOTES

[1]Envoy also accredited to Romania and Serbia; minister resident also held title of consul general.

[2]Minister resident also held title of consul general.

[3]Envoy accredited to five Central American states: Costa Rica, El Salvador, Guatemala, Honduras, Nicaragua.
[4]Envoy also accredited to Paraguay.
[5]Envoy also accredited to Dominican Republic; minister resident also held title of consul general.

II. Consulates general as of 5 April 1890 (additional to combined legations/consulates general)

Apia, Samoan Islands	London, Great Britain
Berlin, Germany	Melbourne, Australia
Bogota, Colombia[1]	Mexico, Mexico
Cairo, Egypt[2]	Montreal, Canada
Calcutta, India	Nuevo Laredo, Mexico
Constantinople, Turkey	Ottawa, Canada
Frankfort, Germany	Panama, Colombia
Guatemala, Guatemala[1]	Paris, France
Guayaquil, Ecuador	Rio de Janeiro, Brazil
Havana, Cuba	Rome, Italy
Halifax, Canada	St. Petersburg, Russia
Honolulu, Hawaiian Islands	Shanghai, China
Kanagawa, Japan	Vienna, Austria-Hungary

Total consulates general = 26, not including 10 minister resident/consul general combined titles (I. above).

NOTES
[1]Consul general also secretary of legation.
[2]Consul general also diplomatic agent.

III. Legations and embassies as of 26 December 1899

Same as I. above, with following modifications:

Berlin, Germany	Raised to embassy
Guatemala, Guatemala	Envoy accredited additionally only to Honduras
Honolulu, Hawaii	Legation closed
London, Great Britain	Raised to embassy
Mexico, Mexico	Raised to embassy
Paris, France	Raised to embassy
Quito, Ecuador	Legation opened
St. Petersburg, Russia	Raised to embassy
San Jose, Costa Rica	Legation opened; envoy accredited also to El Salvador & Nicaragua

Total = 34

NOTE: The ministers or ministers resident at six posts—Athens, Berne, Copenhagen, La Paz, Lisbon, and Port-au-Prince—no longer held titles concurrently as consuls general.

IV. Consulates general as of 26 December 1899

Antwerp, Belgium	Monterrey, Mexico
Apia, Samoan Islands	Montreal, Canada
Barcelona, Spain	Ottawa, Canada
Berlin, Germany	Panama, Colombia
Bogota, Colombia[1]	Paris, France
Cairo, Egypt[2]	Rio de Janeiro, Brazil
Calcutta, India	Rome, Italy
Cape Town, South Africa	St. Gall, Switzerland
Constantinople, Turkey	St. Petersburg, Russia
Dresden, Germany	Santo Domingo, Dominican Republic
Frankfort, Germany	Shanghai, China
Guatemala, Guatemala[1]	Singapore, Straits Settlement
Guayaquil, Ecuador	Stockholm, Sweden & Norway
Halifax, Canada	Tangier, Morocco
Hong Kong, China	Vienna, Austria-Hungary
London, Great Britain	Yokohama, Japan[3]
Melbourne, Australia	
Mexico, Mexico	

   Total consulates general = 34, not including 4 minister resident/ consul general combined titles at Bangkok, Monrovia, Seoul, Tehran.

NOTES
[1]Consul general also secretary of legation.
[2]Consul general also diplomatic agent.
[3]Formerly Kanagawa.

SOURCES: F.S. List, 1890, 1899; Official Register, 1899 (not published in 1889, 1890, 1891).

Appendix C

Annual Compensation of Chiefs of Diplomatic Mission and Consuls General, Selected Posts, 1890, 1899

I. Diplomatic Service[1]

Post	1890	1899
London	$17,500	$17,500
Paris	17,500	17,500
Mexico	12,000	17,500
Peking	12,000	12,000
Santiago	10,000	10,000
Brussels	7,500	10,000
Buenos Aires	7,500	10,000
Athens	6,500	6,500
Copenhagen	5,000	7,500
Port-au-Prince	5,000	5,000
Monrovia	4,000	4,000

II. Consular Service

Post	Salary	1890 Notarial Fees[2]	Total[2]	Salary	1899 Notarial Fees	Total
London	$6,000	$7,134	$13,134	$5,000	$7,609	$12,609
Paris	6,000	9,202	15,202	5,000	8,130	13,130
Havana	6,000	3,916	9,916	6,000	2,256[3]	8,256
Rio de Janeiro	6,000	798	6,798	5,000	757	5,757
Shanghai	5,000	100	5,100	5,000	98[4]	5,098
Yokohama	4,000	751	4,751	4,000	801	4,801
Guayaquil	3,000	96	3,096	3,000	1,312	4,312
St. Petersburg	3,000	88	3,088	3,000	126	3,126
Apia	3,000	597	3,597	3,000	91	3,091
Mexico	2,500	45	2,545	4,000	708	4,708
Bogota[5]	2,000	negl.	2,000	2,000	negl.	2,000
Guatemala[5]	2,000	negl.	2,000	2,000	negl.	2,000

NOTES

[1]The maximum diplomatic pay, $17,500 per annum, remained the same throughout the decade, but the salary at nine lower-paid posts was raised. By 1899 four ambassadors—those at London, Paris, Berlin, and Mexico—received the top pay scale.

[2]Consular salaries were increased by the amount of unofficial fees taken in, usually in the form of notarial charges. Only totals for gross fees received, both official and unofficial, are available for 1890, however. The figures for that year, therefore, are estimated on the basis of the breakdown between official and unofficial fee receipts in 1899. The separate figures are available for the latter year.

[3]For 1898.

[4]Incomplete figure as reported by the post. In any event, data from 1890 indicate that the total was not large.

[5]Incumbent also was secretary of legation.

Sources: F. S. List, 1890, 1899; State *Register,* 1892, 1899; Werking, *The Master Architects,* 5.

Appendix D

Senior Diplomatic and Consular Officers Classified as Without Socioeconomic or Educational Sub-elite Backgrounds, 1890–99

Arthur M. Beaupre	Daniel W. Maratta
Sempronious H. Boyd	Felix A. Mathews
Alfred E. Buck	William L. Merry
Samuel H. M. Byers	Thomas Moonlight
Person C. Cheney	Robert A. Moseley, Jr.
Powell Clayton	Romualdo Pacheco
Oliver H. Dockery	Robert F. Patterson
John G. Donnelly	John R. G. Pitkin
Frederick Douglass	John K. Pollard
Patrick Egan	Eugene Seeger
Wakefield G. Frye	Henry W. Severance
John K. Gowdy	Edmund W. P. Smith
Isaac P. Gray	James G. Stowe
Richard Guenther	Granville Stuart
Samuel Kimberly	Willard D. Tillotson
Adam E. King	Charles E. Turner

Total = 32

NOTE: See chapter 7 for classification criteria.

Appendix E

Placement in Competence Groupings
U.S. Diplomatic and Consular Officers, 1890–99

I. Demonstrably competent or suited to assignment

Thomas Adamson
Eben Alexander
Horace N. Allen
Wendell A. Anderson
James B. Angell
John Barrett
Arthur M. Beaupre
William I. Buchanan
William S. Carroll
Joseph H. Choate
Edwin H. Conger
T. Jefferson Coolidge
Thomas T. Crittenden
Charles de Kay
Charles Denby
Charles M. Dickinson
Frederick Douglass
James T. Dubois
Edwin Dun
Patrick Egan
Wakefield G. Frye
John Goodnow
John K. Gowdy

Richard Guenther
Philip C. Hanna
Thomas S. Harrison
Carl B. Hurst
Darius H. Ingraham
Thomas R. Jernigan
Wallace S. Jones
Julius G. Lay
Fitzhugh Lee
Francis B. Loomis
James C. McNally
George E. Maney
Daniel W. Maratta
Frank H. Mason
Felix A. Mathews
Frederic C. Penfield
Horace Porter
E. Spencer Pratt
Jared L. Rathbone
Whitelaw Reid
W. W. Rockhill
William L. Scruggs
John L. Stevens

Oscar S. Straus
Warner P. Sutton
Hannis Taylor
William W. Thomas, Jr.

Thomas L. Thompson
Andrew D. White
Ramon O. Williams
Stewart L. Woodford

Subtotal = 54

II. Demonstrably incompetent or ill suited

Lewis Baker
Andrew D. Barlow
Thomas F. Bayard
Herbert W. Bowen
James R. Hosmer
W. Godfrey Hunter
Samuel Kimberly
George F. Lincoln
Luther F. McKinney
Samuel Merrill

Lansing B. Mizner
Samuel E. Morss
John K. Pollard
Matt W. Ransom
John M. B. Sill
Jacob Sleeper
Edmund W. P. Smith
Henry M. Smythe
Laurits S. Swenson
Alexander W. Terrell

Subtotal = 20

III. At post too brief a period to leave significant record

a. A few months only:

James H. Blount
Person C. Cheney
Frederick J. Grant

Edward C. Little
Gilbert A. Pierce
David P. Thompson

b. Up to one year:

Robert Adams, Jr.
John A. Anderson
Alexander G. Clark
William B. Hess
William D. McCoy
Romualdo Pacheco

Macgrane Coxe
Seneca Haselton
William Haywood
Thomas W. Palmer
Watson R. Sperry
Edwin F. Uhl

Subtotal = 18

IV. Generally acceptable performance, residual subtotal of 134, out of 226 considered.

NOTE: See chapter 7 for placement criteria.

Notes

Preface

1. Thomas L. Haskell, *The Emergence of Professional Social Science: The American Social Science Association and the Nineteenth-Century Crisis of Authority* (Urbana: Univ. of Illinois Press, 1977), 19.

2. Lawrence Stone, "Prosopography," in *Historical Studies Today*, ed. Felix Gilbert and Stephen R. Grabaud (New York: W. W. Norton, 1972), 114; Elmer Plischke, "Research on the Administrative History of the Department of State," in *The National Archives and Foreign Relations Research*, ed. Milton O. Gustafson (Athens, Ohio: Ohio Univ. Press, 1974), 73, emphasis in original.

3. William H. Masterson, *Tories and Democrats: British Diplomats in Pre-Jacksonian America* (College Station, Tex.: Texas A&M Univ. Press, 1985), xv.

4. Louis Galambos, "The Emerging Organizational Synthesis in Modern American History," *Business History Review* 44, no. 3 (Autumn 1970): 288.

Chapter 1

1. An inward-turning nineteenth-century America is the traditional historical interpretation; see as one example the argument of Charles S. Campbell, *The Transformation of American Foreign Relations, 1865–1900* (New York: Harper and Row, 1976). But a case has been made, usually on economic grounds, that at least America's political and business leadership was oriented toward foreign affairs questions throughout the nineteenth century. Exponents of this revisionist view are usually categorized as the New Left or Wisconsin "school" and include William Appleman Williams, Walter LaFeber, Thomas McCormick, and David Healy. For one representative interpretation along these lines, see Healy, *U.S. Expansionism: The Imperialist Urge in the 1890s* (Madison: Univ. of Wisconsin Press, 1980), especially page 5. On the other hand, David M. Pletcher asserts in another recent volume that American foreign policy during the last four decades of the 1800s was

hesitant and contradictory. See his "1861–1898: Economic Growth and Diplomatic Adjustment," in *Economics and World Power: An Assessment of American Diplomacy Since 1789*, ed. William H. Becker and Samuel F. Wells, Jr. (New York: Columbia Univ. Press, 1984), 119–71. The same volume includes the judgment by one of the editors that "The goals of United States diplomacy in the nineteenth century had been relatively clear cut: minimizing the influence of foreign powers near the United States and the expansion of American sovereignty over the continent"; William H. Becker, "1899–1920: America Adjusts to World Power," in ibid., 173.

2. Robert L. Beisner, *From the Old Diplomacy to the New, 1865–1900* (1975; rev. ed. Arlington Heights, Ill.: Harlan Davidson, Inc., 1986); Jerald A. Combs, *The History of American Foreign Policy* (New York: Knopf, 1986), 1:130. Beisner has an unusually comprehensive and useful bibliographic essay on the subject and period; see *From the Old Diplomacy*, 159–82.

3. Beisner, *From the Old Diplomacy*, 33.

4. Paul A. Varg, "The United States a World Power, 1900–1917: Myth or Reality?" in *Twentieth Century American Foreign Policy*, ed. John Braeman et al. (Columbus: Ohio State Univ. Press, 1971), 240.

5. Henry Cabot Lodge, *George Washington* (Boston, 1889), 1:129.

6. *Washington Post*, 31 Mar. 1893, 4.

7. *Congressional Record* (hereinafter, *Cong. Rec.*), 48th Cong., 2d sess., 1884–85, 16, pt. 1:613 (Sen. William E. Robinson, N.Y.); see also *Cong. Rec.*, 49th Cong., 1st sess., 1885–86, 17, pt. 5:4443 (Rep. John H. Reagan, Tex.), and *Cong. Rec.*, 50th Cong., 2d sess., 1888–89, 20, pt. 2:1247 (Rep. Preston B. Plumb, Kans.).

8. *New York Sun* quoted in Irwin Unger, *These United States: The Questions of Our Past*, 2d ed. (Englewood Heights, N.J.: Prentice-Hall, 1982), 2:571; *Washington Post*, 31 Mar. 1890, 4; Oscar S. Straus, "Reform in the Consular Service," National Civil Service Reform League pamphlet (microfilm), Washington, D.C., Dec. 1894, 4.

9. Warren F. Ilchman, a historian of Foreign Service professionalization, dates America's unpreparedness from 1888 in light of the nation's changing foreign relations; *Professional Diplomacy in the United States, 1779–1939: A Study in Administrative History* (Chicago: Univ. of Chicago Press, 1961), 18.

10. Thomas Jefferson Coolidge, *The Autobiography of T. Jefferson Coolidge, 1831–1920* (Boston: Houghton Mifflin, 1923), 179, passage from his journal entry of 3 Sept. 1892; Straus, "Reform in the Consular Service," 3.

11. George Horton quoted in Nancy Horton, "Quest for a Consulship," *Foreign Service Journal* 62(May 1985):38; *Cong. Rec.*, 53d Cong., 3d sess., 1894–95, 27, pt. 3:1983. The bill, sponsored by Senator Morgan of Alabama and designed to establish a "permanent service of trained men," got nowhere at that time. Its text is on pp. 1986–87.

12. *Cong. Rec.*, 53d Cong., 2d sess., 1893–94, 26, pt. 4:3801; *New York Times*, 27 Aug. 1895, 16.

13. Stephen Skowronek, *Building a New American State: The Expansion of National Administrative Capacities* (New York: Cambridge Univ. Press, 1892), 44; Perry Belmont, "Defects in our Consular Service," *Forum* 4(Jan. 1888):519–26; Robert Adams, Jr., "Faults in Our Consular Service," *North American Review* 156(Apr. 1893):461–66; Francis B. Loomis, "The Foreign Service of the United States" and "Proposed Reorganization of the American Consular Service," *North American Review* 169(Sept. 1899):349–61, and 182(Mar. 1906):356–73. See also an earlier brief editorial note on consular reform in the *North American Review* 149(Dec. 1889):757–59.

14. *New York Times*, 8 July 1889, 4; *Washington Post*, 3 Nov. 1893, 4.

15. *New York Times*, 24 Mar. 1889, 4.

16. Quoted in George Brown Tindall, *America: A Narrative History* (New York: W. W. Norton, 1984), 2:845. Harrison was more circumspect in his inaugural address: "Heads of departments, bureaus, and all other public officers having any duty connected therewith, will be expected to enforce the civil service law fully and without evasion. Beyond this obvious duty I hope to do something more to advance the reform of the civil service. The ideal, or even my own ideal, I shall probably not attain"; Harry J. Sievers, ed., *Benjamin Harrison, 1833–1901: Chronology—Documents—Bibliographical Aids* (Dobbs Ferry, N.Y.: Oceana Publications, 1969), 44.

17. Robert D. Marcus, *Grand Old Party: Political Structure in the Gilded Age, 1880–1896* (New York: Oxford Univ. Press, 1971), 133–34; *New York Times*, 24 Mar. 1889, 4, 8 June 1889, 4, and 8 July 1889, 4.

18. Robert H. Ferrell, *American Diplomacy: A History*, 3d ed. (New York: W. W. Norton, 1975), 7; Richard Hofstadter, *Anti-intellectualism in American Life* (New York: Alfred A. Knopf, 1962, 1963), 171.

19. Richard H. Werking, *The Master Architects: Building the United States Foreign Service, 1890–1913* (Lexington: Univ. Press of Kentucky, 1977), xi; Walter LaFeber, *The New Empire: An Interpretation of American Expansion, 1860–1898* (Ithaca, N.Y.: Cornell Univ. Press, 1963), 377.

20. Ferrell, *American Diplomacy*, 8–10; Pletcher, "1861–1898: Economic Growth and Diplomatic Adjustment," 129; Page Smith, *The Rise of Industrial America: A People's History of the Post-Reconstruction Era* (New York: McGraw-Hill, 1984), vi, 725; H. Wayne Morgan, *From Hayes to McKinley: National Party Politics, 1877–1896* (Syracuse, N.Y.: Syracuse Univ. Press, 1969), 151; Beisner, *From the Old Diplomacy*, 28, 29; Alfred L. P. Dennis, *Adventures in American Diplomacy, 1896–1906* (New York: E. P. Dutton, 1928), 534; Morton I. Keller, *Affairs of State: Public Life in Late Nineteenth Century America* (Cambridge, Mass.: Belknap Press, 1977)1:589.

21. Ilchman, *Professional Diplomacy*, 41. The "worn-out, useless" quotation is attributed to a South Carolina congressman speaking in 1834, and the "party mendicants" phrase, also congressional in origin, dates from 1859. The "frock coat" remark is that of Marine General Smedley D. Butler, cited in Thomas A. Bailey, *The Art of Diplomacy: The American Experience* (New York: Appleton-Century-Crofts, 1968), 47.

22. Harold Nicolson, *Diplomacy* (1939; New York: Oxford Univ. Press, 1963), 129–30.

Chapter 2

1. Richard Olney to Grover Cleveland, 17 Sept. 1895, in *Cong. Rec.*, 54th Cong., 2d sess., 1897, 29, pt. 2:1413–14. By 1895 the Department of State no longer had even a file copy of the 1866 exam.

2. Executive Order, 20 Sept. 1895, text in U.S. Government, *Register of the Department of State* (hereinafter, State *Register*), 1897 and subsequent years. Note that the *Register* was published during this period in 1889, 1892, and annually thereafter (two editions were issued in 1892). Consular positions paying between $1,000 and $2,500 per year were to be filled by transfers within the service or by appointment of persons "selected by the President for examination" who showed themselves to be qualified. The salary range effectively exempted from the order most principal officer positions. About 60 percent of all consular slots nevertheless were affected; Ralph Hilton, *Worldwide Mission: The Story of the United States Foreign Service* (New York: The World Pub. Co., 1970), 159.

3. Standard studies on foreign service reform, in addition to those by Ilchman and Werking already cited, include Walter H. Heinrichs, Jr., "Bureaucracy and Professionalism in the Development of American Career Diplomacy," in *Twentieth Century American Foreign Policy*, ed. Braeman et al., 119–206; and Jerry Israel, "A Diplomatic Machine: Scientific Management in the Department of State, 1906–1924," in *Building the Organizational Society: Essays on Associational Activities in America*, ed. Israel (New York: Free Press, 1972), 183–96. Among other related works, see also Graham H. Stuart, *The Department of State: A History of Its Organization, Procedures and Personnel* (New York: Macmillan, 1949), chaps. 15–19; Gaillard Hunt, *The Department of State of the United States: Its History and Functions* (New Haven, Conn.: Yale Univ. Press, 1924), which contains the texts of the executive orders; William Barnes and John Heath Morgan, *The Foreign Service of the United States: Origins, Development, and Functions* (Washington, D.C.: Department of State, 1961); and Chester Lloyd Jones, *The Consular Service of the United States: Its History and Activities* (Philadelphia: Published for the University, 1906).

We can usefully note here two points on the reform thrust which began in earnest in the early 1900s. The careerist movement was set back in 1913 by the spoils system depradations of President Woodrow Wilson's secretary of state, the former Democratic party standard bearer William Jennings Bryan. Progress toward a career system did not recommence until after the First World War. Secondly, it should be remarked that careerist and merit requirements did not then or later pertain to ambassadors and ministers. Senior appointments are the prerogative of the president, and rules and regulations do not apply to his choices to head up diplomatic missions as his representative to foreign heads of state. See the final chapter of this text for more details.

4. Werking, *Master Architects*, 123, 104, 156. Examples of the questions posed and the subjects covered are in the annual State *Registers* published in the years around 1910. Note that not just anyone could take the Consular or Diplomatic Service exams; to sit for the examinations one had to obtain designation from the White House. Since passage of the Rogers Act in 1924, as modified significantly by the Foreign Service Acts of 1946 and 1980, almost any American who met the age limits has been able to give the difficult test a try. Presidential sponsorship has not been necessary for decades.

5. David Singleton, "Journalists' 'Non-Professional' Status Examined," *Chapel Hill* (N.C.) *Newspaper*, 11 Aug. 1985, 11A.

6. Prof. Karl Llewellyn of Columbia University, in a comment made in 1933, quoted in Paul Wallace, "How Lawyers Monopolize the Law," *The Charlotte* (N.C.) *Observer*, 5 May 1985, B-1. The concept of the law and medicine as professions with exalted status throughout the centuries sometimes is overstated. With respect to the growing pains in colonial America of the law profession, see John M. Murrin, "The Legal Transformation: The Bench and the Bar of Eighteenth-Century America," in *Colonial America: Essays in Politics and Social Development*, ed. Stanley N. Katz and John M. Murrin, 3d ed. (New York: Alfred A. Knopf, 1983), 540–72. On the ambiguous reputation of the medical professions, see George Eliot's *Middlemarch* (1871–72).

7. William J. Goode, "Community Within Community: The Professions," *American Sociological Review* 22 (Apr. 1957), quoted in Wilbert S. Moore, *The Professions: Roles and Rules* (New York: Russell Sage Foundation, 1970), 57–58.

8. Laurence Veysey, "Who's a Professional? Who Cares?" *Reviews in American History* 2 (Dec. 1975):420. As might be deduced from his review article title, Veysey challenges the high valuation put on professionalism in many studies of recent years and even questions the usefulness of the concept.

9. Singleton, "Journalists' 'Non-Professional' Status Examined," 11A.

10. The foregoing several paragraphs, where not otherwise attributed, are drawn largely from Eliot Friedson, *Professional Powers: A Study of the Institutionalization of Formal Knowledge* (Chicago: Univ. of Chicago Press, 1986), and "The Theory of Professions: The State of the Art," in *The Sociology of the Professions: Lawyers, Doctors and Others*, ed. Robert Dingwall and Philip Lewis, eds. (New York: St. Martin's Press, 1983), 19–37. See also Friedson, "Are Professions Necessary?" in *The Authority of Experts: Studies in History and Theory*, ed. Thomas Haskell (Bloomington: Indiana Univ. Press, 1984). The "British disease" term is that of M. Fores and I. Glover, *The Times Higher Education Supplement*, London, 24 Feb. 1978, cited in Friedson, "The Theory of Professions." Friedson prefers the term "Anglo-American disease." The distinction between status and occupational professions is drawn by Philip R. C. Elliott, *The Sociology of the Professions* (New York: Herder & Herder, 1972), 14, 32, also cited by Friedson. Three other noteworthy works on the subject are Gerald L. Geison, ed., *Professions and Professional Ideologies in America* (Chapel Hill: Univ. of North Carolina Press, 1983); William E. Nelson, *The Roots of American Bureaucracy, 1830–1900* (Cambridge, Mass.: Harvard Univ. Press, 1982); and Skowronek, *Building a New American State*. Another useful study is Magali Sarfatti Larson, *The Rise of Professionalism: A Sociological Analysis* (Berkeley: Univ. of California Press, 1977).

11. The advent to the presidency of John F. Kennedy marked an activist era, although short-lived, in which it was thought that experts could solve nearly all of society's problems. The conceptual link with professionalism is obvious.

12. Quoted, disapprovingly, in Veysey, "Who's a Professional?" 419.

13. Robert H. Wiebe, *The Search for Order, 1877–1920* (New York: Hill and Wang, 1967), 111–32, 129.

14. Samuel P. Hays, *The Response to Industrialism, 1885–1914* (Chicago: Univ. of Chicago Press, 1957); Richard Hofstadter, *Social Darwinism in American Thought* (Boston: Beacon Press, 1955), 167; Wiebe, *Search for Order*.

15. Quoted in Louis Galambos, *The Public Image of Big Business in America, 1880–1940: A Quantitative Study in Social Change* (Baltimore: Johns Hopkins Univ. Press, 1975), 4. Note also E. N. Gladden's judgment in this regard, note 22 below. For a sampling of Weber's thought in this context, see S. N. Eisenstadt, ed., *Max Weber on Charisma and Institution Building* (1968; rpt. Chicago: Univ. of Chicago Press, 1974); and Henry Jacoby, *The Bureaucratization of the World* (Berkeley: Univ. of California Press, 1973), esp. 147–52.

16. Kenneth Prewitt and Alan Stone, *The Ruling Elites: Elite Theory, Power, and American Democracy* (New York: Harper and Row, 1973), esp. chap. 6. The authors do not hold, however, that there is elitist cohesion in a democracy, as might be supposed from the restricted selection pool; the group incorporates wide policy and attitudinal differences.

17. Gaetano Mosca, *The Ruling Class*, trans. Hannah D. Kahn (New York: McGraw-Hill, 1939). C. Wright Mills, in *The Power Elite* (New York: Oxford Univ. Press, 1956), has a differing, negative interpretation of elites, the select corps of leading military, political, and business figures. He sees them as a threat to democracy.

18. White married Margaret Stuyvesant Rutherfurd in 1879; after her death, he married Emily Vanderbilt Sloane in 1920. In 1894, as a young but already experienced diplomat who had just been ousted from the ranks of the diplomats by the incoming Democrats, he published an article on the Consular Service in the *North American Review*. Not surprisingly, White, a Republican who later was reappointed under McKinley and Roosevelt, was in favor of reform. He is not included in this group biography because he was named to the status of senior diplomatic envoy after 1900.

19. Several historical studies of American elites are available to the interested student. Edward L. Pessen addresses the subject in a detailed investigation of the political appointment process throughout American history. "Appointees to high judicial, diplomatic, and administrative posts," he finds somewhat surprisingly, "appear to have been cut of even finer cloth than . . . [those] who had had to run the electoral gauntlet." The focus of one compendium of studies is indicated by its title, *The Rich, the Well Born, and the Powerful*, an allusion to the monied backgrounds of elites. Another study, a multivolume work by Philip H. Burch, Jr., singles out as an American elite the members of the cabinet, the Supreme Court justices, and the diplomatic envoys to Britain, France, and Germany. The author comes to positive conclusions, similar to those of Pessen, on the level of abilities and accomplishments of this group. Edward L. Pessen, "Social Structure and Politics in American History," *American Historical Review* 87 (Dec. 1982):1315. See also his related study, *Three Centuries of Social Mobility in America* (Lexington, Mass.: D.C. Heath, 1974); Frederic C. Jaher, ed., *The Rich, the Well Born, and the Powerful: Elites and Upper Classes in History* (Urbana: Univ. of Illinois Press, 1973); Philip H. Burch, Jr., *Elites in American History* (New York: Holmes & Meier, 1981). The Jaher work includes group biographies by the editor and by Richard Jensen, Thomas A. Krueger, and William Glidden.

20. Haskell, *Emergence of Professional Social Science*, 65–68, 163, 176. See also Howard M. Vollmer and Donald L. Mills, eds., *Professionalization* (Englewood Cliffs, N.J.: Prentice-Hall, 1966).

21. Skowronek, *Building a New American State*, 47.

22. E. N. Gladden, *A History of Public Administration* (London: Frank Cass, 1972), 2:318.

23. U.S. Dept. of State, "Inspection Report of Herbert H. D. Peirce, Third Assistant Secretary of State," Confidential (1904), Record Group (RG) 59, entry 596, National Archives, Washington, D.C. Also printed as 59th Cong., 1st sess., 1906, H. Doc. 665.

24. Allan Nevins, *Henry White* (New York: Harper and Brothers, 1930), 97. "Every man in either the diplomatic or consular service," noted astutely one long-term diplomat of the period, "makes a reputation which is as well known as the State Department as a man's reputation in the village where he resides"; Charles Denby, *China and Her People; Being the Observations, Reminiscences, and Conclusions of an American Diplomat* (Boston: L.C. Page, 1906), 2:211.

25. U.S. Dept. of State, Applications and Recommendations for Federal Office, 1897, RG 59, files for H. M. Smythe and W. F. Powell. Hereinafter, these records are cited as Appl. Files, by period and individual concerned. The files for the first Cleveland and the Harrison administrations combined, 1885–93, are in one group; the second Cleveland administration, 1893–97, are in another; and finally, for our purposes, the McKinley years, 1897–1901, are filed together. Files on the same individual often are located in more than one group. These are the closest things to personal records for this era; the diplomatic and consular services established personnel files as such only in 1910—and these are still closed to scholars.

Chapter 3

1. J. G. Martin to Matt W. Ransom, 12 Nov. 1894, Ransom Papers, Southern Historical Collection, University of North Carolina, Chapel Hill (hereinafter, SHC). Martin probably was the son of James Green Martin (1819–78) of Asheville, a Confederate general and a lawyer, like Ransom; Jon L. Wakelyn, ed., *Biographical Dictionary of the Confederacy* (Westport, Conn.: Greenwood Press, 1977), 312–13.

2. Hay quoted in Ferrell, *American Diplomacy*, 9, and Morgan, *From Hayes to McKinley*, 13; Henry Adams, *The Education of Henry Adams*, Modern Hist. Soc. (n.p., 1918, 1931), 794; F. M. Huntington Wilson, *Memoirs of an Ex-Diplomat* (Boston, Bruce Humphries, 1945), 46. He was successful in obtaining appointment as secretary of legation in Japan, largely through his father's influence with the president, and went on to a career as a senior officer in the Department of State and abroad in the early 1900s.

3. The apt comment of a fictional political character is from Gore Vidal, *1876 A Novel* (New York: Ballantine, 1976), 419.

4. Dept. of State, Despatches from United States Ministers to Peru (hereinafter cited as Dipl. Desp., by country), enclosure to no. 515, 24 June 1893, RG 59, microfilm. Hicks returned to a Wisconsin newspaper career, but later served as minister to Chile, 1905–9.

5. *Charlotte* (N.C.) *Chronicle*, 14 Feb. 1890, 3.

6. Appl. Files 1885–93, J. R. G. Pitkin, W. G. Frye; Appl. Files 1897–1901, W. F. Powell, J. R. G. Pitkin.

7. Appl. Files 1893–97, L. Short, W. T. Townes; Appl. Files 1885–93, J. T. Abbott. After his one tour in the foreign service, Townes represented the American Tobacco Company in the Caribbean; W. T. Townes to Robert S. Chilton, Jr., 12 Jan. 1899, Robert S. Chilton, Jr., Papers, Manuscript Division, Duke University Library, Durham, N.C.

8. Appl. Files 1885–93, J. T. Abbott.

9. *New York Times*, 23 June 1893, 12; E. Spencer Pratt to Grover Cleveland, 15 Mar. 1893, 12 May 1893, Appl. Files 1893–97, E. S. Pratt.

10. Charles M. Dickinson, "Reminiscences of Charles M. Dickinson," undated typescript, 50; *Binghamton* (N.Y.) *Press*, clipping from 9 June 1920, Charles Monroe Dickinson Papers, Library of Congress (LOC), Washington, D.C. The press article, while phrased in the third person, almost certainly was written by Dickinson himself.

11. Allan Nevins, *Grover Cleveland: A Study in Courage* (New York: Dodd, Mead & Co., 1933), 193–194, 1. Ransom was nominated and confirmed while a sitting senator, a fact which caused legal complications a few months later. Not surprisingly, the Senate found a way around these problems, but that body had to reconfirm him in the post later in the year. See folder 468, Ransom Papers, SHC. The total of forty-four nations with which the United States had relations as of 1 Jan. 1895 included seven without resident American envoys; State *Register*, 1895.

12. Edward C. Little to Elijah W. Halford, private secretary to the president, 10 Nov. 1892, Benjamin Harrison Papers, LOC; U.S. Dept. of State, "List of U.S. Consular Officers, 1789–1939" (hereinafter, Consular List), RG 59, microfilm; *New York Times*, 16 Nov. 1892, 1; Appl. Files 1885–93, E. C. Little; Judge I. C. Parker to Benjamin Harrison, 6 Feb. 1889, and Sempronius H. Boyd to James G. Blaine, 6 Mar. 1889, Appl. Files 1885–93, S. H. Boyd.

13. U.S. Government, *Official Register of the United States* (Washington, D.C.: Government Printing Office, biennial vols., 1891–1901), hereinafter, *Official Register* by year; Consular List; State *Register*, 1916; and U.S. Dept. of State, "List of U.S. Diplomatic Officers, 1789–1933" (hereinafter, Diplomatic List), RG 59, microfilm. Foreign Service posts continue to be designated as embassies, consulates general, or consulates (there remain no legations). Officers at these posts are designated by diplomatic or consular titles and at embassies sometimes by both. But they, unlike the officers of the 1890s, bear career Foreign Service ranks as well unless they are presidential political appointees. The latter typically are in chief of mission status. It is rare for modern-day Foreign Service officers of senior rank to be assigned to a functional position with a lesser title than the one previ-

ously held at another post.

14. J. Addison Porter to Walden P. Anderson, 22 May 1897, William McKinley Papers, microfilm, LOC; Walden P. Anderson to William McKinley, 14 June 1897, Appl. Files 1897–1901, W. P. Anderson; S. M. Cullom to Benjamin Harrison, 3 Oct. 1892, Harrison Papers, microfilm, LOC. The names of Martin, Anderson, and Hamilton are missing from the comprehensive card file titled, "Name Index to the Appointment of United States Diplomatic and Consular Officers, 1776–1933," Department of State, RG 59. For commentary on Senator Cullom's patronage relations with the next Republican president, see Margaret Leech, In the Days of McKinley (New York: Harper and Bros., 1959), 135–36.

15. I base the sample on my detailed count of files in one-tenth of the containers selected at random in each of the three National Archives groupings. The filing system is such that the first Cleveland and Harrison administrations are lumped together; deriving a separate total for the Harrison administration alone therefore is not feasible.

16. Telegram, Levi P. Morton to James G. Blaine, 29 June 1889, Appl. Files 1885–93, R. G. Lay.

17. Report by William R. Day, Thomas W. Cridler, and Robert S. Chilton, Jr., 6 Dec. 1897, Appl. Files 1897–1901, J. K. Pollard. Pollard earlier managed accidentally to burn the set of consular regulations sent to him and therefore was not as well prepared as he might have been; Pollard to Cridler, 13 Nov. 1897. He served from early 1898 to his death the following year.

18. Julius G. Lay to Robert S. Chilton, Jr., 12 Apr. 1899, enclosing a clipping from the Detroit Free Press of 11 Apr.; Chilton Papers, Duke. The elder Lay, Richard G., served only the four years of the Harrison administration in the foreign service. His son Julius, who was being ousted from Windsor, however, had a long career spanning some four decades, including three years in the Department of State and ending in the 1930s as minister successively to Honduras and Uruguay. Consular List and U.S. Department of State, United States Chiefs of Mission, 1778–1982 (Washington, D.C.: Government Printing Office, 1982). The latter publication is used for this study in conjunction with the Diplomatic List.

19. New York Times, 29 July 1886, 23 June 1893; undated note card in McKinley's writing, Appl. Files 1897–1901, R. A. Moseley, Jr.; Marcus, Grand Old Party, 224–25; William Youngblood to William R. Day, 24 Feb. 1898, Appl. Files 1897–1901, R. A. Moseley, Jr.

20. J. L. Rathbone to James G. Blaine, 4 July 1890, Despatches from United States Consuls, Paris, 1890, microfilm (hereinafter, Cons. Desp. by post). Rathbone's brother, incidentally, as an army major was in the box at Ford's Theater with President Lincoln when he was shot; see Washington Post, 19 May 1887, 4.

Chapter 4

1. An officer of the Foreign Service to this day receives commissions issued in his or her name reading "of Mississippi" or whatever state claimed for residence and home leave purposes at the time of appointment or promotion—a quaint and venerable custom which continues in practice.

2. George E. Mowry commented on the elusiveness of averages when applied to groups of people but nonetheless drew conclusions from his data; The California Progressives (Berkeley: Univ. of California Press, 1951), 291.

3. About two-thirds of the officers in this study have entries in one or more of the

standard biographic reference works. Since they are readily identifiable in these references, factual information from this kind of published source usually is not cited in notes to this study; such citations if detailed would fill dozens of pages. Department of State *Registers* for the years 1910–16 contain brief but relevant biographic sketches on certain officers with more than minimal service abroad in previous years. These and other nonstandard sources are cited. As already noted, a comprehensive and invaluable source of information on many, especially the appointees who do not merit *Who's Who*-type coverage, are the Department of State Applications Files in the National Archives. These documents were used for this chapter and extensively throughout the study.

4. MacVeagh has no Application File at all in the National Archives; he had no need to submit letters or petitions. The mail he received and the news publicity occasioned by his abandonment of the Republican party in October 1892 reflect the furor his action caused; Wayne MacVeagh Papers, Historical Society of Pennsylvania, Philadelphia, Pa. (hereinafter, HSP).

5. In early 1893 Mills, a clerk in the Department of State, accompanied James H. Blount to Hawaii as an aide on the latter's fact-finding mission for Cleveland. Upon return to Washington, Blount got him the Honolulu assignment; *New York Times*, 9 Sept. 1893, 8.

6. Charles A. Beard in his seminal work, *An Economic Interpretation of the Constitution* (1913), found the law profession to be foremost among Constitutional Convention members. Another scholar notes that lawyers were well represented in the Union and Confederate general officer corps. Of the 583 Union generals he identified, one-third previously had been regular army officers, but a substantial 21.6 percent were former attorneys and jurists. Lawyers formed a plurality among 425 Confederate generals, with 30.4 percent of the total; former regulars totalled 29.4 percent. See Ezra J. Warner, *Generals in Blue: Lives of the Union Commanders* (Baton Rouge: Louisiana State Univ. Press, 1964), xix. Donald R. Matthews found that more than one-half of post–World War II senators, 97 of 180 members from 1947 to 1957, were lawyers; *U.S. Senators and Their World* (New York: Vintage, 1960), 282. The law profession through the years has provided a large proportion of the nation's appointed (and elected) governmental leadership.

7. A. L. Conger (President of the Whitman & Barnes Manufacturing Co., Akron, Ohio) to William McKinley, 2 Jan. 1897, Appl. Files 1897–1901, J. G. Stowe; W. S. Dickey (President of the W. S. Dickey Clay Manufacturing Co., Kansas City, Mo.) to James Gardner Stowe, 16 Feb. 1897, Appl. Files 1897–1901, J. G. Stowe; William McKinley to Bart W. Lyon, 29 Oct. 1895, text in *Commercial Traveller*, St. Louis, Mo., Nov. 1896, Appl. Files 1897–1901, J. G. Stowe.

8. Blount did not want the job in the first place and got out of it as soon as possible. See his very first official message to Washington, D.C., as minister, Honolulu despatch no. 1, 24 May 1893, and also no. 4, 1 June 1893, Dipl. Desp., Honolulu. The administration named him to the post largely because he was on the spot as President Cleveland's special emissary when Minister John L. Stevens abruptly departed on 21 May.

9. David J. Rothman, *Politics and Power: The United States Senate, 1869–1901* (Cambridge, Mass.: Harvard Univ. Press, 1966), 157. Because he did not receive an expected cabinet post, one member of this study group was referred to as "poor" Bellamy Storer, who had been "thrown over to the State Dept." and ended up as minister to Belgium; Henry Cabot Lodge to Theodore Roosevelt, 8 Mar. 1897, in Henry Cabot Lodge, ed., *Selections from the Correspondence of Theodore Roosevelt and Henry Cabot Lodge, 1884–1918* (New York: Charles Scribner's Sons, 1925), 1:254.

10. In 1897 Coughlin tried unsuccessfully for the post of minister to Colombia; Appl.

Files 1897–1901, J. Coughlin. He died and was buried at Bogota in 1930; Cons. List.

11. *Dictionary of American Biography*, 4th ed., s.v. "Tower, Charlemagne."

12. Matt W. Ransom to T. R. Ransom, 8 May 1895, Ransom Papers, SHC. Ransom was accompanied to post by a son who served first in an unpaid capacity but who in time received a commission as secretary of legation.

13. U.S. Government, *Abstract of the Eleventh Census: 1890* (Washington, D.C., 1896), esp. 10–11. This possible explanation of the relative lack of appointments from the Deep South still leaves the question why the South Atlantic states, most of which were in the old Confederacy also, were well represented in the service, even with a higher proportion of blacks to whites than the South Central area. One can speculate that the District of Columbia's total of ten and perhaps other appointments in the near vicinity of Washington inflate the regional figure, along with Republican strength in West Virginia, Maryland, and Delaware.

14. The medal was awarded only in 1902. Victor Vifquain, consul general at Panama, 1893–97, also was a Medal of Honor recipient for bravery in action. According to one of Vifquain's supporters, the government made only thirty-eight such awards for valor during the Civil War; A. J. Sawyer to J. Sterling Morton, 12 June 1885, Appl. Files 1893–97, V. Vifquain.

15. The Cleveland administration envoy to Haiti and the Dominican Republic from 1893 to 1897, Henry Maxwell Smythe, however, was a white Virginian.

16. Cleveland nominated C. H. J. Taylor of Kansas to the post of minister to Bolivia and H. C. C. Astwood of New York to the consulate at Calais, both blacks. Reaction was negative; the Senate rejected Astwood on the basis of an adverse report by the Committee on Foreign Affairs and took no action on Taylor's nomination before adjourning early in November 1893. The *Washington Post* opined that the "course is thought to be dictated largely by a disinclination to send colored men as representatives to countries peopled by another race"; *Washington Post*, 4 Nov. 1893, 2. See also W. J. Johnson to Grover Cleveland, 20 Sept. 1893, Grover Cleveland Papers, LOC.

17. John S. Durham to William Pepper, 2 Apr. 1889, William Pepper Papers, Van Pelt Library, University of Pennsylvania, Philadelphia, Pa. Pepper was acting president of the university for many years; Durham looked upon him as a special benefactor.

18. Appl. Files 1885–93, W. D. McCoy.

19. *Abstract of the Eleventh Census*, 10. A study of Civil War generals finds that only 45 of 583 officers of that rank, or 7.7 percent, were born abroad; Warner, *Generals in Blue*, 603.

20. John C. Spooner to James G. Blaine, 16 Mar. 1889, Appl. Files 1885–93, J. Goldschmidt. Blaine appointed Goldschmidt, Spooner's nominee, who served as consul general at Vienna until 1893. Senator John O. Allen of Washington wrote somewhat similarly to Blaine a year later complaining that his state had fewer consular appointments than neighboring Oregon; Allen to Blaine, 2 Aug. 1890, Appl. Files 1885–93, J. F. Gowey.

21. Appl. Files 1893–97, M. Judd; *New York Times*, 23 Mar. 1893, 5; 2 Apr. 1893, 8; 22 Apr. 1893, 9; 21 May 1893, 8. Judd was a partner in a St. Louis cloak manufacturing company and a lumber firm; *Gould's St. Louis City Directory, 1891*, 20th ed., 721 (microfilm,) Appalachian State University Library, Boone, N.C. At Vienna he received his exequatur, in May, thanks in part to the vigorous push for his recognition exerted by the outgoing minister, Frederick D. Grant. His Department of State commission, duly authenticated by the Vienna authorities, now reposes in the Max Judd Papers, Missouri Historical Society, Division of Library and Archives, St. Louis, Mo.

22. Such information as is available on language skills comes from the officers' Appli-

cations Files in the National Archives, standard biographic references, and from scattered comments in correspondence. There is no way now to clarify whether first-person assertions or third-person comments on abilities in a given language reflected a real command of the language or merely a passing acquaintance. Self-assessed language skills in the modern Foreign Service often are viewed with some skepticism, if for no other reason than that constant practice is needed to keep up fluency in an acquired second (or third) language.

23. Beckles Willson, *America's Ambassadors to France, 1777–1927: A Narrative of Franco-American Diplomatic Relations* (London: John Murray, 1928), 360; quotation from Coolidge's journal as minister, ibid., 353. A knowledge of classical Greek was helpful in official circles at the end of the nineteenth century, but would become less so in the decades to come as the vernacular took over. Comments by colleagues indicated that Alexander also was familiar with French; Eben Alexander Papers, SHC.

24. Since this is an all-male study group, I omit information on females in these calculations. A ratio of about one in five constitutes the proportion of school-age male Americans enrolled who went to senior high school or beyond in the school year 1889–90; about 20 percent of the nearly six million male students that year were fifteen years of age or older. All of the rest of the boys in school were youngsters in the lower grades.

What this means is that even though the United States had a literacy rate of nearly 90 percent at the turn of the century, up from 86.3 percent in 1890, the nation was far from being well educated. Many young men barely progressed into high school and comparatively few could seriously entertain the idea of obtaining a higher education. *Abstract of the Eleventh Census*, 73, 62–63, 251; U.S. Government, *Abstract of the Twelfth Census: 1900* (Washington, D.C.: Government Printing Office, 1902), 70, 15, 16.

25. Aside from James H. Mulligan, who was educated partially in Canada, this total includes Romualdo Pacheco of California, named minister to the Central American Republics in late 1890 and accredited to Guatemala and Honduras in 1891. The stepson of a sea captain, Pacheco was educated in Hawaii.

26. *New York Times*, 12 Mar. 1889, 1.

27. *Who Was Who in America* (Chicago: A. N. Marquis, 1942), 1:527.

28. Wisconsin Senator Spooner was insistent on his patronage rights (see note 20 above). In supporting Finch's nomination he asserted that the Montevideo appointment was allotted to his state; Spooner to William McKinley, 15 July 1897, Appl. Files 1897–1901, W. R. Finch.

Chapter 5

1. For one useful survey of the Foreign Service's early history, see Barnes and Morgan, *Foreign Service*, chaps. 2, 3, 5–7, 9, 10, 12, 14, 15, and app. 4. Another is John Bassett Moore, "Beginnings of American Diplomacy," *Harper's Monthly Magazine*, Mar. 1904, 497–507.

2. State *Register*, 1889, 1892; U.S. Government, *Foreign Service Careers*, Department of State Publication no. 9209, June 1984, 2; David F. Trask, "A Short History of the U.S. Department of State, 1781–1981," *Department of State Bulletin*, special supplement, 81, no. 2046 (Jan. 1981): S42; U.S. Government, *Historical Statistics of the United States, Colonial Times to 1970*, 2 parts (Washington, D.C.: Government Printing Office, 1975), 1:9. The information on Belgium's foreign service is drawn from Zara S. Steiner, ed., *The Times Survey of Foreign Ministries of the World* (London: Times Books, 1982), 81; the year in question is 1909.

3. *Historical Statistics*, 1:9; State *Register*, 1899, 1900; Trask, "A Short History of the U.S. Department of State," S35, S18, S42; State *Register*, 1889, 1892–1900. The basic act of 1856 which governed foreign service appointments and compensation did not require that appointees be American citizens.

4. Information in this and succeeding paragraphs is from *State Registers*, 1892 and 1900, and U.S. Department of State, *Diplomatic and Consular Service of the United States* (Washington, D.C.: Government Printing Office, 1890, 1892–99), hereinafter, *F.S. List*), the commonly used title, corrected to 5 Apr. 1890 and 26 Dec. 1899. No *F.S. Lists* were published in 1892. It was issued frequently in some years of the decade, however: for example, five times in 1890, seven in 1891, and four times in 1899.

5. Harold M. Sewall to Jones, 12 Feb. 1887, Appl. Files 1885–93, H. M. Sewall; Charles de Kay to Robert S. Chilton, Jr., 26 Aug. 1897, Chilton Papers, Duke. Chilton at the time was head of the Consular Bureau in the Department of State.

6. State *Register*, 1892; Consular List; *Official Register*, 1899, 1:36–37.

7. Consular List.

8. State *Register*, 1892, 1895, 1899; *F. S. List*, 5 Apr. 1890, 26 Dec. 1899. The consulate at St. Gall evidently was raised to consulate general status in 1892 to accommodate the posting of a Civil War-hero appointee, Samuel H. M. Byers, who had previously been consul general at Rome; see Iowa Senator James F. Wilson to James G. Blaine, 28 Feb. 1891, Appl. Files 1885–93, S. H. M. Byers. Both St. Gall and Apia were reduced to consulates in the early 1900s and finally closed in the 1920s; Consular List.

9. Cons. Desp., Shanghai, no. 96, 7 Jan. 1891; Department of State, "Inspection of Consulates, 1896–1897, Consular Bureau," 1:213–16; Dept. of State, "Reports of Inspections of Consulates, 1899–1900–1901–1902," China, 3:289. Both inspection reports are entry 592, RG 59.

The countries in which extraterritorial courts operated for Americans were China, Korea, Muscat, Morocco, Persia, Samoa, Siam, Tonga, Turkey, Zanzibar, and until 1898, Japan; Denby, *China and Her People* 1:85.

10. Robert S. Chilton, Jr., to Secretary Richard Olney, 8 May 1896, "Miscellaneous Reports & Correspondence on Consular Inspections, 1896–1918," entry 599, RG 59, Dept. of State. George W. Fishback to Olney, 3 Dec. 1896, "Inspection of Consulates, 1896–1897," vol. 1. Having their sons named to consular or diplomatic mission staffs was a widespread practice of senior officers throughout much of the nineteenth century.

11. Wilbur J. Carr testimony, House of Representatives, Foreign Affairs Committee, Diplomatic and Consular Appropriations bill, 1907–8, 18 Dec. 1906, manuscript copy, Wilbur John Carr Papers, LOC.

12. Ibid. Consul General Robert P. Skinner at Marseilles entered the Consular Service by examination in 1897, a product of Cleveland's reform measure of 1895, but he achieved a senior position only in 1902 and is not included in this study group.

13. Andrew D. White, *Autobiography of Andrew Dickson White* (New York: Century, 1905), 2:51–54; Harold F. Peterson, *Diplomat of the Americas: A Biography of William I. Buchanan (1852–1909)* (Albany: State Univ. of New York Press, 1977), 95; twenty-page report dated 1895 but otherwise unidentified, letterbook 1895–96, 263–283, John Barrett Papers, LOC.

14. Thomas S. Harrison, *Homely Diary of a Diplomat in the East 1897–1899* (Boston: Houghton Mifflin, 1917), quoted in Jasper Yeates Brinton, *The American Effort: A Chapter in Diplomatic History in the Nineteenth Century* (Alexandria, Egypt: By the Author, 1972), 129–30. Harrison held a decoration from the khedive of Egypt awarded in 1896 before his tour at Cairo. The late hours that he complained about are still kept in Cairo,

but the secret is that Egyptian life comes to a halt in the afternoon while everyone rests, only to revive in the evening; it is not "something in the air."

15. Merrill sent more than one hundred official messages on other subjects during his tenure. He gives the reader of the Calcutta despatch files the impression of being unhappy and somewhat lost in the assignment. He applied for leave (in effect, home leave) early in 1893, was turned down by Washington, and resigned instead.

During the 1893–94 fiscal year, no American ships called at Calcutta. The leading U.S. consular seaport for shipping that year was Honolulu with 165 vessels. Other heavily travelled ports were Hong Kong (79 ships), Yokohama (65), Rio de Janeiro (64), Liverpool (43), and Southampton and Sydney (each with 29); Bureau of Navigation, *Cong. Rec.*, 53d Cong., 3d sess., 1894–95, 27, pt. 2:1818.

16. One such instance of complexity at Halifax was the seizure by a British cruiser in 1896 of an American schooner, the *Frederick Gerring, Jr.*, for mackerel fishing allegedly inside the three-mile limit; Cons. Desp., Halifax, no. 45, 27 May 1896 and cable same date.

17. One of Mulligan's messages, despatch no. 60 of 18 June 1895, comprises thirty-two pages of text; Cons. Desp., Apia. Assistant Secretary Edwin F. Uhl required his subordinate, A. A. Adee, the longtime assistant secretary, to prepare a précis of the reports for him.

18. Dipl. Desp., Berne, no. 44, 21 May 1890.

19. Finch's despatch no. 14 of 10 Feb. 1898 reporting a coup was preceded by a long despatch on 9 Feb., with news clippings, which predicted an uprising; Dipl. Desp., Montevideo.

Finch was not universally admired. An American woman in Uruguay complained that the minister had no dignity, was ignorant and conceited, went around in tweedy farmers' clothing, looked rough, and was "utterly devoid of any knowledge of tact or diplomacy"; Maria Thurston Pease to Mrs. William McKinley, 23 July 1898, Appl. Files 1897–1901, W. R. Finch. One suspects that Mrs. Pease's criticism was overstated and derived from a social slight of some sort.

20. See Cons. Desp., London, 1889–93. One interesting example of the post's commercial focus is no. 55, 3 Feb. 1890, in response to a departmental circular request: "Refrigerators are used . . . in the larger meat and vegetable warehouses and markets, but to a very limited extent for domestic or household purposes."

21. Dickinson, "Reminiscences," 50–54.

22. Barnes and Morgan, *Foreign Service*, 106–12, 118–23; biennial *Official Register*, 1889–99; *F.S. Lists*, same period. Ministers usually were issued letters of credit against which they could draw their annual salary, plus contingency allowances. For example, the Department of State gave Minister Wayne MacVeagh, upon departure for his post at Rome, a large folio-size document authorizing him to draw against the banking firm of Brown, Shipley & Co. of London. These transactions were audited quarterly by a unit of the Treasury Department called the Office of Auditor for State and Other Departments. MacVeagh Papers, correspondence 1886–95, HSP.

23. *Official Registers, F.S. Lists*. Aside from notarials—taking oaths and witnessing signatures—unofficial fees included taking legal interrogatories and drawing up wills. The long-standing rationale for permitting consular officials to keep these fees was that it was a voluntary service, one that they provided to visiting Americans under no statutory compulsion to do so.

24. Cons. Desp., Shanghai, no. 37, 14 Mar. 1890; Oliver H. Dockery to James G. Blaine, 2 Apr. 1890, Appl. Files 1885–93, O. H. Dockery; John Barrett to Asst. Sec. of

State W. W. Rockhill, 2 Mar. 1896, letterpress book, box 3, Barrett Papers, LOC. In fiscal 1892 the consul general at Rio de Janeiro (Dockery) took in $6,972 in fees, about 90 percent of which was in official receipts and thus remitted to the Treasury Department; F.S. List, 1 Sept. 1892. The combined legation and consulate general at Bangkok had only limited fee receipts.

25. British and German salary figures are respectively from Zara S. Steiner, The Foreign Office and Foreign Policy, 1898–1914 (Cambridge: Cambridge Univ. Press, 1969), 175n, and Lamar Cecil, The German Diplomatic Service, 1871–1914 (Princeton, N.J.: Princeton Univ. Press, 1976), table 5, p. 46. I convert the mark at the rate of 4.25 to the dollar and the pound sterling at $4.87 to the pound; see Thelma Liesner, Economic Statistics, 1900–1983: United Kingdom, United States of America, France, Germany, Italy, Japan (New York: Facts on File Publications, 1985), 32.

26. Cecil, German Diplomatic Service, 54, 56.

27. Washington Post, 19 May 1887, 4; Robert R. Hitt of Illinois, Cong. Rec., 54th Cong. 2d sess., 1897–98, 29, pt. 2:1417. The official who denied the rumors about Paris was assistant secretary James D. Porter, who later, in the midnineties, was minister to Chile.

28. Robert S. Chilton, Jr., to Asst. Secretary of State W. W. Rockhill, 21 Sept. 1896, 14 Oct. 1896, Dept. of State, "Misc. Reports and Correspondence on Consular Inspections 1896–1918," entry 599, RG 59.

29. Ibid. There is no indication in these Department of State inspection files that this practice occurred at consular posts in other European countries. As an indication of the sums involved, however, in 1899 the London consulate general reported fees totalling $66,781.50. Only $7,609 of this sum was in notarial fees, however; F.S. List, 26 Dec. 1899, see appendix C.

30. Reorganization of the Consular Service Act, approved 5 Apr. 1906.

31. Quoted in Neal Allen Brooks, "The Diplomatic Career of Whitelaw Reid" (Ph.D. diss., Case Western Reserve University, 1974), 95–96. A successor to Reid, General Horace Porter, spent his entire annual salary of $17,500 on his palatial residence between the Bois de Boulogne and Avenue Victor Hugo; Elsie Porter Mende, An American Soldier and Diplomat (New York: Frederick A. Stokes Co., 1927), 180.

32. The London American, 8 July 1898, John Hay Papers, LOC. Dining out or attending receptions, the reciprocal of hospitality offered in the line of duty, can be demanding as well. During Hay's first three weeks in England as ambassador he was obliged to decline twenty-six dinner invitations; Hay to John Cabot Lodge, 6 May 1897, Hay Papers, LOC.

33. Oscar S. Straus, "Diplomatic Diary Turkey 1898–99–1900," 219, box 22, Oscar S. Straus Papers, LOC; James M. Swank (gen. mgr., American Iron & Steel Co.) to President Harrison, 20 May 1889, Appl. Files 1885–93, A. L. Snowden.

34. Barnes and Morgan, Foreign Service, 263. An exception was the legation compound at Peking; it was leased over a period of many years. See Dipl. Desp., Peking, no. 86, 10 Aug. 1875 and no. 2910, 13 Apr. 1898.

35. White, Autobiography, 2, 50.

36. François Charles-Roux, Souvenirs Diplomatiques d'un Age Révolu (Paris: A. Fayard, 1956), 10–11, translation by this writer. The diplomatic corps at St. Petersburg in July 1896 consisted of seven ambassadors, fifteen ministers (including the American), one chargé d'affaires, and one separate military representative (from Austria-Hungary); Russian diplomatic list (in French) of that date, box no. 872, Clifton Rodes Breckenridge Papers, LOC.

In 1908 a newspaper correspondent observed that to find an American consulate in a

Chinese city "it is usually necessary to employ a guide," whereas one "never" had to ask the way to the "imposing structures" of the British or the Germans; *Washington Evening Star,* 19 Feb. 1908.

37. *Boston Daily Advertiser* clipping, 20 Mar. 1899, box 33, Joseph Hodges Choate Papers, LOC; Edward Sanford Martin, ed., *The Life of Joseph Hodges Choate: As Gathered Chiefly From His Letters* (New York: Charles Scribner's Sons, 1920), 2:85; K. Baedecker, *London and its Environs* (London, 1894). The Boston newspaper noted as "a national humiliation and scandal" the lack of a suitable permanent residence for the American ambassador.

38. Lloyd C. Griscom, *Diplomatically Speaking* (New York: Little, Brown and Company, 1940), 47, 131, 142; D. N. Demetriades to Robert S. Chilton, Jr., 23 July 1897, Chilton Papers, Duke; Lloyd C. Griscom to Rodman E. Griscom, 3 Nov. 1899, box 2, Lloyd Carpenter Griscom Papers, LOC. Griscom was Straus's secretary of legation at Constantinople.

39. Brooks, "Whitelaw Reid," 57; K. Baedeker, *Paris and Environs* (Leipsig, 1891), 45, (Leipsig, 1898), 50; Willson, *America's Ambassadors to France,* 336, 366. An inventory of the Paris consulate general's furniture in 1890 shows that the facility consisted of an entryway, six officers, a kitchen, and two closets; Cons. Desp. no. 5, 1 Sept. 1890, Paris. There is no mention of the condition of the furnishings, but the inventory covers as well various files, records, and books. Lloyd C. Griscom, who was Ambassador Bayard's private secretary and who later rose to ambassadorial rank himself, remarked that the London embassy on Victoria Street was located on the ground floor of a "gloomy, grimy building"; the ambassador's office was a "small, dark, noisy room" that opened directly onto the street; *Diplomatically Speaking,* 20.

40. Robert S. Chilton, Jr., to Richard Olney, 15 May 1896, "Consular Inspections 1896–1918"; George W. Fishback to Olney, 3 Dec. 1896, "Inspection of Consulates 1896–1897," vol. 1; Cons. Desp., Halifax no. 8, 19 Sept. 1893, and no. 46, 7 Mar. 1896. The annual rent at Halifax went down from $352 to $200.

41. Dept. of State despatch no. 36 to Consulate Smyrna (Consul James H. Madden), 29 Apr. 1896, Dickinson Papers, LOC; George W. Fishback, "Inspection of Consulates, 1896–1897," 1:235–39. Vifquain explained his action by stating somewhat lamely that he understood it was done by all in order to make up other out-of-pocket costs.

42. Chilton to Olney, 8 May 1896, "Consular Inspections 1896–1918"; "Inspection of Consulates 1899– . . . 1902," 3:288, 291–93. News reports of a few years later indicate that the Shanghai consulate general quarters were decidedly second-rate, although it is not clear whether they were the same as those remarked above; *Washington Evening Star,* 19 Feb. 1908.

43. Willis Sutter, "This Was Bangkok at the Turn of the Century," *State* 284 (Dec. 1985): 14–15. The tradition-minded French to this day have their mission at the same location and in the same buildings. The equally tradition-minded British have moved, however.

44. Chilton to W. W. Rockhill, 14 Oct. 1896, 8 Dec. 1896, "Consular Inspections 1896–1918"; Baedeker, *London,* 49; *The Rhine from Rotterdam to Constance* (Leipsig, 1892), 203; *Italy* (London, 1890), 111.

45. Trask, "A Short History of the U.S. Department of State," S18.

46. Peterson, *Diplomat of the Americas,* 78.

47. Dipl. Desp., Austria, no. 7, 28 July 1893 (emphasis added).

48. Dipl. Desp., Chile, no. 10, 29 July 1893, and no. 4, 10 July 1893.

49. Dipl. Desp., Uruguay & Paraguay, unnumbered, 9 July 1897 and 7 Feb. 1898.

50. White to Oscar S. Straus, 14 June 1894, box 2, Straus Papers, LOC; Bayard to Wayne MacVeagh, 7 Mar. 1896, MacVeagh Papers, HSP.

51. Henry M. Smythe (at Port-au-Prince) to Solicitor of Dept. Walter D. Dabney, 4 Apr. 1895, W. D. Dabney Papers, Barrett Library, University of Virginia, Charlottesville, Va.; Oscar S. Straus to John Hay, 2 Apr. 1899, box 3, Straus Papers, LOC. Regarding Straus's post, Constantinople, his secretary of legation complained that "the responsibility of this post is great . . . and it is very easy to get into trouble. The criticism of the missionaries is tremendous if a small mistake is made & the place is full of soreheads who have bones to pick with the Legation." Lloyd C. Griscom to Rodman E. Griscom, 23 Nov. 1899, Griscom Papers, LOC.

52. Eben Alexander to C. M. McClung, 20 Mar. 1894, 8 Aug. 1894, 9 Nov. 1894, Alexander Papers, SHC. Professor Alexander got his spoils-system appointment under unusual circumstances. Out of the blue, with no political background, he asked for the job and was successful. In 1893, deciding that the only way he could ever afford to spend a few years in the land whose language and history had been his lifelong speciality, he went to Washington to ask the new president for the post at Athens. He so impressed Cleveland, according to press accounts, that the president promptly named him to head the legation. See unidentified news clippings, folder 23, Alexander Papers. On Horton, see Nancy Horton, "Quest for a Consulship," *Foreign Service Journal* 62 (May 1985): 38–39.

53. Henry White to John Hay, 6 Mar. 1898, Henry White Papers, LOC. The text reads in part: "I have just had a letter from Rockhill who finds Athens deadly dull. . . . How lamentable that such material of which the value would be inestimable in China should be wasted in Athens." Rockhill's wife died at Athens during the assignment. Ambassador to Italy Wayne MacVeagh of Pennsylvania similarly found Rome dull in 1896. He had favorable comments on the Italian climate and cultural scene in a letter to the family lawyer, but complained, "I fear lack of interesting *work* is nearly getting on my nervous system." MacVeagh to John J. Pinkerton, 19 Apr. 1896, MacVeagh Papers, HSP, emphasis in original.

The diary of White, who was the senior secretary on Ambassador Hay's London staff, is of interest in that it illuminates the pace and style of diplomatic life in that era. His journals in the Library of Congress are complete for some 15 months in the period 1892–94. I selected one week at random—the week of Monday, Feb. 13 to Sunday, Feb. 19, 1893—to get a sense of his workload and activities. Upon return that Monday from the usual weekend in the country, White first went to Christies for a purchase, then briefly to the legation, and soon to the House of Commons to hear Gladstone introduce the Irish Home Rule bill. In the evening he went to a music hall. This set the tone, with some variations, for his week. White dined out four evenings and possibly a fifth (the entry is not clear on this point); he listened to debates in the House on three other occasions; he visited Purdy's, the famed gunmakers; he and the American minister, Robert Todd Lincoln, interviewed the guardian of the heiress to the Hawaiian throne and sent a cable on the conversation to Washington (annexation was an important pending issue at the time). On Saturday White visited a school at Uxbridge to pass on its suitability for his son and on Sunday he attended worship at Westminster Abbey with his family. That week was replete with meetings with political leaders—Haldan, Balfour, Asquith, John Morley—and royalty—the Prince of Wales and the Duke of York. He evidently visited the legation each workday at about 11:30 A.M. for only a short period of time; no punching the time clock for him. See diaries, box 1, White Papers, LOC.

54. Elting E. Morison et. al., eds., *The Letters of Theodore Roosevelt: The Square Deal, 1901–1903* (Cambridge, Mass.: Harvard Univ. Press, 1951), 3:310n.

55. For a reiteration of this point on policy roles by a retired Foreign Service officer, see Leon B. Poullada, "Leaders and Experts: The Professional Solution," *Foreign Service Journal* 63 (Oct. 1986): 24–25.

Chapter 6

1. In 1985 Under Secretary of State Ronald I. Spiers phrased this last responsibility in this manner: "To influence the environment in which the United States acts in ways favorable to the attainment of U.S. policy objectives. . . . " This formulation obviously was designed as a statement appropriate to the 1980s, but it is an elaborate way of saying much the same thing as "showing the flag." U.S. Government, Department of State, Current Policy no. 747, Oct. 1985, "Managing the Department of State," address delivered 26 Sept. 1985 at Washington, D.C.

2. LaFeber, *The New Empire*, chaps. 3 and 4; see also Samuel Flagg Bemis, *The Latin American Policy of the United States: An Historical Interpretation* (New York: Harcourt, Brace & World, 1943), chaps. 7 and 8, and Dexter Perkins, *The Monroe Doctrine, 1867–1907* (Baltimore: The Johns Hopkins Press, 1937), chaps. 1 and 3.

3. Mizner's entry in *The National Cyclopaedia of American Biography* (New York: James T. White Company, 1907), 5:556, asserts that he was at the legation from 1840 to 1844, at a time when he was a teenager, a claim that is supported by a biographic note in his file in the Prints and Photographs Division, LOC. If the information is correct, he was an unpaid clerk; the Diplomatic List for New Grenada, the appellation of Colombia at the time, does not include his name, and the Consular List shows no officers assigned to the post before 1851.

4. See listing in U.S. Government, *Papers Relating to the Foreign Relations of the United States, 1890* (Washington, D.C.: Government Printing Office, 1891), xxxiv–xxxviii; henceforward these documents, published annually in one volume during the period, are cited as *FRUS*, by year.

As useful as the *Foreign Relations* volumes are, criticisms of the series are valid, especially as to the twentieth-century record and the increasing delays in publication of documents. See Richard W. Leopold, "The *Foreign Relations* Series: A Centennial Estimate," *Mississippi Valley Historical Review* 49 (Mar. 1963): 595–612, and "The *Foreign Relations* Series Revisited: One Hundred Plus Ten," *Journal of American History* 59 (Mar. 1973): 935–57. The publication must be used with the recognition that standards for including or excluding material were almost capricious in the early years. But with respect to the period under review in this study, even critic Leopold notes in the first article cited above that "until the War with Spain, nobody seemed to worry whether the series . . . affected current policy"; if the volumes for that era are not especially informative, "the dullness of American foreign policy . . . is partly to blame" (598). In the case of the China records, Professor Michael H. Hunt has suggested to me that they may be dull because "hot" items, or messages that might be politically embarrassing, were expurgated before publication. In my review of the presumably complete 1890s Peking despatch files, however, I found no messages obviously of this type that had been left out.

5. Dipl. Desp., Guatemala, no. 150, 19 Aug. 1890, encl. no. 5.

6. Dipl. Desp., State teleg., 30 Aug. 1890; State despatch no. 206, 18 Nov. 1890. All of the cited messages can be found in *FRUS, 1890*.

Eyewitness accounts of Barrundia's death indicate that he did put up a fight and that he fired the first shot. His days surely would have been numbered if he had been taken into custody, but he was not murdered out of hand, it would seem. See *FRUS, 1890, 86, 108,*

109. After the imbroglio and his dismissal, Mizner returned to California, where he died in 1893 at his daughter's home in the Napa Valley; internal LOC memorandum, 23 June 1941, Lansing B. Mizner subject file, Prints and Photographs Division, LOC.

7. Crittenden's letter file for 1896 alone contains almost five hundred pages of such outgoing correspondence, nearly all handwritten; letterpress 1896, Thomas Theodore Crittenden Papers, Western Historical Manuscript Collection (WHMC), Univ. of Missouri, Columbia. Only the letter file for that year is held in the collection although he was at post from 1893 to 1897. In one message he informed the Senate Appropriations Committee chairman of his need to hire "an operator on the typewriter."

Perhaps Crittenden's chief claim to historical fame is his role in the demise of the Jesse James gang of the 1880s. While governor, he issued the reward proclamation that led to Jesse James's death in April 1882, and it was to him personally that brother Frank surrendered later that year. By cable of 13 June 1893 to Secretary Walter Q. Gresham, Crittenden declined appointment as envoy to the "Sandwich Islands"—Hawaii, that is; Crittenden Papers, WHMC.

8. Some of his 1896 correspondence is in Walter V. Scholes, "Mexico in 1896 as Viewed by an American Consul," *The Hispanic American Historical Review* 30 (May 1950): 250–57. The quoted phrases are from Crittenden to Allison, 11 Feb. 1896, and to F. B. Thurbur, 3 Mar. 1896.

9. Crittenden to H. W. Wheeler, 16 Mar. 1896, Crittenden Papers, WHMC. Scholes does not mention this letter in his article. Foreign Service officers of today frequently are subjected to such unfocussed, comprehensive information requirements, but are not often able to offer his blunt response.

10. Scholes, "Mexico in 1896," 257.

11. The strain derived from riots following a fracas involving crew members of the USS *Baltimore* in Valparaiso harbor in October 1896. Details of the serious disturbances from the United States' point of view are in several legation and U.S. Navy reports; FRUS, *1891*, esp. 204–9. A summary of the Chilean version of events is in a Ministry of Foreign Relations note dated 30 Oct. 1891; ibid., 213–14. H. C. Evans, Jr. *Chile and Its Relations with the United States* (Durham, N.C.: Duke Univ. Press, 1927), 145–52, is a useful brief account of the incident. As background to the strained relations, see Osgood Hardy, "The Itata Incident," *Hispanic American Historical Review* 5 (May 1922): 195–226.

12. Political action and the appointment process are discussed in Thomas N. Brown, *Irish-American Nationalism, 1870–1890* (Philadelphia: Lippincott, 1966), chap. 8. Egan is mentioned frequently in the Irish context in Conor Cruise O'Brien, *Parnell and His Party, 1880–1890* (Oxford: Clarendon Press, 1957); on page 187 he is termed one of "the two greatest non-parliamentary land leaguers."

13. See FRUS, *1891*, 91–284; summaries of the messages are on pages XLVIII–LVII. For the misrepresentation charge see Morgan, *From Hayes to McKinley*, 360. LaFeber is not among Egan's critics, even though he finds little to approve in America's policy toward Chile; *The New Empire*, 130–36.

14. *New York Tribune*, 6 Sept. 1891, clipping in MacVeagh Papers, HSP; David Louis Reading, "The United States Press and the Chilean Civil War of 1891" (master's thesis, University of North Carolina at Chapel Hill, 1971), 69–77.

15. FRUS, *1891*, 194, 196–97; FRUS, *1892*, xiii–xiv. Foreign observers took note. As a British diplomat in Washington reported to the Foreign Office, "What will the United States be like when their fleet is more powerful?" Quotation in Armin Rappaport, *A History of American Diplomacy* (New York: Macmillan, 1975), 184–85.

16. [Irving L. Thompson], Allen Johnson & Dumas Malone, eds., *Dictionary of Amer-*

ican Biography (New York: Scribner, 1931), 3:51–52. The entry also notes his political career in Ireland and the controversy that accompanied his tour in Chile. On the admiration by the British minister, see Campbell, *Transformation of American Foreign Relations*, 172. He is defended generally by Reading and by Osgood Hardy in "Was Egan a 'Blundering Minister'?" *Hispanic American Historical Review* 8 (Feb. 1928): 65–81. John A. S. Grenville and George B. Young note that the archives and the perspective of history "exonerate" Egan; see their *Politics, Strategy, and American Diplomacy: Studies in Foreign Policy, 1873–1917* (New Haven: Yale Univ. Press, 1966), 98.

Egan defended himself against criticism vigorously at the time. As he departed the post for United States, he sent a letter to the editor of the Valparaiso *La Union* of 29 July 1893 in which he gave a detailed justification of his handling of the *Baltimore* affair and in which he attacked one of his critics, the "renegade" Wayne MacVeagh; unidentified newspaper clipping, MacVeagh Papers, HSP.

17. Dipl. Desp., Central American States, Managua cable of 27 Apr. 1895, received in Washington 29 Apr.; Managua cables of 10 June, 19 June, 20 July 1894, see also earlier cables 1 Apr. through 28 May 1894; Managua desp. no. 375, 8 Aug. 1894, no. 378, 30 Aug. 1894, and no. 373, 27 Aug. 1894. The two Americans affected were J. S. Lampton and George B. Wiltbank, local businessmen.

18. Memorandum by Bayard, 23 Nov. 1894, after conversation with Foreign Secretary Lord Kimberley; quoted in Charles C. Tansill, *The Foreign Policy of Thomas F. Bayard, 1885–1897* (New York: Fordham Univ. Press, 1940), 680–84; Dipl. Desp., Managua, no. 412, 11 Oct. 1894; ibid., San José, cable of 13 Apr. 1895; Lewis Baker to Foreign Minister José Madriz, 14 Apr. 1895, Dipl. Desp. San José microfilm reel 80; *FRUS, 1895*, pt. 1:697.

19. LaFeber, *The New Empire*, 222–25; Walter Q. Gresham to Thomas F. Bayard, 2 May 1894, Walter Quentin Gresham Papers, LOC.

20. The reason for Salisbury's delay is unclear, but Bayard reported that Salisbury had been tied up with the Turkish problem, a speech at Brighton, and the death in London of the Turkish ambassador. See Bayard to Olney, 23 Nov. 1895, Thomas F. Bayard Papers, LOC.

21. John Hay, who replaced him at London, found other grounds for criticism: he derided Bayard's "usual blundering gushing style" of speech; quoted in Kenton J. Clymer, *John Hay: The Gentleman as Diplomat* (Ann Arbor: Univ. of Michigan Press, 1975), 104. An example of Bayard's effusive style is to be found in an 1897 letter home. Complaining about the stresses of his ambassadorial job, he wrote: "A man standing alone in such a surging sea of . . . variant interests feels at times a sense of [despair], but swimming along with uplifted eye to the pole star of a plain duty, he at length feels the *aid* of the current." Thomas F. Bayard to William Pepper, 13 Mar. 1897, Pepper Papers, Univ. of Pennsylvania, emphasis in original. Even for the Victorian Age, the metaphors are strained.

22. Cleveland to Charles S. Fairchild, a New York lawyer, 9 May 1895, in Allan Nevins, ed., *The Letters of Grover Cleveland* (New York: Houghton Mifflin, 1933), 392. Two of the several who turned him down wrote the president explaining the personal or professional reasons for their refusal; educator John E. Russell of Massachusetts to Cleveland, 12 Apr. 1895, and New York attorney (and former assistant secretary of state) George L. Rives to Cleveland, 9 May 1895, Cleveland Papers, LOC. After several men refused the post, he named Allen Thomas.

23. As far back as 1865 Stuart published a work that includes a dictionary of the Snake and Chinook tongues; Granville Stuart, *Montana As It Is; Being a General Description of Its Resources, Both Mineral and Agricultural, Including a Complete Description of the Face of*

the Country, Its Climate, Etc. (1865; rpt. New York: Arno Press, 1973).

24. Dipl. Desp., Montevideo, no. 131, 26 Aug. 1897. Stuart's message is seven pages long, handwritten as nearly all despatches still were in the nineties.

25. The published Department of State record of foreign affairs for 1897 does not include Stuart's first-rate eyewitness report of the assassination, illustrating perhaps the uncertain standards of the day for inclusion of documents in the official *Foreign Affairs* series.

26. *New York Times*, 14 Apr. 1896, 5. Williams sent close to three thousand serially numbered despatches during the twelve years he was consul general; *FRUS, 1896*. His reporting through the years "prophetically" highlighted the significance of increasing Cuban-American economic ties; Louis A. Perez, Jr., *Cuba Between Empires, 1878–1902* (Pittsburgh: Univ. of Pittsburgh Press, 1983), 28–30, 123.

27. Cons. Desp., Havana, no. 749, 18 Jan. 1898.

28. Hugh Thomas, *Cuba: The Pursuit of Freedom* (New York: Harper & Row, 1971), 343 (the "firebrand" phrase is Thomas's); *New York Times*, 7 Mar. 1898, 1. Shortly thereafter, in an article on Cuba's plight, Lee described his protection activities on behalf of Americans; "Cuba and Her Struggle for Freedom," *The Fortnightly Review* 63 (1 June 1898): 861–62.

The downward spiral of United States-Spanish relations can be seen in perspective by perusing the published record, the annual *Foreign Relations* series of the Department of State, in addition to diplomatic and consular despatches. In 1896, the first full year after renewed rebellion in Cuba and the year Spain's notorious reconcentration policy was instituted, the published record covers in detail the protection activities of Consuls General Williams and, later, Lee. This consular correspondence and reporting takes up most of the 265 pages of closely printed text devoted to relations with Spain; there are only a few messages included which involve Madrid or the Spanish embassy in Washington. *FRUS, 1896*, 582–847. In the next two years, this emphasis shifted in the published record; United States-Spanish relations took precedence (see note 35 below).

A detailed if sometimes imaginative account of Williams's and Lee's representations on behalf of American citizens in Cuba is in Henry B. Russell, *Our War With Spain* (Hartford, Conn.: Hartford Publishing Company, 1899), chaps. 14, 16, 18, 20, 21. Perez, *Cuba Between Empires*, focusses more on the broad political-economic issues raised by the United States' relations with Spain and Cuba. For a longer-range perspective over the years, see Lester D. Langley, *The Cuban Policy of the United States: A Brief History* (New York: Wiley, 1968), which has less than two hundred pages of text. A very comprehensive study that encompasses those same relations is Thomas, *Cuba*, a volume of almost fifteen hundred pages not including appendixes.

29. *FRUS, 1897*, xi. Despite the importance of the subject matter, the slimmed-down 1897 volume contains only fifty-seven pages of selected materials on the United States' relations with Spain.

30. On Taylor's competence as a diplomatic envoy, see Ernest R. May, *The Imperial Democracy: The Emergence of America as a Great Power* (New York: Harcourt, Brace and World, 1961), 86, and the balanced assessment of Tennant S. McWilliams, *Hannis Taylor: The New Southerner as an American* (University: Univ. of Alabama Press, 1978).

31. George W. Brush (New York state senator) to William McKinley, 11 Jan. 1897, Appl. Files 1897–1901, S. L. Woodford.

32. Richard Olney to Hilary A. Herbert (secretary of the navy), 14 July 1896, Hilary Abner Herbert Papers, SHC. Lee wanted the ship, captained by a "discreet" officer and with a full complement of marines, to stand by under his orders in case of need. The

request did not strike Olney favorably at that time.

33. Herbert Papers, SHC. The quoted phrase is from Lee's cable of 4 Feb. 1898.

34. *FRUS, 1898,* 1024–29.

35. *FRUS, 1898,* 747. The Department of State's published record on Spanish-American relations for 1898 is unusually extensive. The *Foreign Relations* volume includes messages, diplomatic notes, despatches, and telegrams on a wide variety of subjects related to the dramatic course of those relations during the year. *FRUS, 1898* was published in 1901, remarkably speedily by current standards.

36. *The* (Jacksonville) *Times-Union and Citizen,* 23 Apr. 1898, 1; *New York Times,* 22 Apr. 1898, 1, 23 Apr. 1898, 7.

37. Smith, *Rise of Industrial America,* 866. See also Dennis, *Adventures in American Diplomacy,* 68, 75. His correspondence with McKinley is included in Philip S. Foner, *The Spanish-Cuban-American War and the Birth of American Imperialism, 1895–1902,* 2 vols. (New York: International Publishers, 1972). Foner's revisionist orientation is indicated by the title of the work.

38. Alfred T. Mahan, *The Influence of Sea Power upon History, 1660–1783* (Boston, 1890). Capt. Mahan's influential work was first published in Boston by Little, Brown & Company and in England the same year by Sampson Low, Marston and Company. It went through numerous reprintings in subsequent years. A useful recent version is *The Influence of Sea Power Upon History, 1660–1805* (Englewood Heights, N.J.: Prentice-Hall, 1980), which incorporates as abridgment of the 1890 work and extracts from Mahan's *The Influence of Sea Power Upon the French Revolution, 1793–1812* (1892). The gist of his idea is that national strength depends on free access to sea lanes for international trade. Sea power is not simply a mass of warships, but rather is "the sum total of forces and factors, tools and geographical circumstances, which operated to gain command of the sea"; William E. Livezey, *Mahan on Sea Power* (Norman, Okla.: Univ. of Oklahoma Press, 1947), 277. See also Robert Seager II, *Alfred Thayer Mahan: The Man and His Letters* (Annapolis: Naval Institute Press, 1977).

39. *FRUS, 1894,* xi. Appendix 2 to this volume, "Affairs in Hawaii," also published in Washington in 1895, is a compendium of documents furnished to the House and Senate, 53d Congress, 2d sess. Its 1,397 pages of text cover United States-Hawaiian relations from 1820 through the annexation crisis of 1893. The selection of documents by the new Cleveland administration includes a wide range of state papers and reports.

40. *FRUS, 1894,* 169–70, see also 1157–60; Morgan quoted in Joseph A. Fry, "John Tyler Morgan's Southern Expansionism," *Diplomatic History* 9 (Fall 1985): 339; *FRUS, 1894,* 2:1165, 1167.

41. Following are examples of characterizations of Stevens by historians: "An ardent annexationist"; Alexander DeConde, *A History of American Foreign Policy* (New York: Charles Scribner's Sons, 1963), 327. "In 1889 . . . Stevens became the United States Minister to Hawaii. He enthusiastically urged annexation. . . . He did not keep his feelings secret either from Americans in Hawaii or from his sympathetic superiors in Washington"; Wayne S. Cole, *An Interpretive History of American Foreign Relations,* rev. ed. (Homewood, Ill.: Dorsey Press, 1974), 208. "An active partisan for annexation"; Thomas G. Paterson, J. Garry Clifford, Kenneth J. Hagan, *American Foreign Policy: A History* (Lexington, Mass.: D.C. Heath and Co., 1977), 174. He was "a longstanding friend" of Secretary Blaine. "One may assume that Stevens shared Blaine's [annexationist] ideas"; Campbell, *Transformation of America Foreign Relations,* 178. See also LaFeber, *The New Empire,* 141, and standard biographic references which portray him as an enthusiastic advocate of Hawaiian annexation from the time of his appointment.

42. Dipl. Desp., Honolulu, no. 3, 7 Oct. 1889; no. 18, 10 Feb. 1890; no. 10, 4 Nov. 1889; no. 11, 14 Nov. 1889; no. 17, 7 Feb. 1890. The quoted phrase is in despatch no. 10.

43. Ibid., no. 20, 20 Mar. 1890. Stevens had been at post about six months. I too found through the years serving abroad that about six months at a post was sufficient time to settle in and reach a fair understanding of the local scene.

44. Dipl. Desp., Honolulu, no 46, 8 Feb. 1892.

45. Ibid., no. 48, 8 Mar. 1892. In the margin of the summary cover sheet of the Washington copy of this message is the notation, "This despatch was not answered. Alvey A. Adee Dec. 11, 1893." That entry is marked through; substituted for it is the phrase, "No answer was found to this despatch 12/11/93." There is no indication as to who made the second notation, but the assumption of this writer is that an archivist or Department of State clerk wrote the remark; the handwriting is different.

46. Ibid., no. 74, 20 Nov. 1892. Other messages in this series are no. 70, 8 Oct. 1892; no. 72, 31 Oct. 1892; and no. 73, 8 Nov. 1892.

47. Ibid., no. 79, 18 Jan. 1893, received in Washington on 14 Feb. Stevens also sent the text of a cable by ship the same day to San Francisco for transmission to the department; it was received on 28 Jan.

48. Ibid., no. 84, 1 Feb. 1893.

49. FRUS, 1894, Appendix 2, 221, Dept. of State cable, 28 Jan. 1893; ibid; 240–42, Dept. cable 11 Feb. 1893; Dipl. Desp., Honolulu, cable via Navy Dept., 1 Mar. 1893, received 9 Mar. The quoted phrase is the indented comment of Asst. Secretary Alvey A. Adee.

50. Department of State, United States Relations With China (Washington, D.C., 1949), no. 3573, Far Eastern Series 30, pp. 1, 2.

51. On this subject see Michael H. Hunt, The Making of a Special Relationship: The United States and China to 1914 (New York: Columbia Univ. Press, 1983); Marilyn Blatt Young, "American Expansion, 1870–1900: The Far East," in American Expansionism: The Critical Issues, ed. Young (Boston: Little, Brown and Company, 1973), 83–101; John K. Fairbank, " 'American China Policy' to 1898: A Misconception," Pacific Historical Review 39 (1970): 409–20; and David L. Anderson, Imperialism and Idealism: American Diplomats in China, 1861–1898 (Bloomington: Indiana Univ. Press, 1985).

52. Hunt, Making of a Special Relationship, 162.

53. Dipl. Desp., Peking, no. 1074, 28 Mar. 1890; no. 1151, 20 Aug. 1890.

54. Dipl. Desp., Peking, no. 2172, 22 Mar. 1895; Hunt, Making of a Special Relationship, 162–68. "I have devoted a great deal of time and labor to the promotion of railroad projects," Denby wrote shortly before leaving the post; Dipl. Desp., Peking, no. 2905, 5 Apr. 1898.

55. In 1897 Denby caused to be sent to the Department of State numerous identically worded petitions with multiple signatures in support of his desire to stay as minister to China, 127 of which still repose in his file in the National Archives; Appl. Files 1897–1901, C. Denby. Most of these petitions originated in his home state of Indiana, but many were from other far-flung locales, including a number signed by Americans resident in China.

56. Denby's last message was serially numbered 2,958, which meant that he, with his relatively large (for the day) American staff, had sent an average annually of more than 227 despatches over the years he was at post.

57. Beisner, From the Old Diplomacy, 28. "There is a patriotism of race as well as of country," wrote former Secretary of State Richard Olney in his article, "International

Isolation of the United States," *Atlantic Monthly* 81 (May 1898): 588.

58. *FRUS, 1890*, 511–20; the quoted despatch is no. 71 on page 519. As an indication of the surface transit time for communications from Athens to Washington, that despatch was received almost three weeks later, on 5 Jan. 1891.

Official life at one of the usually slow-paced posts, Port-au-Prince, still permitted Minister Frederick Douglass to send a total of seventy-eight despatches to Washington in 1890; Norma Browne, ed., *A Black Diplomat in Haiti: The Diplomatic Correspondence of U.S. Minister Frederick Douglass From Haiti, 1889–1891*, 2 vols. (Salisbury, N.C.: Documentary Publications, 1977).

59. Information in this paragraph is from Cons. Desp., St. Petersburg and Paris, 1890–92; Appl. Files 1889–93, A. E. King. King usually was addressed as "general"; *New York Times*, 5 Oct. 1890, 1, and his Appl. File. He was a brevet brigadier; Warner, *Generals in Blue*, 588.

As one comparison of numbers of despatches sent, in 1890 the Shanghai consulate general forwarded seventy-four such messages, routine and not so routine, to the department; Cons. Desp., Shanghai, 1890–91.

60. Dipl. Desp., Vienna, no. 73, 16 June 1898. Emphasis in original.

61. *New York Times*, 17 May 1889, 1.

62. Appl. Files 1885–93, Z. T. Sweeny.

63. Appl. Files 1893–97, L. Short. Short had travelled abroad previously, but it is not clear to what extent or where. His master's thesis at Michigan appropriately enough was on diplomatic privileges and immunities.

64. Beisner, *From the Old Diplomacy*, 7.

Chapter 7

1. Ernest Satow, *A Guide to Diplomatic Practice*, 4th ed., Nevile Bland, ed. (London: Longmans, Green, 1957); Abba Eban, *The New Diplomacy: International Affairs in the Modern Age* (New York: Random House, 1983); Charles O. Thayer, *Diplomat* (New York: Harper and Brothers, 1959); John R. Wood and Jean Serres, *Diplomatic Ceremonial and Protocol: Principles, Procedures & Practices* (New York: Columbia Univ. Press, 1970); Bailey, *The Art of Diplomacy*. See also Samuel Flagg Bemis, *John Quincy Adams and the Foundations of American Diplomacy* (New York: Knopf, 1956). Consul Wood, incidentally, was at the Paris embassy for well over thirty years and was my chief of section for some months in the late 1950s.

2. Agriculture, fisheries, and mining accounted for the bulk of the workers, some 8.3 million males. No fewer than 7.6 million men and boys were agricultural laborers or farmers, including the comparatively small number of planters and overseers. Trade and transport, the next largest overall category in 1890, included more than a half million clerks, nearly that many unspecified retailers, and well over 365,000 teamsters and draymen. Miscellaneous railway workers other than locomotive engineers and firemen numbered 383,000. *Abstract of the Eleventh Census*, 76–79.

3. John S. Brubacher and Willis Rudy, *Higher Education in Transition: A History of American Colleges and Universities, 1636–1968* (1958; rpt. New York: Harper & Row, 1968), 64, 161; *Abstract of the Eleventh Census*, 73, 62; Henry Steele Commager, "The College in American Education," in *The Past, Present and Future of American Higher Education*, ed. Judyth L. Schaubhut (n.p.: Soc. for College & Univ. Planning, 1978), 5; *Abstract of the Twelfth Census*, 70, 15.

4. The quoted phrase is used by Pessen, "Social Structure and Politics in American

History," 1315. See also note 19, chapter 2.

5. Quoted in Waldo H. Heinrichs, Jr., *American Ambassador: Joseph C. Grew and the Development of the United States Diplomatic Tradition* (Boston: Little, Brown and Company, 1966), 32. Yet Penfield is decsribed as "able" and "tactful" in *Encyclopedia of American Foreign Policy: Studies of the Principal Movements and Ideas*, ed. Alexander DeConde (New York: Charles Scribner's Sons, 1978), 3:1084. His correspondence and reports from the period 1910–13 leave one with a sense, contrary to Grew's assessment, that he was reasonable and good humored; Frederic C. Penfield Papers, HSP.

6. Post Wheeler and Halley Erminie Rives, *Dome of Many-Colored Glass* (New York: Doubleday, 1955), 377; Thomas N. Cridler (Third Asst. Sec. of State) to Wildman, 11 Sept. 1899. See also S. M. Williams to Wildman, 25 July 1898, and William Randolph Hearst cable to Wildman, 2 June 1899. All of the messages to Wildman are in Edwin and Rounseville Wildman Papers, LOC.

7. Appl. Files 1897–1901, H. M. Smythe, W. F. Powell; Appl. Files 1876–85, E. W. P. Smith, H. Clay Whittaker to John Sherman (Sec. of State), 26 Feb. 1897, Appl. Files 1897–1901, V. L. Polk.

8. William Phillips, *Ventures in Diplomacy* (Boston: Beacon Press, 1953), 47–48.

9. William Roscoe Thayer, *The Life and Letters of John Hay* (Boston: Houghton Mifflin, 1915), 2:244; "Inspection Report of Herbert H. D. Peirce." Peirce's long report, including sixty-two pages of exhibits on the Goodnow inspection, reaches no formal conclusions on the allegations against him, but the weight of the evidence leaves one with little doubt that there was substance to the charges.

10. Ernest R. May, *American Imperialism: A Speculative Essay* (New York: Atheneum, 1968), 113; Barbara W. Tuchman, *The Proud Tower: A Portrait of the World Before the War, 1890–1914* (New York: Bantam, 1967), 293.

11. Thomas A. Bailey, "A Hall of Fame for American Diplomats," in *Essays Diplomatic and Undiplomatic of Thomas A. Bailey*, ed. Alexander DeConde and Armin Rappaport (New York: Appleton-Century-Crofts, 1969), 66; Phillips, *Ventures in Diplomacy*, 9.

12. D. N. Demetriades to Robert S. Chilton, Jr., 20 Oct. 1897 and 2 Dec. 1897, Chilton Papers, Duke.

13. Dennis, *Adventures in American Diplomacy*, 451.

14. Ernest May characterizes Coolidge as "a prototype member of what today we call the foreign policy establishment"; *American Imperialism*, 45. He also pins the "robber baron" tag on him (45–46).

15. In an interview upon return from Rio de Janeiro in 1893, Conger demonstrated both a high degree of articulateness and an apparently deep familiarity with the Brazilian political scene; *Washington Post*, 7 Oct. 1893, 1.

16. The quoted phrase is the title of a biography of his father; Leonard Hal Bridges, *Iron Millionaire: Life of Charlemagne Tower* (Philadelphia: Univ. of Pennsylvania Press, 1952).

17. Theodore Roosevelt to Cecil Spring-Rice, 11 Apr. 1908, in *Letters of Theodore Roosevelt* 6:1002. David J. Hill was the relatively impecunious replacement.

18. Joseph C. Grew, *Turbulent Era: A Diplomatic Record of Forty Years, 1904–1945* (Boston: Houghton Mifflin, 1952), 1:38.

19. Robert R. Chilton, Jr., to W. W. Rockhill, 5 Apr. 1897, "Inspection of Consulates 1896–1897," vol. 1. On Mason, see also letter of support from S. L. Clemens (Mark Twain) to Grover Cleveland, 23 Nov. 1892, Carr Papers, LOC.

20. Appl. Files 1885–93, F. A. Mathews.

21. Chilton, "Inspection of Consulates 1896–1897," 1:87, 19; Pletcher, "Economic

Growth," 129; "Inspection Report of Herbert H. D. Peirce," 49.

22. Maratta is an elusive figure in that I can find little useful biographic information on him; see appendix A. In 1897, however, he was heavily supported (to no avail) for retention by the local business community at Melbourne; Appl. Files 1897–1901, D. W. Maratta.

23. Gudger, for instance, rated this praise from an inspector: "[His] office [is] in excellent condition. He is thoroughly efficient and much interested in consular work." See "Inspection of Consulates 1897–1898," 1:102–3.

24. See Appl. Files 1897–1901, J. S. Durham, and Pepper Papers, Univ. of Pennsylvania.

25. A useful, sympathetic sketch of his diplomatic career is Philip S. Foner, ed., *The Life and Writings of Frederick Douglass* (New York: International Publishers, 1955), 4:128–39. See also Louis M. Sears, "Frederick Douglass and the Mission to Haiti, 1889–1891," *Hispanic American Historical Review* 21 (May 1941): 222–38.

26. LaFeber, *The New Empire*, 313, and Cole, *Interpretative History of American Foreign Policy*, 279. For another positive assessment of the red-haired Allen, see Werking, *The Master Architects*, 15. Dr. Allen's contemporary, the acerbic W. W. Rockhill, dissented from any favorable view, calling him "ineffectual" and "a very good, honest fellow with little or no judgment"; quoted in Campbell, *Transformation of American Foreign Relations*, 110.

27. Clippings from the *Mexican Herald*, 14 Nov. 1898, Appl. Files 1897–1901, A. D. Barlow; G. L. Rives to Grover Cleveland, 9 May 1895, Cleveland Papers, LOC.

28. Bernhard Vogel to Benjamin Harrison, 10 Apr. 1890, Appl. Files 1885–93, A. E. King; Wilbur J. Carr to Herbert H. D. Peirce, 13 Jan. 1904, Carr Papers, LOC. King also was rumored, falsely, to have smuggled a silver plate into France when he took up his post in 1890—to what avail this was supposed to have been done was never clear; *New York Times*, 5 Oct. 1890, 1.

29. On Hunter, see clippings in Appl. Files 1897–1901, W. G. Hunter. His financial peccadilloes were said to be a consequence of debts from his failed bid for the Senate in 1896; no charges were proved.

30. A foremost failing of officers of the period was inexperience. One post at least, however, kept a full written account of precedents, forms, usage, and procedures as a guide through the years to incoming chiefs of mission. See the ledger-sized "Advice Book" of the legation at St. Petersburg, David Rowland Francis Papers, Missouri Historical Society, St. Louis, Mo. Entries and additions to the book date from 1894 to 1913. In more recent years, such informal guides have been replaced by voluminous sets of regulations and correspondence handbooks issued by the Department of State.

31. Bernard Bailyn, "Politics and Social Structure in Virginia," in Katz and Murrin, *Colonial America*, 209. Bailyn referred to the seventeenth-century colonial leadership of the "better sort," the gentry and the socially prominent, not a separate class of technicians or careerists. The comment seems to have merit as well in the context of the late nineteenth century and senior diplomatic and consular appointments.

Chapter 8

1. See notes 18 through 21 to chapter 1 of this study.

2. The "broken down men" phrase was used by Congressman Robert R. Hitt, attributed by him to the *New York Evening Post*; *Cong. Rec.*, 53d Cong., 2d sess., 26, pt. 4:3825.

3. Eric F. Goldman, *Rendezvous With Destiny: A History of Modern American Reform* (1952; rpt. New York Vintage Books, 1977), 227.

4. John Bright, speech at Birmingham, 29 Oct. 1858, in James E. T. Rogers, ed., *Speeches on Questions of Public Policy by John Bright, M.P.* (London, 1868), 2:382. Bright repeated the charge in an 1865 speech also at Birmingham: "The foreign policy of this country for the last 170 years has been a system of gigantic out-door relief to the English aristocracy"; ibid., 105.

5. Nicolson, *Diplomacy,* 114; Steiner, *Foreign Office and Foreign Policy,* 185; Steiner, *Times Survey of Foreign Ministries,* 209; J. B. Duroselle, "French Diplomacy in the Postwar World," in *Diplomacy in a Changing World,* ed. Stephen D. Kertesz and M. A. Fitzsimmons (Notre Dame, Ind.: Univ. of Notre Dame Press, 1959), 214. The information on the services of Austria-Hungary, Russia, the Netherlands, Greece, Belgium, and Japan in this and the following paragraph is from Steiner, *Times Survey of Foreign Ministries,* 54–55, 518, 372–73, 264–65, 82, and 328–31, respectively.

6. David Kelly, "British Diplomacy," in *Diplomacy in a Changing World,* ed. Kertesz & Fitzsimmons, 172–203.

7. Nicolson, *Diplomacy,* 114; Steiner, *Foreign Office and Foreign Policy,* 183, 185; Raymond A. Jones, *The British Diplomatic Service 1815–1914* (Waterloo, Canada: Wilfred Laurier Univ. Press, 1983), 217. An interesting, if temporally irrelevant, study is Phylis S. Lachs, *The Diplomatic Corps Under Charles II and James II* (New Brunswick, N.J.: Rutgers Univ. Press, 1965).

8. Cecil, *German Diplomatic Service,* 30, 31–32, 21.

9. Ibid., 21, 328.

10. Ibid., 120.

11. Ibid., 18.

12. Ibid., 97–102.

13. An unexpected exception may have been Austria-Hungary. The middle class was not barred from entry, and by 1918 commoners held 44 percent of the leading diplomatic positions in Vienna's service; Steiner, *Times Survey of Foreign Ministries,* 54–55.

14. Cecil, *German Diplomatic Service,* 21.

15. Paul Gordon Lauren has it, however, that the push for efficiency was engendered by later demands pointed up by World War I. The late nineteenth century was still a "golden age" of small diplomatic and consular staffs and light work loads. Lauren, *Diplomats and Bureaucrats: The First Institutional Responses to Twentieth-Century Diplomacy in France and Germany* (Stanford: Hoover Institute Press, 1976), 2.

16. Steiner, *Foreign Office and Foreign Policy,* 176.

17. Cecil, *German Diplomatic Service,* 328. Rachel West draws similar conclusions, for different reasons, on the American foreign affairs establishment; *The Department of State on the Eve of the First World War* (Athens, Ga.: Univ. of Georgia Press, 1978).

18. *Cong. Rec.,* 53d Cong., 2d sess., 1893–94, 26, pt. 4:3801.

19. "W. F. E.," "The Consul in Kingston," *New York Times,* 27 Aug. 1895, 16. The consul in question was Quincy Oliver Eckford, former chairman of the Mississippi Democratic party commission.

20. Richard Olney to Grover Cleveland, 17 Sept. 1895, quoted in *Cong. Rec.,* 54th Cong., 2d sess., 1897–98, 29, pt. 2:1413.

21. Robert R. Hitt to Wayne MacVeagh, 6 Nov. 1896, MacVeagh Papers, HSP; Theodore Stanton, letter to *New York Times,* 15 May 1893, 3; Chalmers Roberts, "Incidents in American Diplomacy," *The World's Work* 3 (Nov. 1901–Apr. 1902):1660.

22. Quotations from Loomis, "Foreign Service of the United States," 353–55.

23. Nicolson, *Diplomacy*, 90. Nicolson was not complimentary about American diplomats, however; see chapter 1.

24. Quoted in Loomis, "Foreign Service of the United States," 355.

25. John Watson Foster, *Diplomatic Memoirs* (Boston: Houghton Mifflin, 1909), 1:12.

26. Bernard De Voto, *Across the Wide Missouri* (Boston: Houghton Mifflin, 1947), 158.

Chapter 9

1. U. Alexis Johnson, "Caught in the Nutcracker," *Foreign Service Journal*, Sept. 1984, 29–30. The article is an excerpt from his book, written with Jef Olivarious McAllister, *Right Hand of Power: Memoirs of an American Diplomat* (Englewood Cliffs, N.J.: Prentice-Hall, 1984). In 1984 Johnson was one of the founders, with John J. McCloy and Ellsworth Bunker, of the American Academy of Diplomacy, an organization established to screen ambassadorial nominees for the Senate Foreign Relations Committee. Despite membership of up to seventy-five distinguished former ambassadors and secretaries of state, the academy has not been effective; it has never gained the approval or support of the Department of State's political leadership. See *Foreign Service Journal* 62 (May 1985): 22.

2. Johnson, "Caught in the Nutcracker," 30.

3. Ronald I. Spiers, speech, 26 Sept. 1985, in Department of State newsletter *State*, Nov. 1985, 13; Spiers, "The U.S. Foreign Service in a Year of Challenge," speech, 2 May 1986, in Department of State, Bureau of Public Affairs, Current Policy paper no. 831. Some sources show recent higher political appointee ratios; *The Washington Post*, 14 July 1985, 25, for instance, asserts that the Reagan administration in 1982 had 48 percent nonprofessionals as ambassadors. The "historical average" of careerist ambassadors, 1961 to 1986, according to the *Foreign Service Journal*, is 69 percent. This figure fell to a twenty-five-year low of 61 percent in April 1986. See *Foreign Service Journal* 63 (Sept. 1986): 25.

4. Spiers, *State*, Nov. 1985, 13. American Foreign Service Association, "An Injury to the National Interest," *Foreign Service Journal* 67 (Mar. 1987): 3; Sanford J. Unger, "Where Do We Find These Envoy Clowns?" *The Washington Post*, 9 Sept. 1982, B2; John Wills Tuthill, letter to editor, *Foreign Service Journal* 63 (June 1986): 6–7. I served with Tuthill at the Paris embassy in the 1950s. He had a reputation for unusual frankness, if not to say outright profanity, in his speech.

5. Marshall Green, "The Marshall Plan," *Foreign Service Journal*, Feb. 1986, 29.

6. Richard Olney to S. B. Griffin, 26 Mar. 1913, Richard Olney Papers, LOC. The quotation is cited in Gerald G. Eggert, *Richard Olney: Evolution of a Statesman* (University Park: Pennsylvania State Univ. Press, 1974), 318, and in Henry James, *Richard Olney and His Public Service* (Boston: Houghton Mifflin, 1923), 192.

7. One reason that this happens among career diplomats is the usually prolonged residence overseas required of them and a consequent lack of exposure to current domestic views, public and official. As almost poignantly put in behalf of all professionals by an Italian careerist, Daniele Varé (*Laughing Diplomat* [London: J. Murray, 1938], 79):

It is usual to envy diplomats because they travel about the world and meet "the best people" in foreign lands. Admitting this to be an advantage, it has to be paid for, like everything else.

Not all posts abroad are pleasant and healthy, nor are all government and colleagues agreeable to deal with. The circles in which we move are not always brilliant or smart.

When a diplomat comes home, he finds he is out of touch with his own country. His friends have got used to doing without him. The women he might have loved (and who might have loved him) have found other husbands and lovers. At the Club the young men ask each other who the old gentleman with grey hair might be.

Nonprofessionals, on the other hand, fall into this trap largely through inexperience with the practice of diplomacy.

8. Robert R. Hitt to Wayne MacVeagh, 6 Nov. 1896, MacVeagh Papers, HSP. As a young man, Hitt himself served seven years at Paris as a junior diplomat.

9. James B. McCreary, *Cong. Rec.*, 53d Cong., 2d sess., 1893–94, 26, pt. 4:3826; Loomis, "Foreign Service of the United States," 351, 352.

10. Unidentified, undated twenty-two and one-half page typescript biographic sketch of Alexander evidently prepared in early 1911; folder 20, "MSS Biographical Sketches," Alexander Papers, SHC. Internal indications suggest that it was written by Richard H. Battle, secretary and treasurer of the University of North Carolina and brother of University President Kemp P. Battle.

11. Edwin A. Grosvenor, paper delivered at 1898 annual meeting of American Historical Society, *American Historical Review* 4 (Apr. 1899):418–19. His position was disputed in discussion by Prof. S. M. Macvane who asserted that there was a marked decline in the abilities of American diplomats after 1820.

12. *The Meridian* (Miss.) *Star*, 14 May 1982. In a letter to the editor I subsequently defended the training, motives, and patriotism, which were implicitly questioned, of the careerists in the Foreign Service.

13. Michael Dobbs, "Envoy Exits with Call for More Like Him," *The Washington Post*, 14 July 1985, 1, 25.

14. Bailey, *Art of Diplomacy*, 46; James W. Symington, *The Strategy Game* (New York: Macmillan, 1971), 10.

15. Bailey, *Art of Diplomacy*, 46. The thesis that gentleman amateurs have had a valued place in American diplomacy is illustrated by Bailey's personal diplomatic "hall of fame." All six of its members were nonprofessionals. He notes that careerists are at a disadvantage in gaining diplomatic fame because discretion and self-effacement usually are required of them. Even well-known veteran diplomats such as Henry White and Joseph C. Grew thus miss out. Several amateurs of outstanding ability he leaves off his list because they served at posts when nothing much was required of them. Bailey does single out for recognition Benjamin Franklin, Albert Gallatin, Charles Francis Adams, Townsend Harris, Anson Burlingame, and, skipping to the twentieth century, Dwight Morrow. "Though amateurs at the outset, they were diplomats in the finest tradition . . . " Paying tribute to those who adjusted capably to diplomacy after achieving distinction in other fields, Bailey wrote that "no one wants a life-tenure snobocracy." See Bailey, "Hall of Fame for American Diplomats," 55–71, 64.

16. Charles W. Yost, *The Conduct and Misconduct of Foreign Affairs* (New York: Random House, 1972), 176. Yost himself experienced interrupted service. Early in his professional career, he voluntarily departed for a number of years to follow a career in journalism, only to return to the diplomatic field after World War II.

17. Spiers, *State*, Nov. 1985, 13.

18. An FSO involved in the Iranian hostage crisis of 1980–81 speaks of what he terms the "curious insularity" of the career Foreign Service as one explanation for the debacle;

Moorehead Kennedy, *The Ayatolla in the Cathedral* (New York: Hill and Wang, 1986).

19. Henry M. Jackson, Senate subcommittee in 1965, quoted in Bailey, *Art of Diplomacy,* 35.

20. Clare Booth Luce, "The Ambassadorial Issue: Professionals or Amateurs?" *Foreign Affairs* 36 (Oct. 1957): 114. Former ambassador Charles Yost gives an unusually long list of outstanding recent nonprofessionals in both foreign policymaking and overseas diplomatic roles, including Dean Acheson, Adolph Berle, William Benton, Robert Lovett, Averell Harriman, Paul Hoffman, Philip Jessup, Paul Nitze, David Bruce, Walter Bedell Smith, Christian Herter, Chester Bowles, George Ball, Elliot Richardson, George Perkins, Robert Bowie, Gerard Smith, McGeorge Bundy, Harlan Cleveland, Walt Rostow, Roger Hilsman, Henry Kissinger, and Peter Peterson; *The Conduct and Misconduct of Foreign Affairs,* 176–77. Another study compares favorably the post–World War II amateur foreign policy leadership with the current (1980s) bureaucracies; Walter Isaacson and Evan Thomas, *The Wise Men: Six Friends and the World They Made* (New York: Touchstone, 1986).

21. R. T. Curran, "Diplomat, Heal Thyself," *Foreign Service Journal* 62 (May 1985): 23–25. A student of foreign service reform previously cited concedes a similar point with respect to the late nineteenth-century Consular Service. "The principal obstacle [then] to an efficient consular service was not the quality of the appointees, their lack of initial training, or any of [several] other matters." Rather, the administrative system was at fault. Werking, *Master Architects,* 9.

22. Luce, "Ambassadorial Issue," 113.

23. Spiers, *State,* Nov. 1985, 13.

Selected Bibliography

Unpublished Personal Papers

Alexander, Eben. Southern Historical Collection, University of North Carolina, Chapel Hill.

Barrett, John. Manuscript Division, Library of Congress, Washington, D.C.

Beale Family, Decatur House. Manuscript Division, Library of Congress, Washington, D.C.

Breckinridge, Clifton Rodes. Manuscript Division, Library of Congress, Washington, D.C.

Carr, Wilbur John. Manuscript Division, Library of Congress, Washington, D.C.

Chilton, Robert S., Jr. Manuscript Division, Duke University Library, Durham, North Carolina.

Choate, Joseph Hodges. Library of Congress, Washington, D.C.

Cleveland, Grover. Manuscript Division, Library of Congress, Washington, D.C.

Crittenden, Thomas Theodore. Western Historical Collection, University of Missouri, St. Louis.

Dabney, Walter D. Barrett Library, University of Virginia, Charlottesville.

Dickinson, Charles Monroe. Manuscript Division, Library of Congress, Washington, D.C.

Foster, John Watson. Manuscript Division, Library of Congress, Washington, D.C.

Francis, David Rowland. Division of Library and Archives, Missouri Historical Society, St. Louis.

Gresham, Walter Quentin. Manuscript Division, Library of Congress, Washington, D.C.

Griscom, Lloyd Carpenter. Manuscript Division, Library of Congress, Washington, D.C.

Harrison, Benjamin. Manuscript Division, Library of Congress, Washington, D.C.

Hay, John. Manuscript Division, Library of Congress, Washington, D.C.

Herbert, Hilary Abner. Southern Historical Collection, University of North Carolina, Chapel Hill.

Judd, Max. Division of Library and Archives, Missouri Historical Society, St. Louis.

Loomis, Francis Butler. Manuscript Division, Library of Congress, Washington, D.C.

McKinley, William. Manuscript Division, Library of Congress, Washington, D.C.

MacVeagh, Wayne, Historical Society of Pennsylvania, Philadelphia.

Penfield, Frederic Courtland. Historical Society of Pennsylvania, Philadelphia.

Pepper, William. Van Pelt Library, University of Pennsylvania, Philadelphia.

Porter, Horace. Manuscript Division, Library of Congress, Washington, D.C.

Ransom, Matt Whitaker. Southern Historical Collection, University of North Carolina, Chapel Hill.

Scruggs, William Lindsay. Manuscript Division, Library of Congress, Washington, D.C.

Straus, Oscar Solomon. Manuscript Division, Library of Congress, Washington, D.C.

White, Andrew Dickson. Manuscript Division, Library of Congress, Washington, D.C.

White, Henry. Manuscript Division, Library of Congress, Washington, D.C.

Wildman, Edwin and Rounseville. Manuscript Division, Library of Congress, Washington, D.C.

Unpublished Government Documents and Records

U.S. Department of State. Applications and Recommendations for Federal Office, 1861–69, 1877–85. Legislative and Diplomatic Branch, Record Group 59, National Archives. Microform.

_____ . Applications and Recommendations for Federal Office, 1885–93, 1893–97, 1897–1901. Legislative and Diplomatic Branch, Record Group 59, National Archives.

_____ . Despatches from United States Consuls, 1889–1900. Record Group 59, National Archives. Microform.

_____ . Despatches from United States Ministers, 1889–1900. Record Group 59, National Archives. Microform.

————— . "Inspection of Consulates, 1896–1897, Consular Bureau." Volume 1. Entry 592. Legislative and Diplomatic Branch, Record Group 59, National Archives.

————— . "Inspection of Consulates, 1897–1898, Consular Bureau." Volume 2. Entry 592. Legislative and Diplomatic Branch, Record Group 59, National Archives.

————— . "Inspection Report of Herbert H. D. Peirce, Third Assistant Secretary of State," 1904. Entry 596. Legislative and Diplomatic Branch, Record Group 59, National Archives.

————— . List of U.S. Consular Officers, 1789–1939. Record Group 59, National Archives. Microform.

————— . List of U.S. Diplomatic Officers, 1789–1933. Record Group 59, National Archives. Microform.

————— . Miscellaneous Reports and Correspondence on Consular Inspections 1896–1918. Entry 599. Legislative and Diplomatic Branch, Record Group 59, National Archives.

————— . Name Index to the Appointment of the United States Diplomatic and Consular Officers, 1776–1933, and Commissioned Officers of the Federal Government, 1769–1933. Legislative and Diplomatic Branch, Record Group 59, National Archives.

————— . "Reports of Inspections of Consulates, 1899–1900–1901–1902." Volume 3. Entry 592. Legislative and Diplomatic Branch, Record Group 59, National Archives.

U.S. Prints and Photo Division. Subject Files, Library of Congress, Washington, D.C.

Government Publications

Straus, Oscar S. Reform in the Consular Service. Washington, D.C.: National Civil Service Reform League, 1894. Microform.

U.S. Department of State. Diplomatic and Consular Service of the United States. Washington, D.C.: Government Printing Office, 1890, multiple annual issues 1892–99.

————— . Register of the Department of State. Washington, D.C.: Government Printing Office, 1889, annual issues 1892–1900.

————— . United States Chiefs of Mission, 1778–1982. 2d ed. Washington, D.C.: Government Printing Office, 1982.

U.S. Government. Abstract of the Eleventh Census: 1890. Washington, D.C.: Government Printing Office, 1896.

————— . Abstract of the Twelfth Census: 1900. Washington, D.C.: Government Printing Office, 1902.

————— . Biographical Directory of the American Congress. Washington, D.C.: Government Printing Office, 1961.

————— . Congressional Record. 48th–54th Congresses. Washington, D.C.: 1885, 1886, 1889, 1890, 1891, 1893, 1894, 1895, 1899.

_____ . *Correspondence in Relation to the Boundary Controversy Between Great Britain and Venezuela.* Washington, D.C.: Government Printing Office, 1896.

_____ . *Historical Statistics of the United States, Colonial Times to 1970.* 2 parts. Washington, D.C.: Government Printing Office, 1975.

_____ . *Official Register of the United States.* Biennial volumes. Washington, D.C.: Government Printing Office, 1891–1901.

_____ . *Papers Relating to the Foreign Relations of the United States.* Annual volumes. Washington, D.C.: Government Printing Office, 1889–1900.

Theses and Dissertations

Bhurtel, Shyam K. "Alfred Eliab Buck: Carpetbagger in Alabama and Georgia." Ph.D. dissertation, Auburn University, 1981.

Brooks, Neal Allen. "The Diplomatic Career of Whitelaw Reid." Ph.D. dissertation, Case Western Reserve University, 1974.

Carson, Donald K. "Richard Olney: Secretary of State, 1895–1897." Ph.D. dissertation, University of Kentucky, 1969.

LaFeber, Walter F. "The Latin American Policy of the Second Cleveland Administration." Ph.D. dissertation, University of Wisconsin, 1959.

Reading, David Louis. "The United States Press and the Chilean Civil War of 1891." Master's thesis, University of North Carolina at Chapel Hill, 1971.

Talbert, Betty Weaver. "The Evolution of John Hay's China Policy." Ph.D. dissertation, University of North Carolina at Chapel Hill, 1974.

Young, George B. "The Influence of Politics on American Diplomacy During Cleveland's Administrations: 1885–1889, 1893–1897." Ph.D. dissertation, Yale University, 1939.

Reference Works

DeConde, Alexander, ed. *Encyclopedia of American Foreign Policy: Studies of the Principal Movements and Ideas.* 3 vols. New York: Charles Scribner's Sons, 1978.

Findling, John M. *Dictionary of American Diplomatic History.* Westport, Conn.: Greenwood Press, 1980.

Johnson, Allen, et al., eds. *Dictionary of American Biography.* 10 vols. New York: Scribner, 1927–57.

Logan, Rayford, and Michael R. Winston, eds. *Dictionary of Negro Biography.* New York: W. W. Norton & Co., 1982.

McMullin, Thomas A., and David Walker. *Biographical Directory of American Territorial Governors.* Westport, Conn.: Meckler Publishing, 1984.

Morris, Dan and Inez. *Who Was Who in American Politics.* New York: Hawthorn Books, Inc., 1974.

National Cyclopaedia of American Biography, The. 63 vols. New York: James T. White Company, 1888–1984.

New York Times Obituaries Index 1858–1968. New York: New York Times, 1970.

Sobel, Robert, ed. *Biographic Directory of the United States Executive Branch.* Westport, Conn.: Greenwood Publishing Company, 1971.

Whitfield, J. B. *An Official Directory of the State Government. Tallahassee, Fla.:* Floridian Steam Book and Job Office, 1885.

Who's Who in America. Biennial vols. Chicago: A. N. Marquis Co., 1899–1900, 1910–1911.

Who Was Who in America. 5 vols. Chicago: A.N. Marquis Co., 1942, 1950, 1960, 1963, 1968.

Articles

Adams, Robert, Jr. "Faults in Our Consular Service." *North American Review,* Apr. 1893, 461–66.

Bailey, Thomas A. "A Hall of Fame for American Diplomats." In *Essays Diplomatic and Undiplomatic of Thomas A. Bailey,* edited by Alexander DeConde and Armin Rappaport, 55–71. New York: Appleton-Century-Crofts, 1969.

Becker, William H. "1899–1920: America Adjusts to World Power." In *Economics and World Power: An Assessment of American Diplomacy Since 1789,* ed. William H. Becker and Samuel F. Wells, Jr., 173–223. New York: Columbia Univ. Press, 1984.

Belmont, Perry. "Defects in Our Consular Service." *Forum,* Jan. 1888, 519–26.

Blodgett, Geoffrey. "Reform Thought and the Genteel Tradition." In *The Gilded Age,* edited by H. Wayne Morgan, 55–76. Syracuse: Syracuse Univ. Press, 1963; rev. ed., 1970.

Duroselle, J. B. "French Diplomacy in the Postwar World." In *Diplomacy in a Changing World,* edited by Stephen D. Kertesz and M. A. Fitzsimmons, 204–48. Notre Dame, Ind.: Univ. of Notre Dame Press, 1959.

Erikkson, Erik M. "The Federal Civil Service under President Jackson." *Mississippi Valley Historical Review* 13 (Mar. 1927):517–40.

Fossum, Paul R. "The Anglo-Venezuelan Boundary Controversy." *Hispanic American Historical Review* 8 (Aug. 1928):299–329.

Galambos, Louis. "The Emerging Organizational Synthesis in Modern American History." *Business History Review* 44 (Autumn 1970):279–90.

Hardy, Osgood. "The Itata Incident." *Hispanic American Historical Review* 5 (May 1922):195–226.

————. "Was Egan a 'Blundering Minister'?" *Hispanic American Historical Review* 8 (Feb. 1928):65–81.

Heinrichs, Walter H., Jr. "Bureaucracy and Professionalism in the Development of American Career Diplomacy." In *Twentieth Century American Foreign Policy,* edited by John Braeman, Robert H. Bremner, and David Brody, 119–206. Columbus: Ohio State Univ. Press, 1971.

Holbo, Paul. "Economics, Emotion, and Expansion: An Emerging Foreign Policy." In *The Gilded Age,* edited by H. Wayne Morgan, 199–221. Syracuse: Syracuse Univ. Press, 1963; rev. ed., 1970.

Hoogenboom, Ari. "Civil Service Reform and Public Morality." In *The Gilded Age*, edited by H. Wayne Morgan, 77–95. Syracuse: Syracuse Univ. Press, 1963; rev. ed., 1970.

Kelly, David. "British Diplomacy." In *Diplomacy in a Changing World*, edited by Stephen D. Kertesz and M. A. Fitzsimmons, 172–203. Notre Dame, Ind.: Univ. of Notre Dame Press, 1959.

Lee, Fitzhugh. "Cuba and Her Struggle for Freedom." *The Fortnightly Review*, 1 June 1898, 855–66.

Leopold, Richard W. "The *Foreign Relations* Series: A Centennial Estimate." *Mississippi Valley Historical Review* 49 (Mar. 1963):595–612.

————. "The *Foreign Relations* Series Revisited: One Hundred Plus Ten." *Journal of American History* 59 (Mar. 1973): 935–57.

Loomis, Francis B. "The Foreign Service of the United States." *North American Review*, Sept. 1899, 349–61.

————. "Proposed Reorganization of the American Consular Service." *North American Review*, Mar. 1906, 356–73.

Luce, Clare Booth. "The Ambassadorial Issue: Professionals or Amateurs?" *Foreign Affairs* 36 (Oct. 1957):105–121.

Lyman, Charles. "Ten Years of Civil Service Reform." *The North American Review*, Nov. 1893, 571–79.

Pessen, Edward L. "Social Structure and Politics in American History." *American Historical Review* 87 (Dec. 1982):1290–1325.

Pletcher, David M. "1861–1898: Economic Growth and Diplomatic Adjustment." In *Economics and World Power: An Assessment of American Diplomacy Since 1789*, edited by William H. Becker and Samuel F. Wells, Jr., 119–71. New York: Columbia Univ. Press, 1894.

Plischke, Elmer. "Research on the Administrative History of the Department of State." In *The National Archives and Foreign Relations Research*, edited by Milton O. Gustafson, 73–102. Athens, Ohio: Ohio Univ. Press, 1974.

Sears, Louis. "Frederick Douglass and the Mission to Haiti, 1889–1891." *Hispanic American Historical Review* 21(May 1941):222–38.

Stone, Lawrence. "Prosopography." In *Historical Studies Today*, edited by Felix Gilbert and Stephen R. Grabaud, 107–40. New York: W. W. Norton, 1972.

Taylor, Hannis. "A Review of the Cuban Question in Its Economic, Political, and Diplomatic Aspects." *The North American Review*, Nov. 1897, 610–35.

Trask, David F. "A Short History of the U.S. Department of State." *Department of State Bulletin* 81 (Jan. 1981), special supplement no. 2046.

Varg, Paul A. "The United States a World Power, 1900–1917: Myth or Reality?" In *Twentieth Century American Foreign Policy*, edited by John Braeman et al., 207–40, Columbus: Ohio State Univ. Press, 1971.

Veysey, Lawrence. "Who's a Professional? Who Cares?" *Reviews in American History* 3 (Dec. 1975):419–23.

Books

Anderson, David L. *Imperialism and Idealism: American Diplomats in China, 1861–1898.* Bloomington: Indiana Univ. Press, 1985.

Aronson, Sidney H. *Status and Kinship in the Higher Civil Service: Standards of Selection in the Administrations of John Adams, Thomas Jefferson, and Andrew Jackson.* Cambridge, Mass.: Harvard Univ. Press, 1964.

Bailey, Thomas A. *The Art of Diplomacy: The American Experience.* New York: Appleton-Century-Crofts, 1968.

Barnes, William, and John Heath Morgan. *The Foreign Service of the United States: Origins, Development, and Functions.* Washington, D.C.: Department of State, 1961.

Beisner, Robert L. *From the Old Diplomacy to the New, 1865–1900.* 2d ed. Arlington Heights, Ill.: Harlan Davidson, Inc., 1986.

Bottomore, T. B. *Elites and Society.* Baltimore: C. A. Watts, Pelican, 1964.

Brinton, Jasper Yeates. *The American Effort: A Chapter in Diplomatic History in the Nineteenth Century.* Alexandria, Egypt: By the Author, 1917.

Browne, Norma, ed. *A Black Diplomat in Haiti: The Diplomatic Correspondence of U.S. Minister Frederick Douglass From Haiti, 1889–1891.* 2 vols. Salisbury, N.C.: Documentary Publications, 1977.

Burch, Philip H., Jr. *Elites in American History.* 3 vols. New York: Holmes & Meier, 1980-81.

Campbell, Charles S. *The Transformation of American Foreign Relations, 1865–1900.* New York: Harper and Row, 1976.

Cecil, Lamar. *The German Diplomatic Service, 1871–1914.* Princeton, N.J.: Princeton Univ. Press, 1976.

Charles-Roux, Francois. *Souvenirs Diplomatique d'un Age Revolu.* Paris: A. Fayard, 1956.

Clymer, Kenton J. *John Hay: The Gentleman as Diplomat.* Ann Arbor: Univ. of Michigan Press, 1975.

Cohen, Naomi Weiner. *A Dual Heritage: The Political Career of Oscar S. Straus.* Philadelphia: Jewish Publishing Society of America, 1969.

Coolidge, T. Jefferson. *The Autobiography of T. Jefferson Coolidge, 1831–1920.* Boston: Houghton Mifflin Company, 1923.

Cortissoz, Royal. *The Life of Whitelaw Reid.* 2 vols. New York: Charles Scribner's Sons, 1921.

Crane, Katherine E. *Mr. Carr of State: Forty-seven Years in the Department of State.* New York: St. Martin's Press, 1960.

Denby, Charles. *China and Her People: Being the Observations, Reminiscences, and Conclusions of an American Diplomat.* 2 vols. Boston: L. C. Page & Company, 1906.

Dennett, Tyler. *John Hay: From Poetry to Politics.* New York: Dodd, Mead & Company, 1933.

Dennis, Alfred L. P. *Adventures in American Diplomacy, 1896–1906.* New York: E. P. Dutton, 1928.

Dingwall, Robert, and Philip Lewis, eds. *The Sociology of the Professions: Lawyers, Doctors and Others.* New York: St. Martin's Press, 1983.

Divine, Michael J. *John W. Foster: Politics and Diplomacy in the Imperial Era, 1873–1917.* Athens, Ohio: Ohio Univ. Press, 1981.

Dobson, John M. *Politics in the Gilded Age: A New Perspective on Reform.* New York: Praeger, 1972.

Eggert, Gerald G. *Richard Olney: Evolution of a Statesman.* University Park: Pennsylvania State Univ. Press, 1974.

Eisenstadt, S.N., ed. *Max Weber on Charisma and Institution Building.* Chicago: Univ. of Chicago Press, 1968.

Elliott, Philip. *The Sociology of the Professions.* New York: Herder & Herder, 1972.

Evans, Henry Clay, Jr. *Chile and Its Relations with the United States.* Durham, N.C.: Duke Univ. Press, 1927.

Faulkner, Harold U. *Politics, Reform and Expansion, 1890–1900.* New York: Harper and Bros., 1959.

Fish, Carl Russell. *The Civil Service and the Patronage.* Cambridge, Mass.: Harvard Univ. Press, 1920.

Friedson, Eliot. *Professional Powers: A Study of the Institutionalization of Formal Knowledge.* Chicago: Univ. of Chicago Press, 1986.

Foner, Philip S. *A History of Cuba and Its Relations with the United States.* Vol. 2. New York: International Publishers, 1963.

Foster, John Watson. *Diplomatic Memoirs.* 2 vols. Boston: Houghton Mifflin Company, 1909.

Geison, Gerald L., ed. *Professions and Professional Ideologies in America.* Chapel Hill: Univ. of North Carolina Press, 1983.

Gladden, E. N. *A History of Public Administration.* 2 vols. London: Frank Cass and Company, 1972.

Goldman, Eric F. *Rendezvous With Destiny: A History of Modern American Reform.* New York: Vintage Books, 1952; reprinted 1956, 1977.

Grenville, John A. S., and George B. Young. *Politics, Strategy, and American Diplomacy: Studies in Foreign Policy, 1873–1917.* New Haven, Conn.: Yale Univ. Press, 1966.

Gresham, Matilda. *Life of Walter Quentin Gresham, 1832–1895.* Chicago: Rand, McNally & Company, 1919.

Grew, Joseph C. *Turbulent Era: A Diplomatic Record of Forty Years, 1904–1945.* 2 vols. Boston: Houghton Mifflin, 1952.

Griscom, Lloyd C. *Diplomatically Speaking.* New York: Little, Brown and Company, 1940.

Harrington, Fred H. *God, Mammon and the Japanese: Dr. Horace N. Allen and Korean-American Relations, 1884–1905.* Madison: Univ. of Wisconsin Press, 1944.

Haskell, Thomas L. *The Emergence of Professional Social Science: The American Social Science Association and the Nineteenth-Century Crisis of Authority.* Urbana: Univ. of Illinois Press, 1977.

_____ , ed. *The Authority of Experts: Studies in History and Theory.* Bloomington: Indiana Univ. Press, 1984.

Hays, Samuel P. *The Response to Industrialism, 1885–1914.* Chicago: Univ. of Chicago Press, 1957.

Healy, David. *U.S. Expansionism: The Imperialist Urge in the 1890s.* Madison: Univ. of Wisconsin Press, 1970.

Heinrichs, Waldo H., Jr. *American Ambassador: Joseph C. Grew and the Development of the United States Diplomatic Tradition.* Boston: Little, Brown and Company, 1966.

Hunt, Gaillard. *The Department of State of the United States: Its History and Functions.* New Haven, Conn.: Yale Univ. Press, 1914.

Hunt, Michael H. *The Making of a Special Relationship: The United States and China to 1914.* New York: Columbia Univ. Press, 1983.

Huntington Wilson, F. M. *Memoirs of an Ex-Diplomat.* Boston: Bruce Humphries, 1945.

Ilchman, Warren F. *Professional Diplomacy in the United States, 1779–1939: A Study in Administrative History.* Chicago: Univ. of Chicago Press, 1961.

Israel, Jerry, ed. *Building the Organizational Society: Essays on Associational Activities in America.* New York: Free Press, 1972.

Jaher, Frederic C., ed. *The Rich, the Well Born, and the Powerful: Elites and Upper Classes in History.* Urbana: Univ. of Illinois Press, 1973.

James, Henry. *Richard Olney and His Public Service.* Boston: Houghton Mifflin Company, 1923.

Jones, Arthur G. *The Evolution of Personnel Systems for U.S. Foreign Affairs: A History of Reform Efforts.* Carnegie Endowment for International Peace, 1965.

Jones, Chester Lloyd. *The Consular Service of the United States: Its History and Activities.* Philadelphia: Published for the University, 1906.

Jones, Raymond A. *The British Diplomatic Service 1815–1914.* Waterloo, Canada: Wilfred Laurier Univ. Press, 1983.

Keller, Morton I. *Affairs of State: Public Life in Late Nineteenth-Century America.* Cambridge, Mass.: Belknap Press, 1977.

LaFeber, Walter. *The New Empire: An Interpretation of American Expansion, 1860–1898.* Ithaca, N.Y.: Cornell Univ. Press, 1963; 5th ed., 1975.

Larson, Magali Sarfatti. *The Rise of Professionalism: A Sociological Analysis.* Berkeley: Univ. of California Press, 1977.

Lauren, Paul Gordon. *Diplomats and Bureaucrats: The First Institutional Responses to Twentieth-Century Diplomacy in France and Germany.* Stanford: Hoover Institute Press, 1976.

Leech, Margaret. *In the Days of McKinley.* New York: Harper and Brothers, 1959.

Lodge, Henry Cabot, ed. *Selections from the Correspondence of Theodore Roosevelt and Henry Cabot Lodge, 1884–1918.* 2 vols. New York: Charles Scribner's Sons, 1925.

McWilliams, Tennant S. *Hannis Taylor: The New Southerner as an American.* University: Univ. of Alabama Press, 1978.

Marcus, Robert D. *Grand Old Party: Political Structure in the Gilded Age, 1880–1896*. New York: Oxford Univ. Press, 1971.

Martin, Edward Sanford, ed. *The Life of Joseph Hodges Choate: As Gathered Chiefly from His Letters*. 2 vols. New York: Charles Scribner's Sons, 1920.

May, Ernest R. *American Imperialism: A Speculative Essay*. New York: Atheneum, 1968.

_____ . *Imperial Democracy: The Emergence of America as a Great Power*. New York: Harcourt, Brace and World, 1961.

Mende, Elsie Porter. *An American Soldier and Diplomat*. New York: Frederick A. Stokes Co., 1927.

Moore, Wilbert S., ed. *The Professions: Roles and Rules*. New York: Russell Sage Foundation, 1970.

Morgan, H. Wayne. *From Hayes to McKinley: National Party Politics, 1877–1896*. Syracuse, N.Y.: Syracuse Univ. Press, 1969.

Mosca, Gaetano. *The Ruling Class*. Translated by Hannah D. Kahn. New York: McGraw-Hill, 1939.

Nelson, William E. *The Roots of American Bureaucracy, 1830–1900*. Cambridge, Mass.: Harvard Univ. Press, 1982.

Nevins, Allan. *Henry White*. New York: Harper and Brothers, 1930.

Nicolson, Harold. *Diplomacy*. New York: Oxford Univ. Press, 1939; Galaxay, 1964.

Norris, James D., and Arthur H. Shaffer, eds. *Politics and Patronage in the Gilded Age: Correspondence of James A. Garfield and C. E. Henry*. Madison: State Historical Society of Wisconsin, 1970.

Ostrogorski, Moisei. *Democracy and the Organization of Political Parties*. Vol. 2. Edited and abridged by Seymour Martin Lipset. New Brunswick, N.J.: Transaction Books, 1982.

Perez, Louis A., Jr. *Cuba Between Empires, 1878–1902*. Pittsburgh: Univ. of Pittsburgh Press, 1983.

Perkins, Dexter. *The Monroe Doctrine, 1867–1907*. Baltimore: The Johns Hopkins Press, 1937.

Peterson, Harold F. *Diplomat of the Americas: A Biography of William I. Buchanan (1852–1909)*. Albany: State Univ. of New York Press, 1977.

Plischke, Elmer. *United States Diplomats and Their Missions: A Profile of American Diplomatic Emissaries Since 1778*. Washington: American Enterprise Institute for Public Policy Research, 1975.

Pratt, Julius W. *Expansionists of 1898: The Acquisition of Hawaii and the Spanish Islands*. Baltimore: The Johns Hopkins Press, 1936; Chicago: Quadrangle, 1964.

Prewitt, Kenneth, and Alan Stone. *The Ruling Elites: Elite Theory, Power, and American Democracy*. New York: Harper and Row, 1973.

Russell, Henry B. *Our War With Spain*. Hartford, Conn.: Hartford Publishing Company, 1899.

Scruggs, William L. *The Venezuela Question: British Aggressions in Venezuela, or the Monroe Doctrine on Trial: Lord Salisbury's Mistakes; Fallacies of the British*

"Blue Book" on the Disputed Boundary. Atlanta: The Franklin Printing and Publishing Company, 1896.

Skowronek, Stephen. *Building a New American State: The Expansion of National Administrative Capacities.* New York: Cambridge Univ. Press, 1982.

Spaulding, E. Wilder. *Ambassadors Ordinary and Extraordinary.* Washington: Public Affairs Press, 1961.

Sproat, J. G. *The Best Men: Liberal Reformers in the Gilded Age.* New York: Oxford Univ. Press, 1968.

Steiner, Zara S. *The Foreign Office and Foreign Policy, 1898–1914.* Cambridge: Cambridge Univ. Press, 1969.

————. ed. *The Times Survey of Foreign Ministries of the World.* London: Times Books, 1982.

Straus, Oscar S. *Under Four Administrations: From Cleveland to Taft.* Boston: Houghton Mifflin Company, 1922.

Stuart, Graham H. *The Department of State: A History of Its Organization, Procedures and Personnel.* New York: Macmillan Company, 1949.

Tansill, Charles C. *The Foreign Policy of Thomas F. Bayard, 1885–1897.* New York: Fordham Univ. Press, 1940.

Tate, Merze. *The United States and the Hawaiian Kingdom: A Political History.* New Haven, Conn.: Yale Univ. Press, 1965.

Thayer, Charles W. *Diplomat.* New York: Harper and Brothers, 1959.

Thayer, William Roscoe. *The Life and Letters of John Hay.* 2 vols. Boston: Houghton Mifflin Company, 1915.

Trask, David F. *The War With Spain in 1898.* New York: Macmillan Company, 1981.

Vollmer, Howard M., and Donald L. Mills, eds. *Professionalization.* Englewood Cliffs, N.J.: Prentice-Hall, 1966.

Werking, Richard H. *The Master Architects: Building the United States Foreign Service, 1890–1913.* Lexington: Univ. Press of Kentucky, 1977.

West, Rachel. *The Department of State on the Eve of the First World War.* Athens, Ga.: Univ. of Georgia Press, 1978.

Wheeler, Post and Hallie Erminie Rives. *Dome of Many-Colored Glass.* New York: Doubleday, 1955.

White, Andrew D. *Autobiography of Andrew Dickson White.* 2 vols. New York: The Century Company, 1905.

White, Leonard D. *The Republican Era, 1869–1901.* New York: Macmillan Company, 1958.

Wiebe, Robert H. *The Search for Order, 1879–1920.* New York: Hill and Wang, 1967.

Williams, R. Hal. *Years of Decisions: American Politics in the 1890s.* New York: Wiley, 1978.

Williams, William Appleman. *The Tragedy of American Diplomacy.* Rev. ed. New York: World Publishing, 1962.

Willson, Beckles. *America's Ambassadors to England (1785–1928): A Narrative of Anglo-American Diplomatic Relations.* London: John Murray, 1928.

_____ . *America's Ambassadors to France, 1777–1927: A Narrative of Franco-American Diplomatic Relations*. London: John Murray, 1928.

Yost, Charles W. *The Conduct and Misconduct of Foreign Affairs*. New York: Random House, 1972.

Young, Marilyn Blatt, ed. *American Expansionism: The Critical Issues*. Boston: Little, Brown and Company, 1973.

Index